Lilies That Fester

Lilies That Fester

Abortion and the Scandal of Christian Discipleship

JOHN BOSSERT BROWN JR.

RESOURCE *Publications* • Eugene, Oregon

LILIES THAT FESTER
Abortion and the Scandal of Christian Discipleship

Copyright © 2022 John Bossert Brown Jr. All rights reserved. Except for brief quotations in critical publications or reviews, no part of this book may be reproduced in any manner without prior written permission from the publisher. Write: Permissions, Wipf and Stock Publishers, 199 W. 8th Ave., Suite 3, Eugene, OR 97401.

Resource Publications
An Imprint of Wipf and Stock Publishers
199 W. 8th Ave., Suite 3
Eugene, OR 97401

www.wipfandstock.com

PAPERBACK ISBN: 978-1-6667-5340-0
HARDCOVER ISBN: 978-1-6667-5341-7
EBOOK ISBN: 978-1-6667-5342-4

03/17/23

Unless otherwise mentioned all Scripture is taken from the HOLY BIBLE, Revised Standard Version. Harper Study Bible. Copyright 1952, 1962, 1964. Used by permission of Harper & Row, Publishers, All Rights Reserved.

Scripture marked NIV is taken from The NIV Study Bible, New International Version. Copyright 1973,1978, 1983 Used by permission of Zondervan Bible Publishers. All rights reserved.

Scripture marked NEB is taken from The New English Bible with the Apocrypha. Copyright 1970. Used by permission of Oxford University Press, Cambridge University Press. All rights reserved.

Scripture marked GNB is taken from The Good News Bible, The Bible in Today's English Version. Copyright 1976. Used by permission of the American Bible Society. All rights reserved.

Scripture marked NIVASB is taken from the NIV Archaelogical Study Bible. Copyright 2005 by the Zondervan Corporation. NIV Study Bible, New International Version copyright 1973, 1978, 1984 by International Study Bible. Used by permission of Zondervan. All rights reserved.

To my wife. Carol, the love of my life, for her encouragement with this book, and her love and companionship for over half a century. She is my faithful companion, my unswerving and patient encourager, and my creative helpmate. She has accompanied my efforts with this book with her efforts in making beautiful clothing for children around the world. She's very practically pro-life, and I am deeply grateful for her love and support.

For sweetest things turn sourest by their deeds;
Lilies that fester smell far worse than weeds.

—William Shakespeare, Sonnet 94

Contents

Acknowledgements | ix
Introduction | xiii

1 A Troubling Surprise: Giga-death | 1
2 Ideologies Gone Rogue | 32
3 Lilies That Fester: The Scandal of Discipleship | 75
4 Jesus, Discipleship, and Worldviews | 130
5 Making Disciples: Shaping Hearts, Minds, and Behavior | 177
6 Home Discipleship | 209

Bibliography | 237
Name Index | 253

Acknowledgements

TO ACKNOWLEDGE ALL THOSE who helped with this book, who in some way encouraged me over the years, is impossible. I have been thinking about the ideas and issues in this book for decades, though it has been only in the last five years or so that I began putting some of those thoughts into book form. Working quickly is not my forte. This process was helped along by many people, some through personal conversations, others through their books and articles. Much of the help that influenced my thinking came from those whose faith, commitment, and knowledge, were greater than mine. I think in particular of C. S. Lewis, who taught me the importance of truth, and the realization that the Christian faith and worldview is of value to the extent that it reflects reality. It is also true that help sometimes came from those with whom I disagreed. I have learned much from those with different views, both in terms of the knowledge they shared, as well as in challenging me to think more deeply about my own ideas.

I owe much to my colleagues of the National Pro-Life Religious Council (NPRC), past and present, for all they have taught me, and for the encouragement they—and the Christian organizations they represent—have given me and the pro-life movement by their courageous example and steadfast support. I am also appreciative of the National Right to Life Committee (NRLC) for the wealth of knowledge, wisdom, courage, and practical support they have given to our country—and her churches—in building a culture of life. Hundreds of thousands of individuals owe their very lives to the work of the NPRC, the NRLC and their affiliates.

The United Church of Christ Friends for Life Committee, the prolife group in the United Church of Christ, with whom I served for nearly 30 years, also taught me a great deal. Special mention goes to Robin Fox and Mary Ellen Stone, our executive directors during many of those years, and whose hard work, intelligence and friendship, was always to be counted on.

Being a pastor brings with it challenges and blessings. The greatest blessing is the hope that in some small way one has cooperated with God in the furthering of his purposes in the lives of others. Another is the opportunity to make lasting friendships with the wonderful people of the three congregations my wife and I served. They are the United Church of Christ of North Troy, Vt, the United Methodist Church of Newport Center, Vt, and Shepherd of the Hills (now Calvary Chapel) of Bechtelsville, Pa. Our family has been richly blessed by the love and encouragement of these friends, and by my fellow pastors at Shepherd, then and now. Many of the ideas expressed in this book were worked out with their help and support. It is a joy to think that we shall be friends forever.

The prayers and support given to me by family and friends for this book has been a constant source of encouragement. Those who read and commented on the book and prayed for me include numerous family members. My wife, Carol, to whom the book is dedicated. My brothers, David and Jan, and their wives, Rose Marie and Dixie. My daughters, Jenniffer Lantz, and Kathryn Moore, my son John and his wife, Stefanie, and my nephew, Nick Korchowsky. Many friends also contributed to the process: Dale Bangs, Richard Banning, Ron and Barbara Christman, Rosalie Ellis, Rev. Dr. Bob Gerhart, Navin Mathews, Les McDougall, Rev. Dr. Brad Mellon, Lance Lewis, John Ludy, Dave Shalaway, Brad Smith, Janet Smithson, and Sandra Volgger-Balazinski, A number of National Pro-Life Religious Council colleagues also contributed, in many ways through countless discussions regarding the ideas involved. They include: Fr. Frank Pavone, Rev. Paul Stallsworth, Georgette Forney, Ernest Ohlhoff, and Rev. Dr. Dennis DiMauro. Another group worthy of mention for their prayers and encouragement are the friends who belong to the small group that meets in our home. Should I have inadvertently omitted someone, my apologies.

Acknowledgements

Special thanks to those who helped with editing: Richard Banning, Bob Gerhart, Nick Korchowsky, Jenniffer Lantz, Les McDougall, Brad Mellon, and Janet Smithson.

In and through the many contributions made to this book has been the influence of the Holy Spirit, to illuminate, to strengthen, to prod me along the way. As many a writer has (rightfully) said: Soli Deo Gloria.

Introduction

SEVERAL YEARS AGO WHILE working on this book it began to snow. Our Cocker Spaniel, Blackie, and I decided it was time for a walk. It proved to be a delightful time. The falling snow added a touch of beauty to everything—to trees, lawns, and the fields that edged the dark, quiet stream that meanders through the woods near our home. Later than evening I noticed that the snow had stopped. The skies had cleared, and a full moon lighted the landscape. All was silent and still. I breathed a prayer of gratitude for the beauty that surrounded me. All that day and evening, however, on television and talk radio the news was focused on the killing of an Iranian general by an American airstrike. Most of those interviewed considered the killing justified, saying the man was a terrorist with American blood on his hands. But there was also talk of the likelihood of retaliation, and the possibility of war. The situation was obviously serious, but what struck me that evening was that there was no mention of the beauty of the day. It was not surprising. After all, most news programs do not focus on the weather unless disaster is unfolding somewhere. But I thought then, and many times since then, that violence has a way of destroying beauty and shattering the dreams of individuals, families, neighborhoods, even nations. Nature, and animals, are not unaffected. The misery and suffering resulting from human violence in modern times is ugly and ubiquitous.

Violence and conflict are everyday events in locations around the world, and often lead the headlines of the daily news. In February 2022 the world was outraged by Russia's invasion of Ukraine, a grinding conflict now in its seventh month, and the first European war since the end of World War II. Meanwhile, tensions between China and Taiwan are increasing, and there is talk of the possibility of war. In the United States multiple mass shootings have become commonplace. It is early September as I write, and already there have been 314 mass shootings in the United States.[1] The two deadliest incidents occurred in May. In the first incident ten men and women, all people of color, were murdered in a grocery store in Buffalo NY. Just days later, in Uvalde, TX, nineteen children and two teachers were killed by a teen-aged shooter in an elementary school. Today—and tomorrow, and every day after that—many thousands of unborn children here and in dozens of other nations will be violently destroyed by abortion. But there will be no media coverage, for killing an unborn child in many countries and in some American states is legal. The defenders of abortion in America, as the clamorous response to the recent *Dobbs* decision by the Supreme Court makes clear, are determined to sustain and extend its legality.

At the birth of the twentieth century, by way of contrast, the world seemed relatively peaceful. Expectations for progress in science, industry, medicine, health, and religion, were high. Some of those expectations were met and exceeded. Lifespans have increased, certain diseases have been largely curtailed, space exploration has put a man on the moon, America has become history's greatest superpower, and Christianity has become the world's largest religion. There were, however, surprises. Perhaps the most troubling surprise to a number of historians (and to me as my understanding increased) was the massive scale of violence.

When I became the pastor of two small congregations in northern Vermont (this was in 1969), I found it difficult to preach about certain subjects. I tended to avoid, or treat lightly, topics that I thought might be upsetting. Then came the Supreme Court's *Roe v. Wade* decision on

---

1. A mass shooting is the shooting of four people, injured or killed, other than the shooter. As of this writing there have been over 22,000 homicides in the USA thus far. See https://www.insider.com/number-of-mass-shootings-in-America-this-year-2022-25. Accessed August 30, 2022. Some scholars, e.g., Steven Pinker, argue that the world is safer and less violent. And yet, from 1969 to 2019 there were nearly 600,000 murders in the United States of people naturally born. See "United States Crime Rate." Available at https://www.disastercenter.com/crime/us.crime.htm. Accessed September 18, 2022.

abortion. The more I learned, the greater the sense of conviction that I should speak about it. But for a long while I lacked the courage necessary to do so. The pastor friends I talked with weren't eager to deal with the issue either. "Don't rock the boat," was a common response. Eventually, after much prayer and prodding by the Holy Spirit (our congregation had become involved in the charismatic renewal at that time), I shared my concern that abortion was a grave sin that the church should face. It proved to be a turning point for me, a small step forward in obedience.

Abortion remained an important issue for me, and studying the issue gradually led me to see it in the larger context of twentieth century violence, along with the efforts to dehumanize people that often preceded the violence. The scale, variety, and brutality of violence surprised me. I had known nothing about the massacre of Armenian Christians in World War I, or the disastrous eugenics movement in America, and very little about Germany's euthanasia program and the Holocaust, to name just a few of twentieth century horrors. Racism was an issue while I was in seminary (1966–69). I remember hearing more than once the comment that the most segregated hour of the week was Sunday morning.[2]

One of the first things that struck me in my reading was learning of the enormous number of twentieth century victims. I was amazed to learn that *several hundred million* people had been destroyed through wars, planned famines, mass executions, euthanasia, and terror since the beginning of World War I. Many of these victims were civilians and non-combatants who were deliberately targeted, a new feature of modern warfare. Through my ongoing study on abortion I eventually learned that when the victims of abortion are included in the death total—and few historians do—this number *quadruples*. Worldwide, from Russia's authorization of abortion in 1920 until the present day, over *one billion* unborn children have been killed by this brutal method. The number is astonishing, all the more so because it involves the willingness of parents to seek and pay for the execution of their own preborn children. Media outlets pay close attention to acts of violence, but there is little mention of abortion. It is a silent holocaust. It is also an invisible holocaust, as videos and images of the victims are not shown.

Perhaps equally disturbing was learning that Christian resistance to instances of mass violence was often limited, even at times supportive. The commitment to the sanctity of human life that is rooted in the

---

2. This remark may have originated with Martin Luther King Jr.

Gospel often seemed absent. Christians in many nations provided a measure of support for the eugenics movement. During the Holocaust most German Christians were bystanders. Perhaps two hundred thousand Hutu Christians took part in the Rwandan genocide. Here in the United States sixty-four million unborn children have been destroyed by abortion since 1973, perhaps as many as 50 percent of them sought by women who identify as *Christian*.

Many questions come to mind in pondering these matters. What motivated the perpetrators? What were the reasons for the massive bloodshed? How was it possible to kill millions of people? Was it prejudice, fear, or love of power? The biblical answer to these questions stems ultimately from the rejection of God and his Word. This is a view—a destructive worldview—common to the humanist ideologies of the last century or so. Without God it is not difficult to deny that certain human beings are made in God's image (e.g., Armenians, Jews, Tutsis, unborn children), and it is easy to dehumanize them. Killing dehumanized human beings—those considered subhuman, non-persons, and disposable—is justified because their death purifies society and makes it better. In their view, might makes right.

There are questions for Christians too. Why have so many Christians remained bystanders in the presence of racism or violence? Why have so many Christian mothers (and fathers) ignored the command not to kill? How has abortion affected the unity of the churches? Our modern world is incredibly complex, but I wonder: Might the decline of churches in Western nations be connected in some way with the failure of so many Christians to resist the dehumanization and violence of our time? Can Christians be righteous?

Thinking about these things has troubled me. Can those who have acquiesced or participated in violence really be Christians? It is easy to believe the answer is no. The lack of empathy for others, the unwillingness to speak out against injustice, the refusal to help when help was needed, all seem completely contrary to the faith and behavior one would hope to see among fellow believers. Part of the problem I believe is that multitudes of people thought to be Christian were (or are) only conventional Christians. They are outwardly observant, but inwardly lack the faith, commitment and presence of the Holy Spirit. There are other multitudes who are Christians, genuine believers in Jesus, alive in the Spirit in some sense, but immature. They are ignorant and unsure of the biblical worldview, and without confidence or courage when it comes to facing the challenges before them. They have been influenced by the utopian ideologies of modern times that promise progress and pleasure, that defy and downplay the reality of God, and overlook the subtle but radical sinfulness that lies at the root of human evil. In this book I do not make judgments as to who was, or is, a Christian and who is not. We cannot know another's heart. Judgment must be left to God. What is certain is that the Christians churches must become more effective with the spiritual formation of their people.

That all human beings, including those not yet born, are made in God's image is fundamental to the health of society. This truth is rooted in the biblical story and worldview, but it must be practiced for it to be appreciated, and it can only be practiced when Christian churches and their leaders take Jesus's command to make disciples seriously. They must *teach* the Gospel in all its fullness clearly and unapologetically and they must *act* accordingly. The need of our time is for disciples who know the biblical story, and are committed to Jesus as Savior and Lord. Disciples who are able to think Christianly, who can discern truth from untruth, and have the faith, discipline and the courage to actually obey what Jesus taught. This must include the willingness to love those in need, with actions as well as words. Support for mothers and children is paramount, as is counseling for those wounded by abortion.

Making discipleship a priority must also include a serious effort in helping parents in discipling their children. Children belong to the next generation. If they are to take up responsibility for sharing the Gospel and building a culture of life, they must become disciples of Jesus Christ. Biblically, the primary moral responsibility to disciple children belongs to parents. Practically, there is no substitute for the thousands of hours parents have to spend with their children, along with the hundreds of learning and discipling opportunities that everyday life provides. The human family remains the basic building block of every society, as well as every Christian church.

In the first half of this book I attempt to place abortion in the context of twentieth century mass violence, and shine a light on some of the ideologies that have contributed to it. This is followed by a look at the response of many Christians to the violence highlighted in the first chapters. Despite the great good that the followers of Jesus have contributed to the world, the appeasement or perpetuation of violence forms a darker strain in the life of many modern churches which suggests that some Christians—to use Shakespeare's metaphor— are like "lilies that fester, that smell far worse than weeds."³ It is a failure of discipleship.⁴ A failure I consider to be a scandal.

The second half of the book is a call to take Jesus's emphasis on discipleship with greater seriousness. It includes my reflections on the importance of the biblical story and worldview for developing personal maturity, and the unity among believers which makes the Gospel message credible. The book concludes with ideas parents could use in the process of discipling their children.

I pray that readers will be encouraged to take discipleship for themselves, their children, and their church communities with greater seriousness, and to see their life stories as a part of the great biblical story of creation, fall, redemption and restoration. Each of us has a role to play that once understood gives life significance and meaning. Effective discipleship will not bring an end to the violence and suffering caused by abortion, but it can make a genuine difference, and it can help restore credibility to the Gospel. The world is watching.

You may contact the author at:
Info@liliesthatfester.org

---

3. They have power to hurt and will do none. Sonnet 94. Available at https://www.poetryfoundation.org/45100/sonnet-94-they-that-have-power-to-hurt-and-do-none. Accessed September 16, 2022

4. Abortion is far from the only cause of disunity in Christian churches. Nor is it the only sign of ineffective discipleship. There are numerous studies which show that many Christians, including millions of conservative Christians who are most concerned for biblical authority and doctrine, live in ways nearly indecipherable from their non-Christian neighbors.

1

A Troubling Surprise
Giga-death

Contrary to its promise, the twentieth century became mankind's most bloody and hateful century, a century of hallucinatory politics and of monstrous killings. Cruelty was institutionalized to an unprecedented degree, lethality was organized on a mass production basis. The contrast between the scientific potential for good and the political evil that was actually unleashed is shocking. Never before in history was killing so globally pervasive, never before did it consume so many lives, never before was human annihilation pursued with such concentration of sustained effort on behalf of such arrogantly irrational goals

—Zbigniew Brezinzski[1]

If abortion counts as a form of violence, the West has made no progress in its treatment of children. Indeed, because effective abortion has become widely available only since the 1970s (especially, in the United States, with the 1973 Roe V. Wade Supreme Court decision), the moral state of the West hasn't improved; it has collapsed.

—Steven Pinker[2]

---

1. Brzezinski, *Out of Control*, 4–5.
2. Pinker, *Better Angels of Our Nature*, 426.

When the Lord saw that man had done much evil on earth and that his thoughts and inclinations were always evil, he was sorry that he had made man on earth, and he was grieved at heart... Now God saw that the whole world was corrupt and full of violence. In his sight the world had become corrupted, for all men had lived corrupt lives on earth.

—Genesis 6.5–6, 11(NEB)

He who finds me (Wisdom) finds life and obtains favor with the Lord, but he who misses me, injures himself; all who hate me love death.

—Proverbs 8.35–36

GREAT EXPECTATIONS

Historians note that the twentieth century began with great expectations for human progress. The continent of Europe was at peace. The industrial revolution was in full stride. The development and applications of electricity—many demonstrated at the Chicago World Fair in 1893—were expected to make life easier and better. Transportation was becoming cheaper and more accessible. Medical improvements were contributing to longer and healthier lives. Scientific discoveries promised a deeper understanding of the universe and human nature. There was a growing concern for the welfare of children and the poor. Prior to 1800 abortion was unsafe and rare. In the nineteenth century the number of abortions grew in response to the increase in medical knowledge and skill that made them safer. A better understanding of conception and pregnancy also sparked a small movement among physicians and journalists who respected the sanctity of life ethic rooted in the Judeo-Christian worldview, and led to the prohibition of abortion in scores of nations by 1900.

There were, however, substantial changes in philosophy underway. Some of these changes would lead to an erosion and reversal of the sanctity of life ethic. Philosophers of the Enlightenment had become increasingly critical of religious and political authorities. Charles Darwin's theory of evolution, and his ideas on natural selection and the survival of the fittest, first published in 1859, complemented their views, as did the writings of Herbert Spencer. Spencer developed a comprehensive evolutionary philosophy that envisioned a social Darwinism that would include ideas on economics, politics, geology, and sociology, among other things, all of them part of a powerful and continuous upward movement contributing to the survival of the fittest.[3] Francis Galton, a cousin of Darwin, would give the name "eugenics" to this movement. A growing number of scholars and scientists embraced these ideas in the last decades of the nineteenth century, not least because they were thought to undermine the biblical view of creation and the authority of the Bible, a view they considered outmoded. These individuals would help shape a secular worldview in the twentieth century, and greatly enhance the prestige and authority of science. These ideas would also bring substantial changes to the value and worth of human life.

Many liberal churchmen in America—most of them Protestants—who were at the vanguard of the social gospel movement, and critical of biblical authority, were comfortable with the growing prestige of science. Proponents of the social gospel, such as Josiah Strong, Walter Rauschenbusch and Washington Gladden, were enthusiastic about social justice efforts in the cities of America, in dealing with poverty, overcrowding, crime, and needed labor reforms. That eugenics was considered a scientific discipline bent on the improvement of the human race made it a movement somewhat easier for them to embrace. They believed that in doing so the eugenics movement would benefit not only the country but the Kingdom of God.[4]

Christians of a more conservative bent, while concerned about these changes, also looked ahead to the twentieth century with a sense of optimism.[5] In the mid-1800s, along with calling for the end of slavery, evangelical Christians were at the forefront of a variety of social ministries directed toward helping the poor, founding schools and colleges, and supporting mission efforts in cities across the country. In the twentieth century, however, disagreements between conservatives (or fundamentalists as they became known) and liberals over the issues of biblical authority and doctrine would lead to divisions within denominations and educational institutions. While liberals would increasingly assume a stronger stance with regard to social programs, conservatives would increasingly concentrate on biblical doctrine and evangelism. John R.

3. Dorrien, *Social Ethics in the Making*, 71.
4. Rosen, *Preaching Eugenics*, 14–17.
5. See Metaxas, *Amazing Grace*, for a popular accounting of the life of William Wilberforce and friends in their efforts to end the slave trade.

Mott, a noted Christian leader, speaking in Edinburgh in 1910 to a world conference of the Student Christian Movement (SCM), foresaw the evangelization of the whole world.[6]

Some of these expectations were realized. Industrialization, science and technology were to make many extraordinary advances in the twentieth century, much of it made possible by vast increases in energy production. Advances in health, communication, and medicine would extend the lifespan of countless numbers. The free market economic system would lift hundreds of millions out of poverty. The embrace of some form of democracy would empower citizens in many nations to speak up, get an education, and give voice to a support for human and civil rights. New transportation systems including air travel would make travel cheaper and safer for countless numbers. Decades later the contraceptive pill would contribute to a sexual revolution, the delay of marriage, smaller families, and a growing acceptance of abortion. The development of computers would help put a man on the moon, and put laptops and smart phones in the hands of billions. The corporations that developed these innovations would become global enterprises, making the world smaller, and the pace of life faster. America would become the world's, and history's, largest superpower.

Supporters of the social gospel would initiate many social programs around the country, and contribute to the goals of the eugenicists, e.g., in discouraging the immigration of people from southern and eastern Europe who might affect the American gene pool negatively. Though John Mott's challenge to evangelize the world was not completely fulfilled, the Christian churches of the world would undergo a huge expansion in terms of numbers. Surprisingly large increases would occur in South America, Africa and Asia. There may be as many as one hundred million Christians in Communist China. Churches in western countries, however, following considerable growth earlier in the twentieth century, have declined markedly in recent decades. At present about one third of the world's population is thought to be Christian.

A TROUBLING SURPRISE

While these advances have amazed people, the astonishing and astronomical scope of human violence unleashed early in the twentieth

---

6. Graves, "Founder of World Mission, John Mott."

century proved to be a particularly troubling surprise. Jonathan Glover in his book on the moral history of the twentieth century had this to say:

> It is a myth that barbarism is unique to the twentieth century: the whole of human history includes wars, massacres, and every kind of torture and cruelty: there are grounds for thinking that over much of the world the changes in the last hundred years or so have been towards a psychological climate more humane than at any previous time. But it is still right to say that much of twentieth-century history has been a very unpleasant surprise . Technology has made a difference. The decisions of a few people can mean horror and death for hundreds of thousands, even millions of other people. These events shock us not only by their scale. They also contrast with the expectations, at least in Europe, with which the twentieth century began.[7]

The moral calamity that was World War I involved destruction, human slaughter, and upheaval on a scale not seen before. A back cover comment from historian Christopher Clark's book, *The Sleepwalkers*, puts it succinctly: "On the morning of June 28, 1914, when Archduke Franz Ferdinand and his wife, Sophie Chotek, arrived at Sarajevo Railway Station, Europe was at peace. Thirty-seven days later, it was at war. The conflict that resulted would kill more than fifteen million people, destroy three empires, and permanently alter world history." The ineffectiveness of the national leaders involved in World War I—the "sleepwalkers" as Clark referred to them[8]—in staunching the bloodletting of this terrible war is illustrative of the fact that the achievements of the twentieth century did not include a significant advance in moral maturity.

The devastation of World War II, in terms of property damage, disruption of national boundaries, and loss of human life, turned out to be far greater. It included the Jewish Holocaust, the deliberate murder of over 5 million Jewish men, women and children, as well as the murder of half a million Gypsies (Roma). As historian Neil Ferguson noted, "Significantly larger percentages of the world's population were killed in the two world wars than had been killed in any previous conflict of comparable geopolitical magnitude."[9]

---

7. Glover. *Humanity*, 3.

8. See Clark, *The Sleepwalkers*, summary comment on back cover.

9. Ferguson, *War of the World* , xxxiv. Professor Steven Pinker disagrees, arguing that earlier conflicts such as the Mongol Conquests in the thirteenth century, and the An Lushan Revolt in China in the eighth century, extrapolated to the twentieth

Conflicts in Europe, Russia, China, the Ukrainian famine imposed by Stalin, and the Spanish Civil War, consumed the lives of millions between the wars. In the decades following World War II, there were to be other instances of violence in which millions of people lost their lives, such as occurred in India, Korea, Vietnam, the Congo and Rwanda. In his book, *Out of Control*, Zbigniew Brzezinski wrote that the scale of the twentieth century's mass murders was so great that it was difficult to comprehend, but thought that a statistical accounting could provide a sense of perspective. According to his tabulation (published in 1993) over 87 million people, both soldiers and civilians, died in twentieth-century military conflicts.[10] The huge number of civilians killed were the result of "the pervasive inclination of all combatants to view enemy civilians as legitimate targets."[11] Brzezinski also sets down the great number of civilians killed by starvation, gassing, shooting, and collectivization, apart from explicit military actions, and sets that number at 80 million people. Taken together these figures add up to 167,000,000 men, women and children killed by political and military actions.[12] Later studies tabulated by Milton Leitenberg, a specialist in arms control, and which included all of the twentieth century, put the number of deaths resulting from a "human decision" at 231 million.[13]

The numbers have continued to mount. As I write there are several conflicts in Africa with sizable casualties, as well as Russia's invasion of Ukraine, the first war in Europe since 1945. Loss of life there has been substantial, and the United Nations says over 3 million Ukrainians have become refugees. There is no end to the war in sight, and there is talk of a possible use of nuclear weapons by Russia.[14] Brzezinski's summary of twentieth century violence remains apt.

---

century were far more deadly. See his book, *Better Angels of Our Nature*, 192–200. Pinker, as with other historians, does not include abortion in the death tolls he cites.

10. Brzezinski, *Out of Control*, 7–17.

11. Brzezinski, *Out of Control*, 10.

12. Brzezinski, *Out of Control*, 17. This figure includes the estimated 60 million people who died largely of starvation during China's Great Leap Forward, and the one million Armenians murdered by the Turks during World War. It was considered by many as the century's first genocide.

13. Leitenberg, *Deaths in War and Political Conflicts in the 20th Century*, 14.

14. A study done for the United Nations points out that since 2011 there has been a sharp increase from 41 armed conflicts in 2014, to 50 such conflicts in 2015, most of them in the Middle East and Africa. Nearly 90 percent of the casualties have been civilian. See Marc, "Conflict and violence in the 21st century." During the George W.

Contrary to its promise, the twentieth century became mankind's most bloody and hateful century, a century of hallucinatory politics and of monstrous killings. Cruelty was institutionalized to an unprecedented degree, and lethality was organized on a mass production basis. The contrast between the scientific potential for good and the political evil that was actually unleashed is shocking. Never before in history was killing so globally pervasive, never before did it consume so many lives, never before was human annihilation pursued with such concentration of sustained effort on behalf of such arrogantly irrational goals.[15]

GIGADEATH

The massive loss of life tabulated by Brzezinski, Leitenberg, and other scholars with regard to modern violence is horrendous. But it is notable for a significant omission: the deaths due to *abortion*.[16] It is right that these lives should be included, for each unborn child killed by abortion is a human being made in the image of God. According to the data collected by W. Jacobson and William Robert Johnston in their book, *Abortion Worldwide Report (AWR)*, in the period from 1920, when abortion was first legalized in Russia, until 2015, there have been 1.02 billion abortions. Jacobson and Johnson say of their work, "[T]his is a sacred accounting of their lives, presented from a Judeo-Christian and moral perspective of the sanctity of human life."[17] We must make an effort to remember, and to honor, the preborn lives because they matter. They should matter to

---

Bush administration, violence in the Sudan eventually led to Secretary of State Colin Powell to label the violence there—largely Muslim attacks on Christians living in the southern part of the country—"genocide." Sadly, the Christian community in the West paid it relatively little attention.

15. Brzezinski, *Out of Control*, 4–5. Psychologist Steven Pinker disagrees. He argues that the twentieth century is to be noted not for violence, but for progress brought about by the Enlightenment. See Pinker, "Enlightenment Is Working," WSJ, C1. (his emphasis)

16. See for example Johnson, *Modern Times*, Snyder, *Bloodlands*, Ferguson, *War of the World*.

17. Jacobson and Johnston, *Abortion Worldwide Report*, 85. This report is the result of many years of meticulous effort to compile data and ensure its accuracy. Such a compilation also has many other applications, e.g., for relating to the demographic, health, and other policy consequences of abortion. Part IV includes information on how the data on abortion was obtained, such as official government sources, intergovernmental organizations (e.g., the United Nations), and peer-reviewed publications.

us, and most certainly they matter to God. He remembers them: "Can a woman forget her sucking child, that she should have no compassion on the son of her womb? Even these may forget, yet I will not forget you. Behold, I have graven you on the palms of my hand (Isaiah 49.15–16a)." One of the best ways to honor the preborn dead is to give our best and prayerful efforts to ending the scourge of abortion.

Jacobson and Johnson calculate that globally there are approximately 15 million abortions a year, for an average of nearly 40,000 preborn human beings destroyed every single day. Each one is a living human being, deliberately destroyed in cold blood.[18] The death toll resulting from abortion in this century far exceeds that of any other period in history. Brzezinski referred to the twentieth century as the century of *megadeath*, the death of millions, but it was in fact the century of *gigadeath*—the death of a *billion* or more individuals. There has never been anything like this authorized, bureaucratized, mechanized destruction of human life in the history of the world.

Abortion is a form of violence that is often personal and hands-on, in which an abortionist (usually a physician) uses one of a variety of procedures to kill a living preborn human being growing within the mother's womb. Every procedure is brutal. Saline abortions, used in the eighties and early nineties, introduced a salt solution into the uterus which killed the preborn child by burning its skin and lungs. Suction abortions, done up to 12 weeks, tear the body of the preborn baby apart through the force of the suction device. Dilation and evacuation abortions dismember the preborn baby piece by piece through use of a clasping device. Chemical abortion is used in the first 70 days, and involves two pills, one which prevents the preborn child from attaching to the uterus and receiving nourishment, and a second which causes the womb to expel the dead fetus. This is now the most popular procedure, because a woman can use it at home without medical assistance.[19]

18. Thomas Jacobson, in a phone call with me (October 2, 2020), noted that changes in reporting from China have led them to revise the figure of 12 million abortions worldwide in a year given in their report, upward to about 14.6 million. Jacobson and Johnston emphasize that their figures, as much as possible, rely on hard data and not estimates. The World Health Organization gives a figure of 56 million abortions worldwide a year, while the Guttmacher Institute figure is 73 million abortions yearly, both based on estimates that Jacobson considers to be unreliable. Jacobson, who worked with the United Nations on behalf of Focus on the Family, has worked with Johnston in establishing a data bank that is truly reliable.

19. "Abortion Techniques," National Right to Life. See https://www.nrlc.com/abortion/medicalfacts/techniiques/.

Dilation and extraction abortions (often called partial-birth abortions), done in the third trimester, are particularly controversial because they can be performed up to the time of birth. They are complicated procedures, and are relatively rare. This procedure moves the preborn child through the birth canal until only the head remains inside the mother. The abortionist then punctures the head with scissors, and suctions out the brain, allowing the skull to collapse and be removed. This procedure was banned by President Bush in November 2003, but was largely limited in practice to federal facilities. It remains in practice in eight states: Alaska, Colorado, New Hampshire, New Mexico, Oregon, Vermont, New York and the District of Columbia.[20]

There is a debate as to when fetal pain is first felt, but there is little question that very large numbers of preborn human beings die in pain. As one abortionist noted of saline abortions, the thrashing about of the fetus in the womb once the saline is introduced is clear evidence of the distress it experiences.[21] Human Life International, commenting on fetal pain, says, "These inhumane death procedures would not be acceptable for any animal, yet they are used regularly to kill the most innocent and fragile human beings."[22]

The brutal destruction of preborn human beings is a massive violation of human rights which, morally and legally, should concern every citizen and every Christian. This is important not only in terms of their inherent status as human beings, but in order that the human dignity and worth of all human beings, now and in the future, be accorded the protection and respect due them as creatures made in the image of God. The continued legalization of abortion gives momentum to the efforts to legalize infanticide, as well as the euthanizing of those who are terminally or even chronically ill. At present seven nations have authorized euthanasia in some form. The United States has not legalized euthanasia, though eight American states and the District to Columbia have right-to-die laws, in which individuals may request medical help in dying.[23] This state

20. Brown, "Late-term abortion: It happens and it needs to stop." See https://www.liveaction.org/news/late-term-abortion-needs-to-end-in-america/.

21. "What are the Different Types of Abortion?" See https://choicesresource.com/fetal-pain-is-a-reason-to-end-abortion?; https://womenscaremedicalcenter.org/what-are-different-types-of-abortion?'

22. "Fetal Pain Is a Reason to End Abortion," See https://www.hli.org/resources/fetal-pain-reason-to-end-abotion/

23. See *World Population Review,* at https://worldpopulationreview.com/state-rankings/right-to-die-states.

of affairs was not always the case. In Part II of the *AWR* the editors document the fact that during the period from 1803 to 1918 seventy nations enacted laws prohibiting abortion. This number eventually climbed to 86 by the year 2015, either strengthening an earlier law, or enacting their first prohibition. However, beginning with the Soviet Union's authorization of abortion in 1920, forty-two of these nations would reverse their position and authorize abortion, including most countries in Europe, and the United States. As of 2016 one hundred thirty-six nations have authorized abortion in some manner.[24] Communist regimes account for nearly 65 percent of all the abortions documented by Jacobson and Johnston.[25]

In the United States the rights of unborn children were honored in most states until the *Roe v Wade* and *Doe v Bolton* decisions by the Supreme Court on January 22, 1973 removed them in favor of an expansion of options for pregnant women.[26] Since those decisions there have been 64 million unborn children destroyed by abortion; a horrific shedding of innocent blood. This is all the more horrific given the fact that over half of these abortions were sought by mothers (and many fathers) who consider themselves to be Christians, which is an issue to be explored more fully in later chapters.

The Court's *Roe* decision asserted that the fetus—the preborn individual—had *no constitutional rights*, though it did establish some limits to abortion. In the first trimester, the state provided *no protection* for the preborn; in the second trimester the state may regulate abortion to protect *only the mother's health*; in the third trimester the state could regulate, and even prohibit, abortion out of concern for the preborn's "potential life," though abortion even then was permitted should the mother's health or life be endangered.[27]

---

24. Jacobson and Johnston, *Abortion Worldwide Report*, 43–45.

25. Jacobson and Johnston, *Abortion Worldwide Report*, 201. In Part VII of the *AWR* it is reported that in the People's Republic of China 381.4 million abortions took place between 1956 and 2015. The Soviet Union, while it lasted, recorded 278.5 million abortions between 1920 and 1991.

26. Arizona, California, Colorado, and North Carolina were considering abortion laws less restrictive in the late 1960s. Alaska, Hawaii, Washington and New York by 1970 had passed laws that basically legalized abortion on demand. See Young, "Life Before Roe." Accessed 7/16/22 at https://www.ewtn.com/catholicism/library/life-before-roe-a-brief-survey-of-us-abortion-laws-before-the-1973-decision-12100.

27. U. S. Conference of Catholic Bishops. "Summary of Roe v. Wade and other key abortion cases," 1.

In *Doe v. Bolton* the Court ruled that if a woman sought an abortion for reasons of health, it could not be prohibited. The definition of health used by the Court was inclusive: "[A]ll factors—physical, emotional, psychological, familial, and the woman's age—are relevant to the well-being of the patient." This broad view of health (ultimately determined by the woman herself) allowed abortion throughout the pregnancy—even into the ninth month. This opened the door to what became known as partial-birth abortion, a procedure that allowed a fetus to be partially delivered before killing it.[28]

Prolife challenges on the state and federal levels led in succeeding decades to a number of restrictions on abortion. The appointment of several conservative judges to the Supreme Court during the presidency of Donald Trump, prompted multiple states to codify laws that would maintain the legality of abortion. New York State, for example, due to concerns over possible restrictions on abortion, fashioned a law that would permit abortions for any reason up to 24 weeks, and up to the time of birth if a woman's health or pregnancy was at risk. This law, which became effective on January 22, 2019, the forty-sixth anniversary of the *Roe v Wade*, also moved abortion from the penal code to the section dealing with health statutes, and authorized midwives and physicians' assistants to perform certain abortions.[29]

The recent Supreme Court decision in *Dobbs v. Jackson Women's Health*, in overturning earlier decisions—*Roe v. Wade* and *Planned Parenthood v. Casey*—did not prohibit abortion, but returned the abortion issue to all 50 states. Since the decision, there has been a flurry of activity including protests, marches, and attacks on crisis pregnancy centers by those angered by this decision. Among those opposed is President Biden, who signed an executive order on July 8, 2022 designed to protect health care workers (those who work at facilities which do abortions) and to safeguard access to healthcare centers (facilities where abortions take place). Other federal agencies also mandated similar actions. Health and Human Services, for example, cautioned the nation's pharmacies to

---

28. A partial-birth abortion, or dilation and extraction abortion, as noted above is rare. This is primarily due to the fetus's larger size, which may weigh a pound or more. Because of he increased risk of compilations not many physicians do them, though a few have actually specialized in them. One who did was Dr. William Rashbaum, who claimed he had done 19,000 abortions between 1979 and 1996. See https://healthresearchfunding.org/18-amazing-partial-birth-abortion-statistics. Accessed February 28, 2023.

29. O'Kane, "New York passes law allowing abortion at any time if mother's health is at risk."

provide requested medications regarding healthcare, meaning medications that could be used for chemical abortions.[30]

States favoring abortion, including New York, Illinois and California, are prepared to take steps legislatively and through the courts, to sustain the legality of abortion.[31] In the states where abortion was legal, abortion continues. Some advocates are willing to go to extreme lengths. In 2019 Amelia Bonow, in response to an effort in Congress to defund Planned Parenthood, helped found a social media movement (now worldwide) called Shout Your Abortion through which women can share their personal story. This movement encourages the normalization of abortion, and continued access to it—whether or not it is legal.[32]

States favoring the protection of unborn life have celebrated the decision. A number of states, among them Kentucky, South Dakota, Mississippi, Utah and Wyoming, had trigger laws ready to be activated should Roe be overturned. A number of other states also favor protection of the unborn. Fortunately, some of the new restrictions and laws in states where the sanctity of life ethic prevails will save thousands of preborn lives.

The basic argument in support of abortion is that it does not involve the taking of a human life, or if it does, it cannot be taken to mean the death of a human *person*, given the primitive state of the preborn child at the time of its destruction. But the argument made here, on the basis of medical science, is that the unborn or preborn child—zygote, blastocyst, embryo, fetus—is a human being.[33] Though primitive biologically, the preborn individual is *ontologically* the same being throughout its life span—from conception to natural death. As such every preborn human being is a bearer of rights that deserve to be protected by law, as was the case in most Western nations until the mid-twentieth century. Being human, their lives deserve to be honored, and their destruction deserves to be noted and lamented along with the millions of others lost to mass

---

30. See Kiesewetter, "The Federal Government's Response in the Wake of the Dobbs v Jackson Women's Health Supreme Court Decision, Foreword, July 15, 2022, at htpps://2022/07/the-federal-governments-response-in-the-wake-of-the-dobbs-v-jackson-womens-health-supreme-court-decision/. Accessed July 20, 2022.

31. See https://statecapitollobbgyist.com/2022/07/07/states-reaction-ti=supreme-courts-dobbs-ruling-abortion-access-trigger-laws-more/. Accessed July 20, 2022.

32. Available at https://shout yourabortion.com. Accessed July 20, 2022.

33. *The Human Life Review* has promoted the sacredness of human life since its founding in 1975. J. C. Willke, Francis Beckwith, Hadley Arkes, John Noonan, Jean Garton, Marvin Olasky, Michael Gorman, Frank Pavone, and Ronald Reagan, are just a few of the notable authors who have written for this journal.

killings. To do so is to bear witness to the depth of understanding that the gospel of Jesus Christ gives to the sanctity of human life.

To take note of the mass killings of the modern world, including those of the preborn, particularly in Western lands, necessarily means taking seriously Brzezinski's observation of a "massive collapse of moral values," a phenomenon associated with the declining role of religion in defining and upholding moral values.[34] In America this has meant a dismissal and denigration of moral law widely held from the time of founders until the late nineteenth and early twentieth centuries. This view of moral law, often referred to as the natural law, was thought to be understandable through human reason, and compatible with divine law. Thomas Jefferson, in the eloquent opening words of the *Declaration of Independence,* affirmed this truth: "We hold these truths to be self-evident, that all men are created equal, that they are endowed by their Creator with certain unalienable rights." Abraham Lincoln considered the *Declaration of Independence* with its assertion that all people are created equal the moral bedrock of the American experiment. Many Americans who hold to the sanctity of human life believe that this assertion also applies clearly to the right of the preborn child to live.[35]

Steven Pinker, neither pro-life nor an advocate of natural law, noted in his book, *The Better Angels of Our Nature,* that in 2003 there were about 17 million abortions worldwide, and added this telling comment:

---

34. Brzezinski, *Out of Control,* x.

35. Protestant Christians have often ignored, or downplayed, natural law, which many consider a Catholic issue. This was not generally true of the Reformers, such as Luther, Calvin Zwingli and Melanchthon, who affirmed the natural law as rooted in biblical theology. St Paul, in his letter to the Christians in Rome, in his consideration of God's judgment of those who have the law, the Jews, and those who do not, the Gentiles, wrote: "When Gentiles who have not the law do by nature what the law requires, they are a law to themselves, even though they do not have the law. They show that what the law requires is written on their hearts, while their conscience also bears witness and their conflicting thoughts accuse or perhaps excuse them on that day when, according to my gospel, God judges the secrets of men by Christ Jesus" (Rom 2.14–16). Though the human heart is corrupt, it does not mean that human beings are totally incapable of moral reasoning. Those who uphold this view of moral law see it as common ground, a place where Catholics and Protestants can stand together in defending the right of the preborn child to live. J. Darryl Charles in an article on the thought of Abraham Kuyper—the well-known Reformed public intellectual and politician (1837–1920)—argues that Kuyper's affirmation of natural law, which he understood to be an important biblical insight, meant that Protestants and Catholics—despite their genuine theological differences—could work together on issues of common concern. See Charles, "The Kuyperian Option," 25–26.

"If abortion counts as a form of violence, the West has made no progress in its treatment of children. Indeed, because effective abortion has become widely available only since the 1970s (especially, in the United States, with the 1973 *Roe V. Wade* Supreme Court decision), the moral state of the West hasn't improved; it has collapsed."[36] Pinker does *not* in fact believe that this is the case, citing the tendency for many proponents of abortion to think that only with the arrival of consciousness does the life of the fetus count. Still, as he admits, "we might expect a general distaste for the destruction of any kind of living thing to turn people away from abortion even when they don't equate it with murder."[37]

Abortion, whether considered murder or not, is the most effective source of violence in the world. Few of the victims targeted by it escape, for they cannot speak for or protect themselves. Those who should—their parents and the governing authorities—support the executioners. The upholders of the ethic of life—the faith communities—often remain bystanders. The brutal treatment of the preborn is a silent, invisible holocaust which has affected the soul of nations and cultures. It has lessened respect for life in general, and has calloused the hearts and minds of untold numbers of people around the world.

The harmful influence of abortion is pervasive. In the words of Ryan Anderson and Alexandra DeSanctis, abortion is "tearing us apart." Their newly published book of that title provides a detailed overview of the ways in which abortion distorts and harms the institutions of our country.[38]

The citing of statistics regarding the large-scale violence of modern times (no matter how it occurred) obscures the personal losses that were, and are, involved. To make sense of these things—for numbers in the millions and billions cannot adequately be comprehended—a look is required at the experience of individuals and their personal stories. In his book, *Bloodlands,* Historian Timothy Snyder makes this point in writing of the millions of individuals murdered by Stalin and Hitler in Eastern Europe. I believe that his words also apply to the great number of individuals destroyed by abortion:

> "Each record of death suggests, but cannot supply, a unique life. We must be able not only to reckon the number of deaths but to reckon with each victim as an individual. The one very large

---

36. Pinker, *Better Angels of Our Nature,* 426.
37. Pinker, *Better Angel of Our Natures,* 427.
38. See Anderson and DeSanctis, *Tearing Us Apart.*

number that withstands scrutiny is that of the Holocaust, with its 5.7 million Jewish dead, 5.4 of whom were killed by the Germans. But this number, like all of the others, must be seen not as 5.7 million, which is an abstraction few of us can grasp, but as 5.7 million *times one*."[39]

Few of the billion or so preborn human beings destroyed by abortion have been given a name. But they were—like those lost in the killing fields of Poland and Ukraine—individual human beings conceived, knit together and nurtured in their mother's womb, as all human beings are. There are survivors who can bear witness.

Several years ago my wife, Carol, and ID met a young woman who had survived an abortion. Her name is Melissa Ohden. An abortion meant to destroy her before birth—before she could be known and loved as every child should be—had failed. I remember looking at this young woman and thinking that, at the most vulnerable point in her life and innocent of any wrong-doing, there was a deliberate attempt by a highly trained medical team at a reputable hospital in Iowa to kill her.

Several years ago Melissa spoke at our church and shared the story of her birth mother's unexpected pregnancy, and her maternal grandmother's determined effort to see that her daughter had an abortion. Melissa's grandmother, a nurse, was present when Melissa, very unexpectedly, was delivered alive. The saline infusion abortion having failed to kill her, her grandmother wanted the newborn—her own granddaughter—to be left alone to die (not an uncommon fate for many children who survive an abortion). Providentially, another nurse, noticing the newborn gasping for breath, rushed the baby to the hospital neonatal intensive care unit. It was determined that Melissa was well over two pounds in birth weight, and very probably seven months in gestational age. Despite a number of complications, Melissa thrived. When strong enough to leave the hospital, she was placed in a foster home, and was later adopted by a loving family. Only at age 14 did she learn that had survived abortion. Eventually she found and met her birth mother and other family members. From them she learned that her mother had in fact wanted to have her baby, but had been strongly pressured by her own mother to undergo

---

39. Snyder, *Bloodlands*, 407–8. The "Bloodlands" is a word Snyder has given to the area in Eastern Europe (Central Poland, Western Russia, Ukraine, Belarus and the Baltic States) where over a period of ten or twelve years 14 million human beings were put to death by the Nazi and Soviet regimes.

the abortion. Despite the trauma of abortion, Melissa Ohden is healthy, married, the mother of two children, and an author.

Not surprisingly, Melissa is strongly prolife. In 2012 she founded the Abortion Survivors Network. Though very rare, there are survivors of abortion, and they deserve support. An outspoken pro-life feminist, she has appeared before Congress, on various media programs, and before audiences throughout the nation. She tells her story in the book, *You Carried Me*. Every human being who is aborted is an individual who, like Melissa Ohden, bears the image of God, and if allowed to survive, has their own unique contribution to make to their family and the world.

The struggles Melissa faced with emotional pain were severe—shame and hurt at having been aborted, guilt at having survived when so many millions have not, and eventually joy when reconciliation with her birth mother and others of her family became a reality. In describing her experience she referred to the words Joseph used upon meeting the brothers who had left him for dead: "As for you, you meant evil against me; but God meant it for good, to bring it about that many people should be kept alive, as they are today (Genesis 50.20)." It is Melissa Ohden's hope and prayer that her experience, and those of other abortion survivors, will enable many to see abortion for the deadly and ungodly procedure that it is, and contribute to a world in which abortion is unthinkable, and truly rare.

No one can foretell what any individual might make of their lives, whether born or pre-born, nor the joy he or she might bring to others, but it is obvious that their death ends every possibility. Human beings are the greatest resource we have. The cold-blooded and assembly-line destruction of millions upon millions of human beings, and the contributions they would undoubtedly have made through their relationships with family and friends, and the use of their intelligence and creativity, constitutes an enormous loss to the human community.

In remembering the humanity of the unborn child, we must never forget the mother and father. Facing an unplanned and unexpected pregnancy can be extraordinarily difficult, especially for the mother who will carry the child. A pregnancy brings great responsibilities, and pregnancy sooner or later becomes public. While the stigma of pregnancy outside of marriage has decreased sharply, there are many women who would be embarrassed or ashamed at having their pregnancy become known. Maintaining the pregnancy and being mindful of all that makes for the health of mother and child is no small matter. The cost of a pregnancy is also no small matter, and the child once born (if not given in adoption) will require many years of support for food, clothing, shelter, health-care, recreation, and education. This is often a concern for couples as well as many unmarried women. Dealing with the interruption of personal plans, such as for education or career, can be wrenching. Many relationships, perhaps more frequently for single women who become mothers, are shaken. Significant numbers of men, particularly (but not only) unmarried men, are very reluctant to assume the responsibilities of fatherhood. Many pressure the woman by threatening to leave the relationship if she will not abort their child. There may also be pressures from parents, grandparents, and friends, who think abortion is the better choice, for any number of reasons.

That abortion is legal is another factor which contributes to the stress involved in facing an unplanned pregnancy. Why, say its advocates, should a woman or man feel guilty or grieve over something that is not unlawful? Why should they be troubled over the elimination of a tiny, primitive human being if, as many believe, it is not a person, but just a "product of conception," and an intolerable burden? Moreover, every child should be wanted, and if they are not, it would be better for them not to exist than to enter life and be unwanted and unloved. Furthermore, should a pregnancy test suggest an abnormality, the point is made that life for a handicapped child would be very difficult. An abortion would forestall their suffering, not to mention the cost and difficulty of caring for such a child. These are just a few of the arguments that are given to mothers and fathers faced with an unplanned pregnancy. Another factor, particularly for unwed mothers who identify with a Christian community in some way, is the thought that their church community would be more inclined to judge her than help her.[40] This too is part of the scandal of Christian discipleship, to be explored further in later chapters.

Author Frederica Matthews-Green, today pro-life, was once a passionate advocate of abortion. In a series of conversations with women from different backgrounds and circumstances in cities around the country, she learned something that all who uphold the sanctity of human life must always keep in mind: abortion is harmful to women, and deeply hurtful. As she learned from these conversations, "There was nearly always a complex nest of problems, affecting both [the mother's] material situation and her emotional well-being." Another theme that became

---

40. This will be discussed further in chapter three.

clear was that "In nearly every case the abortion was undertaken to fulfill a felt obligation to another person, a parent or boyfriend ... the woman felt bound to please or protect some other person, and abortion was the price she felt she had to pay."[41]

Whatever the motivations, it is clear that many individuals who have experienced an abortion are troubled and suffer from some form of post-traumatic stress. There is a growing body of documented evidence demonstrating that a great many of those who choose to have an abortion are devastated by the experience.[42] One such study reported in the *British Journal of Psychiatry* was a meta-analysis of 22 studies worldwide done between 1985 and 2009. The study, carried out by Priscilla Coleman, was carefully crafted to avoid bias by comparing mental problems of different groups, e.g., women who had abortions, women who did not, women who carried a child to term, and women who got pregnant unintentionally and carried their child to term. These studies altogether involved 877,181 women, of whom 163,831 had abortions. The results were significant: women who had experienced abortion suffered greater mental health problems, including higher rates of depression, alcohol and drug abuse, and suicidal tendencies. Coleman's conclusion:

> This review offers the largest quantitative estimate of mental health risks associated with abortion available in the world literature. Calling into question the conclusions from traditional reviews, the results revealed a moderate to highly increased risk of mental health problems after abortion. Consistent with the tenets of evidence-based medicine, this information should inform the delivery of abortion service.[43]

---

41. Mathewes-Green, *Real Choices*, 33. This book offers some of the deepest insights into the decisions women make regarding abortion, as well as providing a number of practical suggestions for helping them.

42. Depression, self-loathing, food disorders, and the use of drugs and alcohol are not uncommon. Theresa Burke, while in graduate school studying to become a psychotherapist, led a support group for women who were struggling with eating disorders. The group took an unexpected turn when one member of the group revealed that she was disturbed by memories of an abortion. Her confession sparked that of others. As it turned out, six of the eight women in the group had had an abortion. Further discussion and research led Dr. Burke to the conclusion that some of the personal struggles that women who've aborted face, such as eating disorders, are tied to the abortion. Burke, et al, believes that sexual trauma can also lead to a variety of sexual struggles. See Burke with Reardon, *Hidden Grief,*, xiv.

43. Coleman, "Abortion and Mental Health: quantitative synthesis and analysis of research published 1995—2009," abstract.

Coleman's follow-up literature review of all studies done worldwide on the effect of abortion on the mental health of women between 1993 and 2018 found that 49 of the 75 studies reviewed showed a definite correlation between abortion and adverse mental health outcomes.[44] Several pro-abortion scholars replicated her studies and found that there was indeed an association between abortion and an increased risk of "anxiety, alcohol misuse, illicit drug use/misuse, and suicidal behavior."[45] Hopefully such research will become widely publicized, and give both abortion providers and the women (and men) seeking an abortion serious pause for thought.

Studies and statistics are of great importance in understanding the harm that abortion causes, but stories are also helpful in showing the personal, and lasting, impact of abortion. In 1988, writer Monica Miller and several friends discovered the bodily remains of over one thousand aborted children on the loading dock of a pathology lab in a northern Illinois town. They retrieved the bodies and gave them a Christian burial, entrusting them to God. A few weeks later Miller returned to the cemetery and the grave site of these innocents. The flowers they had left at the site, though shriveled, remained. With them there was now a small plastic bag in which was a toy rabbit. Attached to the rabbit's paw was a note from a young mother written to the baby she had aborted.

> Please forgive me and maybe someday I can forgive myself. I'll always wonder what you would have been, what you would have become. I can't stop hating myself right now, regretting the hardest decision I've ever made in my life, wishing now I could do it differently. But I can't. I will always remember this. It was a tough lesson to learn. I pray to God and to you to forgive me so I can go on with my life, and I swear to you and the Lord that I will never ever do it again. Please forgive me so I can let go and go on.[46]

In my own experience as a pastoral counselor I met and worked with a number of women and men who expressed regret over an abortion. Finding forgiveness, healing and peace is often difficult for them, for memories remain despite the desire to forget. Drugs, alcohol, self-harm,

---

44. See American Association of Pro-Life Obstetricians and Gynecologists, "Abortion and Mental Health," Practice Bulletin No.7, December 2019, 4, https://aaplog.org/wp-content/uploads/2019/12/FINAL-Abortion-Mental-Halth.PB&.pdf.
45. Anderson and DeSanctis, *Tearing Us Apart*, 87–88.
46. Miller, "Severed ties," 26.

and self-loathing are not uncommon. Two individuals I worked with recounted experiences that predated the Supreme Court's Roe v Wade decision by decades. Both had driven a considerable distance to meet with me, a stranger, concerned that their secret remain hidden from family and friends. The first was a woman in her seventies. Though a Christian for most of her life, she confessed that as a young wife she had an affair with her physician which resulted in her becoming pregnant. To hide the affair—and save her marriage—she consented to have her physician/lover abort their child. The marriage was saved, but her emotional distress (by the time I met her) had persisted for over forty years. Though she had confessed everything to God on her own she remained troubled. I was the first person she had ever actually spoken with about the affair and the abortion. Though deeply embarrassed, she found that being able to talk openly about her experience was a relief. Her repentance and confession, and the assurance of God's forgiveness, eventually brought her the healing and peace she needed.

The other individual was a man, also in his seventies, burdened with a secret that had troubled him greatly for much of his life. Decades earlier, when in his thirties, he had performed abortions even though he lacked medical training. The abortions were done in a local funeral parlor to which he had access. What particularly tormented him was the fact that one of the abortions he had performed killed the preborn infant he himself had fathered, and whose tiny body he burned after the abortion to destroy it completely. Though a Christian at the time we met, his guilt over these actions was such that he found it difficult to live with himself. As with the older woman, he had never revealed these experiences to another person. Talking things out was a painful process, but thankfully, through confession, repentance and prayer, this man was also able to experience God's forgiveness and healing. It is fair to say that stories such as this are far from untypical.

The reality of post-traumatic stress resulting from abortion has been met with a number of supportive ministries. Two of the leaders in the forefront of providing support for those women and men affected by some form of post-abortion trauma in the United States are Theresa Burke and David Reardon. Burke, founder of Rachel's Vineyard, a post-abortion training and healing ministry, and Reardon, a post-abortion researcher, put their concerns and insights into the book, *Hidden Grief*. The book does not make the claim that all women or men who have gone through an abortion respond in the same way. They do claim, as do other therapists and scholars, that abortion does have a profoundly negative impact—usually a long-term impact—on large numbers of those who have experienced it. They emphasize, further, that the Christian churches have a great responsibility to help bring hope and healing to those who are struggling with the aftermath of aborting their own preborn child.[47] Another ministry that provides support is Silent No More, co-founded by Georgette Forney and Janet Morana in 2002. Forney found that sharing her abortion story brought a measure of healing. Seeing that doing so encouraged others, she and Morana developed a format that provided a way for women and men grieving from abortion to share their stories, as well as demonstrate to those who listened that abortion is a devastating experience. Nearly 7000 women, and a growing number of men, have shared their abortion testimonies in gatherings held in all 50 states, and 17 other countries. Thousands of these testimonies are available for viewing on their website.[48]

Another side of abortion is the physical danger it poses to women. A study first published in *The Lancet* (published in 2006), and later by the World Health Organization, stated that there are millions of unsafe abortions worldwide every year, a problem they labeled as a "preventable pandemic." Such abortions are usually lacking in hygiene, medical expertise, and medical treatment. Difficulties such as infection, perforated organs, and failure to remove all parts of the fetus, are common, and often life-threatening. Great numbers of women are left with lasting health issues, including infertility. This study claims that nearly 68,000 women die each year from unsafe abortions, most of them in developing countries.[49] This, and related studies acknowledge that these figures are estimates, and may be inflated due to the inability of governing authorities to provide accurate statistics. The World Health Organization and the United Nations, not surprisingly, recommend more lenient laws pertaining to abortion.[50]

---

47. See also Burke, et al., *Redeeming a Father's Heart*; Condon and Hazard, *Fatherhood Aborted*; Pierson, *Mending Hearts, Mending Lives*; Reardon, *The Jericho Plan.*; Reardon, *Aborted Women. Silent No More*; Shaver, *Gianna*; Stanford, *Will I Cry Tomorrow?*

48. Forney is President of Anglicans for Life, and Morana the Executive Director for Priests for Life. *The Human Life Review* recently carried an interview with Forney that details the efforts of the Silent No More Awareness Campaign. "Silent No More": An Interview with Georgette Forney, Spring 2022, 32–36. See https://silentnomoreawarenessawareness.org.

49. Grimes, "Unsafe Abortion," 1-2.

50. Grimes, "Unsafe Abortion," 1-2. See also, UN News, "Some 25 million unsafe

All authorities, including those who oppose abortion, would argue that better education, better health care, and the wise use of contraception would be helpful.

Health care in the United States and Europe is significantly better than that provided in developing countries. Still, many abortions in western nations are done in abortion facilities where the standard of care is lower than that of certified medical centers. In a number of them woman face a serious risk to their physical well-being. The story of Karnamaya Mongar, a young Indian woman living in Virginia, is a case in point. In November 2009, Ms. Mongar went to a small clinic in Philadelphia to get an abortion. She and her family were immigrants to the United States from Bhutan. In early November she learned she was pregnant. Believing her family could not support another child she decided on an abortion. Unable to obtain one in Virginia where she lived, and being over fourteen weeks pregnant, she learned of the clinic run by Dr. Kermit Gosnell at 3801 Lancaster Avenue in West Philadelphia. On the evening of November 20, Dr. Gosnell performed the abortion. During the procedure Mongar developed breathing difficulties. Eventually an ambulance was called and she was taken to the University of Pennsylvania Hospital where, despite heroic efforts, she died. It would be determined that her death was due to the medical incompetence of Gosnell and his staff.[51]

The clinic at 3801 Lancaster Avenue turned out to be a little house of horrors. When police raided the clinic looking into illegal drug sales, they discovered an abortion clinic in which many other illegal activities had taken place. It was unbelievably filthy, and managed by a staff of men and women who were untrained and unlicensed by the Pennsylvania Department of Health. It would be determined that there had been multiple violations of drug and medical care, including many illegal late-term abortions. Pennsylvania law at that time allowed abortions to be performed up to twenty-three weeks and six days. Gosnell had done numerous abortions after the legal limit, stating that he thought abortions were legal up to twenty-six weeks.[52]

One can argue that clinics like Gosnell's are atypical. But there is evidence that many other such clinics across the United States have failed

---

abortions occur each year UN health agency warns."

51. McElhinney and McAleer, see chapter 5, "The Indian Woman." Though death is rare, physical damage to women's reproductive health is not uncommon.

52. McElhinney and McAleer, *Gosnell*, see chapter 1, "From Drug Bust to House of Horrors."

to meet modern medical standards. According to a recent report by the Pennsylvania Family Institute, 60 percent of the state's abortion facilities failed a health safety inspection in 2019.[53] An abortion facility not far from the state capitol in Harrisburg, PA was closed in 2017 due to continuing violations of Pennsylvania health laws, despite the fact that they were given extra time to clean up their operations following a warning from the Department of Health.[54] I believe that one reason for the shoddy clinical and medical care that is not uncommon in such facilities is due to the fact that the work being done there is focused on death, carried out by personnel whose worldview not only precludes respect for the dignity and worth of preborn human beings, but is also quite willing to kill them. Another reason reported by abortionists is that doing abortions is profitable. OB-GYN physician, Dr. Kathi Aultman in an op-ed for *USA Today* admitted that doing abortions—including dismemberment abortions for which she had sought training—was more profitable than work as an ER physician. Now prolife, she shared her concern over treatment at abortion facilities, which she claims is often shoddy, and made more problematic because follow-up for women who may have complications is non-existent in many states.[55]

Abby Johnson's story provides yet another perspective on the harm that abortion brings. As the successful director of a Planned Parenthood facility in Texas, and a post-abortive woman, she found the work meaningful until the day she was asked to assist with an abortion procedure by handling an ultrasound probe. Though reluctant, she consented. Holding the probe on the mother's abdomen once the procedure started she recognized a perfectly formed profile of a baby. "Thirteen weeks," said the nurse who assisted the doctor. It reminded her of seeing an ultrasound of her own child born several years before. Then the image of the abortion cannula appeared, clearly visible on the ultrasound screen. Horrified, and yet fascinated by what she was seeing, she observed the cannula probe the baby's side. In Abby Johnson's words:

---

53. "PFI Briefing: 2020 State of Abortion in Pennsylvania." Available at https://pafamily.org/wp-context/2020/05/2020-State—of-Abortion-in Pennsylvania-Report-pdf/.

54. The health and safety violations of the Hillcrest abortion facility covered 44 pages. Htpps://vimeo.com/231514526.

55. Aultman, "Why I am no longer an abortionist," Focus on the Family, January 16, 2020. https://focusonthefamily,com/pro-life/kathi-aultman-why-i-am-no-longer-an-abortionist.

My head was working hard to control my responses, but I couldn't shake an inner disquiet, that was quickly mounting to horror as I watched the screen. The next movement was the sudden jerk of a tiny foot as the baby started kicking, as if trying to move away from the probing invader. As the cannula pressed in, the baby began struggling to turn and twist away. It seemed clear to me that the fetus could feel the cannula and did not like the feeling. And then the doctor's voice broke through, startling me. "Beam me up, Scotty," he said lightheartedly to the nurse. He was telling her to turn on the suction—in an abortion the suction isn't turned on until the doctor feels he has the cannula in exactly the right place. I had a sudden urge to yell, "Stop!" To shake the woman and say, "Look at what is happening to your baby! Wake up! Hurry! Stop them!" But even as I thought those words, I looked at my own hand holding the probe. I was one of "them" performing this act. My eyes shot back to the screen again. The cannula was already being rotated by the doctor, and now I could see the tiny body violently twisting with it. For the briefest moment it looked as if the baby were being wrung like a dishcloth, twirled and squeezed. And then the little body crumpled and began disappearing into the cannula before my eyes. The last thing I saw was the tiny, perfectly formed backbone sucked into the tube, and then everything was gone. And the uterus was empty. Totally empty. I was frozen in disbelief.[56]

Witnessing the actual death of a preborn child proved to be a profoundly disturbing experience that eventually led Johnson to resign, convinced that her work with Planned Parenthood had been in support of a lie, of an ideology that said that helping mothers destroy their own unborn children was a good thing—for her, for society.[57] Abby Johnson is today a powerful opponent of abortion. As she explains, "My mission—my team's mission—is simple: We're in the fight for life because we're pro-love. We see that every life, from the child in the womb, to the elderly—and in-between, including the abortion clinic worker's life, have incredible worth and value."[58]

---

56. Johnson with Lambert. *unPlanned*, 5–6.

57. Abby Johnson's experience has now been made into a movie, as was released in 2019.

58. From her mission statement at abbyjohnson.org. Johnson's story is now available as a movie—*unPlanned*. It is disturbing to watch, including as it does the scene quoted above, but very thought-provoking. One hopes that it will be seen by millions, and contribute to changed hearts and a changed culture.

That over a billion such deaths have been recorded in the last century is witness to the fact that abortion is an unusually efficacious procedure. This is not surprising when it is understood that many abortions are carried out by physicians trained in abortion procedures, and whose intended victims cannot defend themselves. To note this is to see that abortion has in significant ways corrupted modern medicine.

Who could have predicted it? In the nineteenth century physicians in the United States, working with state legislatures, helped pass laws that protected the life of the unborn child as well as their mother. Similar laws, with the help of physicians the world over, were enacted in dozens of other nations. The practice of medicine and medical technology made enormous strides in the twentieth century, from more effective diagnostic and surgical techniques, to organ transplants, to the development of medicines that have greatly ameliorated diseases such as diabetes, cancer, smallpox and HIV. These developments have contributed much to the quality of life and the lifespan of billions of people. There is a great deal to be thankful for.

But it is also true that in the course of the last hundred years some branches of medical science took a turn toward the dark side. German medical societies largely supported the heinous euthanasia program developed in the nineteen thirties that murdered over 300,000 people, most of whom were gassed in psychiatric hospitals. The technology used for gassing those deemed unfit was later applied to the murder of the Jews. The world, and the world's medical societies, condemned these actions as morally reprehensible. Still, the doctors and scientists committed to a eugenicist worldview who took part in those activities contributed in a lasting way to the erosion of the sanctity of life ethic.[59] From that worldview and the growing secularization of the West, has come a concern for overpopulation, the acceptance of a more hedonistic attitude to life, and the promotion of abortion.

The intimate connection with abortion that has developed during the last fifty years of medical school education, as well as the huge numbers of abortions performed in hospitals and abortion facilities, have

---

59. The American Medical Association was founded in 1847 and opposed abortion until 1967, when a committee on human reproduction convinced the AMA to adopt a more lenient policy. This policy would allow abortion in the case of rape, incest, possible fetal abnormalities, and threats to the mother's life or health. It would also encourage the idea that such decisions should be made with the help of physicians, an idea cited favorably by Supreme Court Justice Harry Blackman in writing the *Doe v. Bolton* decision. See Anderson and DeSanctis, *Tearing Us Apart*, 132–33.

been accompanied by the desire of certain organizations to use the bodies of aborted victims as material for experimentation. The vast majority of abortion victims have been discarded as just so much garbage, ash-heap lives, of little or no significance, unless, of course, the "trash" can be sold. For some people preborn human beings are apparently worthless when alive, but quite valuable as a source of fetal body parts and tissue once they are dead. For the perpetrators of abortion this is another indication of their disrespect for the humanity and dignity of the lives they so carelessly destroy and desecrate. Evidence of this was discovered in 2015 when the Center for Medical Progress (CMP), a pro-life activist organization, videoed interviews with Planned Parenthood officials who stated their willingness to sell body parts to medical researchers. The videos aroused tremendous controversy and triggered a series of lawsuits. There is good reason, however, to think that the videos were credible.[60] In the summer of 2021 a series of reports emerged claiming that the University of Pittsburgh Medical Center had been harvesting baby parts from aborted children for research purposes with the use of funds ($2.7 million) supplied by the National Institutes of Health. The University has denied these reports, but serious questions remain, in part due to the fact that the Magee-Women's Hospital with the University of Pittsburgh Medical Center performs more abortions than any other facility in Pennsylvania.

Many pro-choice proponents argue that abortion is a form of health care for women. Medical societies, hospitals, and abortion facilities all claim they are focused on health (e.g., the facility named in the recent Supreme Court decision is entitled Jackson Women's Health). In truth, considering abortion as health care is to be taken in by a euphemism. The primary purpose of an abortion is to destroy a preborn human being because they are usually unwanted, an embarrassment, a burden,

60. David Daleiden, founder of the Center for Medical Progress (CMP), made public several undercover videos in 2015 that he claims show Planned Parenthood executives discussing the sale of fetal body parts which is illegal under federal law. In response to the public outcry, Planned Parenthood sued the CMP, arguing that the videos were illegally made. They won a two-million dollar settlement. The CMP has sued Planned Parenthood in turn, claiming that the videos are valid. Meanwhile, there are media reports that the Fifth Circuit Court of Appeals (a federal court in the southern United States), has made use of these undercover videos, and that the executives in question admitted *under oath* that they had in fact violated federal law regarding the sale of fetal body parts obtained through partial-birth abortions. See investigative videos, including sworn testimony videos, at https://centerformedicalprogress.org. For information on Planned Parenthood suit, see Williams, "Planned Parenthood awarded $2.3 million for secret videos."

disposable, and unworthy of respect. After all, abortion is legal, and there are powerful political, cultural and medical authorities in the United States ever ready to support mothers and fathers willing to destroy their own offspring. The words of Terrence des Pres in describing the Nazi death camps seem equally appropriate with regard to facilities and medical wards that do abortions: "The dedication of life's energies to the production of death is a demonic principle of the first degree."[61]

Perhaps the most important function of law and government is to foster a just society in which the life and well-being of every citizen is protected. This is no longer the case. In his book, *A New Birth of Freedom*, Harry Jaffa describes how the works of European philosophers, and modern science—which owed much to the work of Charles Darwin—gradually introduced into Western (and American) society the idea that there was no such thing as an inalienable right endowed by God. Unalienable rights, as the American founders understood them, were moral laws given by God to provide order to a free society and protection for the innocent. As the nineteenth century gave way to the twentieth, and the sanctity of life ethic began to erode, the whole foundation of law shifted, and rights came to be seen as conditional, and dependent on the desires of cultural elites. Law, cut loose however gradually from a moral grounding in God, has given way to the idea that *might makes right*.[62]

The practice of abortion implements the idea that might makes right, and in so doing has helped perpetuate the inequality that is rooted in the worldview of the eugenics movement. The goal of eugenicists, most of whom were white male racists, was to purify the human race by preventing the birth of those deemed unfit for physical and mental reasons, and to strengthen the race through encouraging the reproduction of those they considered superior (for the most part, white children of Northern European extraction). Setting immigration quotas and legalizing the sterilization of the unfit proved largely ineffective, and abortion (though attractive in principle to some eugenicists), was not acceptable during the heyday of the eugenics movement. Its eventual authorization, however, has enabled those imbued with the elitist and racist mindset of the eugenicists to target unwanted groups (females, the handicapped, people of color, those who would lead to overpopulation) and prevent their birth through abortion.

61. des Pres, "Introduction," in Steiner, *Treblinka*, x.
62. See Jaffa, *A New Birth of Freedom*, 94—96.

A study done several years ago, and reported in the *Proceedings of the National Academy of Science*, found that in China, India, and a dozen other Asian nations, there was a serious gender imbalance. The availability of ultrasound technology enabled physicians to determine the sex of a baby before birth. In societies where male babies are preferred the use of this technology has contributed to greater numbers of female fetuses being aborted, leading to the gender imbalance. Though such targeting is now illegal in most places, determining the motivations of the parents can be difficult.[63]

Targeting preborn children identified with Down syndrome is legal and quite acceptable in a number of countries. In Iceland, for example, Down syndrome children are nearly non-existent. At a United Nations meeting in January of this year Iceland was criticized for its attitude toward children with Down Syndrome. Prenatal testing was introduced in the early 2000s. Nearly 100 percent of Danish women since that time terminated their pregnancy once a prenatal test revealed that their preborn child tested positive for Down syndrome. A number of other countries also have a high abortion rate with regard to Down Syndrome. Denmark's rate is about 98 percent, and that of the UK about 90 percent. Accurate statistics for the United States are unavailable, but it is thought the rate is over 60 percent.[64]

Those within the African-American community who value the sanctity of human life have found it disturbing that the abortion rate for African-Americans is far higher proportionately than their numbers within the American population as a would suggest.[65] Are blacks being targeted? Claims have been made that Planned Parenthood has targeted the black population by establishing some of their abortion clinics within areas with a dense African-American population. A study done by the Life Issues Institute found that over 60 percent of Planned Parenthood

---

63. Pandey, "Selective Abortion Killed 22.5 Million Female Foetuses [sic] in China, India, *Down To Earth*. "April 17, 2019. https://www.downtoearth.org.in/news/health/selection-abortion-killed-22-25-million=femal-foetuses-in-china-india-64043. Accessed September 9, 2022.

64. Cook, "Iceland lashed over Down syndrome at UN." Feb 15, 2022. https://bioedge.org/disability/Iceland-lashed-on-down-syndrome-record-at-un/. Accessed September 15, 2022.

65. Blacks compose 13 percent of the American population, but obtain over 36 percent of the abortions, five times the rate of white women. Since the Roe v. Wade Supreme Court decision in 1973 over 19 million black babies have been aborted. See Blackman, "Abortion: The Overlooked Tragedy for Black Americans."

facilities that provide abortions are within walking distance of black neighborhoods. Planned Parenthood has denied the claim of racism, stating that it is just business.[66] True enough, given their willingness to abort preborn children of all ethnic backgrounds. But it is a fact that Margaret Sanger, the founder of Planned Parenthood, though never on record as supporting abortion, was very much in favor of discouraging pregnancies among African-American and other low-income populations considered by her and other eugenicists as more likely to be poor, possibly of lesser intelligence, and less "fit" for bettering the human race.[67]

Dr. Dolores Bernadette Grier, founder of the Association of Black Catholics Against Abortion, was inspired to join the pro-life movement because of the example of Rev. Jessie Jackson—a black politician who—for a time—opposed abortion. In a speech given in 1989 Dr. Grier said this:

> Abortion is racism. It is a way of pruning, if you will, the black population . . . In 1973, shortly after the civil rights struggles, when there were more benefits for black people, all of a sudden we were given this free, free thing from the society of America: abortion. Seventy-eight percent of your abortion clinics were placed in black and urban areas, for the purpose of something free of charge from a racist society. To put it in the words of one pro-abortionist, "We don't need so many Negroes anymore. There's no more cotton to pick."[68]

This, admittedly, is a very strong statement. But if blacks are not targeted as such, it is nonetheless true that the abortion rate is very high among women of color. In New York City there are more abortions than live births among black women. This is true in other locales as well. This was not true prior to the *Roe* decision in 1973 when most black Americans disapproved of abortion. Today, more black Americans favor abortion than any other ethnic group. Black American women have more than five times as many abortions as white.[69] One doubts that Margaret Sanger would have been displeased.

It is not surprising that abortion is also harmful to the understanding of freedom. Historically freedom has meant the absence of coercion,

---

66. Reported in Goldberg, "Abortion: Devastating Impact of Black Americans," at https://www.thepublicdiscourse,com/2019/02/43594/.

67. Franks, *Margaret Sanger's Eugenic Legacy,* 40–50.

68. Cited by Horowitz, *Dark Agenda,* 93–94.

69. Reported in Goldberg, "Abortion: Devastating Impact of Black Americans," at https://www.thepublicdiscourse,com/2019/02/43594/.

usually from a government's misuse of power. To be free meant the ability to act voluntarily, without being pushed around or forced to act in a certain way. But for freedom to work in an organized society requires order, a system of laws that are just and fairly applied.[70] It also requires individual responsibility and self-restraint in making wise decisions, which make cooperation with others possible. If, however, laws become unjust, and individuals insist on doing as they please, order breaks down and injustice increases. These changes, as noted by Jaffa above, are now well along in many societies. The monstrous violence of the twentieth century owes much to laws which removed the rights of certain groups. American segregation laws targeted people of color for many decades, and though these laws have been struck down, racism persists. In 1900 coercive sterilization was illegal in the United States. By 1930 a number of states had legalized this practice, and thousands of men and women were forcibly sterilized. In Germany prior to the installation of the Nazi government it was against the law to kill handicapped people—until the law was changed making it legal to do so. At the beginning of the twentieth century women in numerous western nations were not free to abort their unborn child because the law protected the unborn child's right to live. But as the century unfolded many of those nations changed their laws giving women—including millions of Christian women—the freedom to dispose of their child.

Freedom is essential to human flourishing. But is killing the handicapped or the unborn a wise use of freedom? Os Guinness in his book, *The Magna Carta of Humanity*, writes, "freedom fails when free societies become so caught up in the glory of freedom that they justify anything and everything done in its name, including things that quite clearly contradict freedom—such as the abuse of others."[71] The apostle Paul, writing to the Christians in Galatia, advised them to be careful with freedom: "For you were called to freedom, brethren; only do not use your freedom as an opportunity for the flesh . . ." (Gal 5.13) Millions upon millions of men and women have misused their freedom by aborting an unborn child it was their moral responsibility to love.

Law is fundamental to the ordering of society, but laws have often been unjust. Martin Luther King, protesting segregation laws in Birmingham, Alabama, was jailed for demonstrating and picketing against them.

---

70. Evans, *The Theme Is Freedom*, 23–25.

71. Guinness, Magna Carta Of Humanity, 124.

Local (white) religious leaders expressed concern over the fact that he and the protesters had broken a number of such laws. King responded in a letter: "How does one determine when a law is just or unjust? A just law is a man-made code that squares with the moral law or the law of God. An unjust law is a human law is that out of harmony with the moral law . . . Any law that uplifts human personality is just. Any law that degrades human personality is unjust.[72]

As we can see, abortion is profoundly destructive. It kills unborn children in astonishing numbers. It wounds untold numbers of mothers physically and psychologically, and also deeply affects many fathers. Their suffering adds to the effect that abortion has on modern culture—to medicine, health, equality, freedom and law. These things in turn have had a profound effect on Christian men and women, and the churches to which they belong. When a Christian woman—a Christian mother—gets an abortion the relationship with the father (married or not) is often shaken, and the fellowship to which they belong is also affected. Abortion severs the deep bond so natural between mother and child. It also breaks the sixth commandment—"You shall not kill"—and violates Jesus's command to love others. Breaking these commands also breaks the unity of believers for which Jesus prayed. A unity so important that the credibility of the Gospel would be called into question were it to be broken.

The defiance of God, and the erosion of the moral underpinnings of law, freedom, medicine, and religion have unleashed an enormous wave of violence around the world which has destroyed well over a billion human beings, the vast majority of them unborn children. It raises the question: In what way are the destructive ideas and events of the twentieth century related to the decline of the churches in Western countries that we see today?

---

72. King, "Letter From a Birmingham Jail," reprinted in *Annotations On A Letter*, 142.

2

Ideologies Gone Rogue

[T]he main responsibility for the century's disasters lies not so much in the problems as in the solutions, not in impersonal forces but in human beings, thinking certain thoughts and as a result performing certain actions.

—Robert Conquest[1]

The dedication of life's energies to the production of death is a demonic principle of the first degree.

—Terrence des Pres[2]

Ideas have consequences.

—Richard Weaver[3]

What comes out of a man is what defiles a man. For from within, out of the heart of man, come evil thoughts, fornications, theft, murder, adultery, coveting, wickedness, deceit, licentiousness, envy, slander, pride, foolishness. All

---

1. *Reflections on a Ravaged Century,* Preface.
2. Introduction to Steiner, *Treblinka,* x.
3. *Ideas Have Consequences.* Title of his book.

these evil things come from within, and they defile a man.

—Jesus, Mark 7.21–23

All who hate me (Wisdom) love death.

—Proverbs 8. 36b

INTRODUCTION

At the present moment the issue of abortion is very much in the public eye. The Supreme Court's *Dobbs* decision some months ago (June 24, 2022) has sparked the interest and concern of millions here and abroad. Those who defend life believe this decision to return abortion to the states will save lives by allowing state legislatures and the voters who support them to pass laws protecting unborn children. Those who support abortion view this decision as a major setback. They have promised to redouble their efforts to keep abortion legal. Criticism has been strong, even harsh, from the White House, members of Congress, foreign heads of government, business and entertainment leaders, and millions of women who view abortion—the killing of their unborn children—as a civil right.

It is odd to think that leaders of the American government, and millions of women (a majority of whom are Christians) are angry because the Supreme Court has stated that the U. S. Constitution does not include a right for women to dispose of their children. But then, when we take a serious look at the massive violence of the twentieth century, and the extraordinary number of people that have been disposed of because certain other people decided to eliminate them, perhaps not so odd.

Defiance of God, the willingness to break the biblical command not to kill, the denial of the truth that all people are made in God's image, and the view that *might makes right* is a stance common to several ideologies that have led to unprecedented levels of violence and suffering in the last century. Due to their vicious and destructive nature Soviet scholar Robert Conquest referred to them as *rogue* ideologies.[4] Abortion, though

---

4. Conquest, *Reflections on a Ravaged Century,* xi. Some writers distinguish between *ideologies* and *worldviews,* while others use them interchangeably (.e.g., Naugle, *Worldview,* 234) as I do in this book. I take them to mean a body of ideas, concepts, or theories that orient an organization, society, or individual with regard to reality, meaning and purpose.

it takes place out of the public eye, and despite its popularity, is almost unfailingly destructive. It should be understood in the context of twentieth century violence and the ideologies which have given rise to it. This chapter focuses on several of these rogue ideologies, and their victims.

EUGENICS

Charles Darwin through his studies on a voyage around the world, developed a theory of evolution. He believed that evolution was a process that involved humans as well as animals in an on-going struggle for existence (particularly in their need for food), in which the strong would survive and the weak would perish. Though opposed to slavery, Darwin, like many of his contemporaries, was a racist, and in his book, *The Descent of Man* (published in 1871), stated his conviction that over time superior races would flourish, while inferior races would eventually succumb, and perish.[5] Darwinism, the philosophy that developed from his ideas, would influence others with political power, including V. I. Lenin, and Adolph Hitler. His theory also undermined confidence in the biblical doctrine of creation, and the idea that human beings were made in the image of God.

Darwin's theory that evolution was an on-going natural process that included human society was widely accepted throughout Europe and the United States. Discussions in scholarly circles in the last decades of the nineteenth century and early decades of the twentieth led to the idea that the process of evolution could, and should, be controlled by human beings. Francis Galton, a cousin of Darwin, was much impressed with Darwin's theory, and became a leading proponent of a movement that would apply Darwin's ideas to bettering humanity, and to which he gave the name, "eugenics." As he explained, "What nature does blindly, slowly, and ruthlessly, man may do providentially, quickly and kindly."[6]

Ironically, the eugenics movement would in fact prove to be anything but kind. Its elitist, racist, and coercive methods would cause enormous human suffering through its support for immigration policy, coercive sterilization, euthanasia, war, and eventually abortion. Influential German biologist Ernest Haeckel as early as 1904 proposed that adults should be euthanized if diagnosed with certain disabilities or infirmities. As he said, "The value of human life appears to us today, on the

---

5. Weikert, *Darwinian Racism*, 21–24.
6. Weikert, *Darwinian Racism*, 81.

firm ground of evolutionary theory, in an entirely different light that it did fifty years ago."⁷

Though this movement owed much to Europeans such as Darwin, and given a name by Darwin's cousin, Francis Galton, it was in the United States that it first took root and gained momentum. This was due in part to political support and government assistance—particularly that of the United States Department of Agriculture, the Labor Department, and the U. S. Army. Wealthy Americans who were committed to the aims of the eugenics movement, such as John D. Rockefeller and Andrew Carnegie, provided further assistance through substantial financial contributions.⁸

> It [Eugenics] was conceived at the outset of the twentieth century and implemented by America's wealthiest, most powerful and most learned men against the nation's most vulnerable and helpless. Eugenicists sought to methodically terminate all the racial and ethnic groups, and social classes, they disliked and feared. It was nothing less than America's legalized campaign to breed a super race—and not just any super race. Eugenicists wanted a purely Germanic and Nordic super race, enjoying biological dominion over all others.⁹

The American eugenicists were certain that they could make human life and society healthier if there were more "healthy" people and fewer "unhealthy" people. It was a vision they were determined to implement through science, law—and religion. Chapter three focuses on the fact that among those who supported this new movement and its worldview in the United States were a number of well-known religious leaders. They were Protestant and Jewish for the most part, and embraced eugenic ideas quite wholeheartedly.

A common distinction made by eugenicists was that between "positive eugenics" and "negative eugenics."¹⁰ The "positive eugenics" approach, which many liberal Christians supported, consisted of encouraging favored ethnic groups, such as those from northern European countries, and the Anglo-Saxon population in the United States, to have

---

7. Weikert, *Darwinian Racism,* 84. Today the advance of diagnostic technology has made possible the diagnosis, and abortion, of unborn children with certain disabilities. Iceland, for example, has largely eradicated children with Down syndrome, through aborting them before birth.

8. Black, *War Against the Weak,* 296.

9. Black, *War Against the Weak,* 7.

10. Franks, *Margaret Sanger's Eugenic Legacy,* 40.

more children. But as substantial numbers of Anglo-Saxon Americans chose to have fewer children, it did not work well. That it would eventually lead to evils such as sterilization, euthanasia, and abortion seems to have been little understood or anticipated by them.

The "negative eugenics" approach focused on coercive efforts to limit the reproduction of groups and individuals considered in some way inferior (e.g., the poor, the handicapped, the mentally slow, alcoholics, people of color), and would prove to be much more effective because of government support and financial assistance from wealthy organizations.[11] One focus involved passing laws to limit the immigration of individuals or groups considered undesirable.[12] Another was the development of intelligence tests by which to discern who was intellectually fit—and eugenically acceptable—and who was not. Margaret Sanger, a prominent feminist and eugenicist, pioneered a third effort, that of contraception. She also encouraged a liberalization of sexual conduct. She founded the American Birth Control League in 1916 (the name changed to Planned Parenthood in 1942), as a means of promoting her views.[13, 14]

Yet another focus was incarcerating individuals considered defective in institutions. In a number of states, through the concerted efforts of eugenicists, the sterilization of those considered unfit was made legal by their legislatures. The Supreme Court ratified this practice in 1927 in their infamous Carrie Buck decision.

---

11. Franks, *Margaret Sanger's Eugenic Legacy*, 40.

12. Hitler in his book, *Mein Kampf*, noted appreciatively that the USA had passed immigration laws to keep out certain races, as well as those who were sick; cited by Black, *War on the Weak*, 275.

13. Planned Parenthood has proved to be one of most influential organizations in the world in the promotion of eugenicist ideas, particularly that of abortion. Though not encouraged by the religious leaders in the early decades of the twentieth century, many in the mainline denominations would come to accept a liberalization of sexual mores as the sexual revolution of the 1960s gained momentum. Approval of and support for the legalization of abortion was followed by a growing acceptance of easy divorce, sex before marriage, the ordination of homosexuals, and eventually support for homosexual marriage.

14. Sanger was also adamantly opposed, as were many eugenicists, to charities that helped the poor, believing that they enabled the poor to flourish, when, in her view, they constituted a threat to the health of American society. Like many others in the eugenicist movement, she was an elitist, believing that the future of the human race should belong to the strong. Margaret Sanger, interestingly enough, was not in favor of abortion, though she strongly supported coercive sterilization.

Carrie Buck was a young woman who at age seventeen became pregnant, claiming she had been raped. The year was 1923. The parents of the man she accused of the rape claimed that she was feebleminded. Doctors agreed with this claim, and she was committed to a home, as her mother had been. Her child received a similar label. Several eugenicists, seeing in Carrie Buck, her mother, and her child, three generations of feeblemindedness, and wanting to encourage Virginia to legalize sterilization of those considered unfit, used her as a legal test. Her lawyer claimed that she had a right to be a mother, and had been denied due process. Her case went from a local court, to the Virginia Court of Appeals, and eventually to the Supreme Court.

Supreme Court Justice Oliver Wendell Holmes, who was to write the Court's decision, had been deeply influenced by the writings of social Darwinism. He opposed charities and "do-gooders," and did not believe in the sacredness of human life.[15] In his decision for the Court, announced on May 2, 1927, he agreed with those who considered Carrie Buck (and her ancestors) mentally unfit, and in a phrase which resonated widely, wrote: "Three generations of imbeciles is enough."[16] In all, twenty-nine states enacted forced sterilization laws; and "by the end of 1940, no fewer than 35,878 men and women had been sterilized or castrated—almost 30,000 of them after *Buck v. Bell*."[17] The final toll according to historian Edwin Black would be the forcible sterilization of more than 70,000 men and women.[18]

America's expertise in eugenics was embraced in some measure by a number of other countries[19]—Finland, France, Italy, Hungary, Romania,

---

15. A favorite comment given to British scholar Harold J. Laski: "As I have said, no doubt, often, it seems to me that all society rests on the death of men. If you don't kill 'em one way you kill 'em another—or prevent their being born." Black, *War Against the Weak* 120.

16. Black, *War Against the Weak*, 117-21.

17. Black, *War Against the Weak*, 121-23. North Carolina continued this practice until 1979.

18. Sterilizations continued in the United States into the 1970s; it is estimated that over 70,000 men and women were eventually sterilized, Black, *War Against the Weak*, 398.

19. England, despite much discussion and controversy never fully legalized compulsory sterilization, though the son of Charles Darwin, Major Leonard Darwin, presiding at the first International Eugenics Conference held in London in 1912, proposed that the British government develop traveling squads of scientists, with the power to make arrests, who would travel about the country identifying and arresting the "unfit." Those classified as such would be segregated in special colonies or

Norway, Sweden, Russia and Germany among them.[20] Germany and the Scandinavian countries were particularly interested, in part because of the emphasis given the alleged superiority of Nordic peoples. Several of these nations would also derive support from religious leaders.

The German government and medical community, drawing on the work of eugenicist intellectuals, as well as generous financial support from American foundations, went further than any other nation following Adolph Hitler's election as German chancellor in 1933.[21] Correspondence between American and German eugenicists was extensive even before Hitler came to power. The Germans acknowledged that American eugenicists had provided the early leadership in the eugenics movement.

Hitler was impressed with American eugenicists and their emphasis on racial health long before he became chancellor of Germany, and corresponded with several of them. In a letter to prominent eugenicist Madison Grant, Hitler referred to his book, *The Passing of the Great Race,* as his Bible."[22] The book made clear Grant's negative eugenicist worldview:

> Mistaken regard for what are believed to be divine laws and a sentimental belief in the sanctity of human life tend to prevent both the elimination of defective infants and the sterilization of such adults as are themselves of no value to the community. The law of nature requires the obliteration of the unfit and human life is valuable only when it is of use to the community or race.[23]

A number of German philosophers, scientists, physicians and jurists were very much in agreement. In 1920 Lawyer Karl Binding and psychiatrist Alfred Hoche had made similar arguments for the destruction of those considered "unworthy of life" as being therapeutic for the nation.[24] Hitler himself strongly endorsed infanticide in a speech to the Nuremberg Party Congress in 1929, saying "If Germany would produce

---

sterilized. Legislation was eventually proposed, but never became law. Nonetheless, many sterilizations were carried out utilizing various "voluntary" methods.

20. Over 41,000 forced sterilizations occurred in Norway, over 63,000 in Sweden. Black, *War Against the Weak,* 244–45.

21. The Carnegie and Rockefeller Foundations provided millions of dollars in support of Germany's eugenic program. Black, *War on the Weak,* 283–84.

22. Black, *War Against the Weak,* 259–60.

23. Black, 259.

24. Lifton, *Nazi Doctors,* 46. See T*he Release of the Destruction of Life Devoid of Value,* by Alfred Hoche and Karl Binding.

a million children and dispose of 700,000 to 800,000 of the weakest, then in the end the result would possibly even be an increase in strength."[25]

In response to these influences, the German legal and medical community moved to expand their eugenics program. Between 300,000 and 400,000 men and women, once classified as "unfit," were sterilized. It is estimated that 75,000 more people were sterilized in countries conquered by the German Army.

In 1939 murder—euthanasia—was added to the German eugenics repertoire.[26] They began with children—children with names, but expendable, unwanted newborns and young infants with severe mental problems or deformities. The first was a child whose name was Knauer. He was born blind, with mental and physical deficiencies. He was unwanted by his family and the state, and was euthanized. After all, as one SS officer stated, "the solution of the problem of the mentally ill becomes easy if one eliminates these people."[27] The problems presented by 300,000 physically and mentally handicapped men, women and children in Germany and countries they occupied were "solved" by their being put to death, most asphyxiated by gas.[28]

The killings, unlike the sterilizations, though authorized by Hitler and carried out by German courts and the German psychiatric community, were actually illegal under German law, and thus were carried out by a series of machinations designed to keep the program secret.[29] There were six killing centers, each fitted out with gas chambers and a crematorium, one in an old castle, the others in what were once hospitals. In time, the killings, despite the attempt at secrecy, became more widely known. Public awareness was aroused through the smell of the crematoriums, and questions raised by family members of victims, and by lawyers who had legal authority for them.[30]

Hitler, concerned about such criticisms, stopped the killings in Germany for a time, though they were later resumed with greater secrecy,

25. Weikart, *The Death of Humanity*, 229.

26. *Holocaust Encyclopedia*. "Euthanasia Program."

27. Lifton, *Nazi Doctors*, 50.

28. See Lifton, *Nazi Doctors*, chapter 2 & 3 for an overview. This number is an estimate of historians. See https://www.dw.com/en/remembering-the-forgotten-victims-of-nazi-euthanasia-murders/a-37286088.

29. See Friedlander, *Origins of Nazi Genocide*, and Lifton, *The Nazi Doctors*, for two of the best studies on the German euthanasia program.

30. Freidlander, *Origins of Nazi Genocide*, 116–17.

usually in local hospitals. They also continued in Poland (divided between Germany and Russia after the September 1939 invasion), and were expanded further as new territories were conquered. The emphasis on secrecy enabled some of these centers to continue operations until the very end of the war.[31] However, when Germany attacked Russia in June 1941 the major focus of attention turned to the Jews; hundreds of thousands were shot, and millions (utilizing the technology used in the euthanasia murders) were gassed during what became known as the Holocaust.[32] This technology was also used, secretly of course, on some badly wounded German soldiers, for they too, once no longer useful, were also expendable.[33]

COMMUNISM

Karl Marx and Fredrick Engels were contemporaries of Charles Darwin.[34] Their writings, including *The Communist Manifesto,* included a condemnation of capitalism and religion, and the dream of a classless society. These ideas, when modified decades later by V.I. Lenin and Joseph Stalin and their associates, led to a worldwide social catastrophe of staggering proportions.

Another, whose ideas on revolution and the importance of violence would have a considerable influence on Lenin and Communism was Sergey Nechayev, a Russian anarchist and nihilist. In Nechayev's pamphlet, *The Catechism of a Revolutionary,* he wrote about violence: "The revolutionist knows only one science, the science of destruction, which does

---

31. United States Holocaust Museum. "Euthanasia Program." The Holocaust Museum estimates that 250,000 people were murdered altogether, though the number could be significantly higher. Some records have been unattainable. Of those murdered by the German euthanasia program between 50,000 and 100,000 were German—all "worthless eaters," see Black, *War Against the Weak,* 317.

32. By war's end over 5 million Jews, half a million Gypsies (Sinta, Roma), and thousands of Russian POWs had been murdered, many through use of the technology developed in the euthanasia program. See Rubenstein & Roth, *Approaches to Auschwitz,* chapter 5.

33. Lifton, *Nazi Doctors,* 78. Another aspect of technology had to do with the early computing systems which made it possible to identify and correlate millions of names with details about nationality, health, etc. Much of this technology was developed in the United States by IBM. See Black, *War on the Weak,* 289–91; also Black, *IBM and the Holocaust,* chapter 1.

34. Marx, born 1818, Engels, 1820, Darwin, 1809.

not stop at lying, robbery, betrayal, and torture of friends, even murder of one's own family."[35]

The ideology of Communism required replacing the existing government of Russia and the influence of the Russian Orthodox Church, with the goal of creating a "new man," in an atheistic and classless society. The Communist Party redefined morality, and put their ideas into practice with brutal and unrelenting use of force.[36]

It is quite probable that the extraordinary use of violence that would become so typical of Communist rule was influenced by the brutality and destruction of the first World War, a conflict that unleashed violence on a global scale. A war that opened the door to ever greater horrors and violence. Karl Kautsky, a German socialist, wrote in 1920 of the desensitization many experienced in the war, a desensitization that contributed markedly to a declining respect for religion and the sacredness of human life as the twentieth century unfolded.

> The real cause of the change ... into a development toward brutality is attributable to the world war ... When, therefore, the war broke out and dragged in its train for four years practically the whole of the healthy male population, the coarsening tendencies of militarism sank to the very depths of brutality, and to a lack of human feeling and sentiment. Even the proletariat could no longer escape its influence. They were to a very high degree infected by militarism and, when they returned home again, were in every way brutalized. Habituated to war, the man who had come back from the front was only too often in a state of mind and feeling that made him ready, even in peacetime and among his own people, to enforce his claims and interests by deeds of violence and bloodshed. That became, as it were, an element of civil war.[37]

---

35. Quoted in Micelli, *Roots of Violence*, 34. Nechayev acted on his beliefs, murdering with the help of friends a young student who criticized his ideas. He was arrested for this crime, found guilty, and died in prison in 1882.

36. There are thousands of volumes on the Communist movement. The Courtois (et. al) volume provides a country by country look at the violence unleashed by the Communist movement. Other recent volumes worthy of note: the three volumes of the *Gulag Archipelago* by Solzhenitysn; Applebaum: *Red Famine; Iron Curtain; Gulag;* Hollander, *From the Gulag to the Killing Fields,* and Snyder, *Bloodlands.*

37. Kautsky, *Terrorism and Communism*, 149, 152, cited in Courtois, *Black Book of Communism*, 734.

The Bolshevik revolution which began in 1917 was a continuation of the world war that in Russia became a civil war, and would lead to the foundation of the Union of Soviet Socialist Republics (USSR) in 1922. The brutal civil war which led to the founding of the USSR was also notable for becoming the first modern nation to authorize abortion.[38] There will be more about this in the section below which focuses on this.

Joseph Stalin assumed leadership of the Communist party in what became the USSR following Lenin's death, and vastly increased the scale of violence and murder.[39] In fact, the Communist movement, wherever it took root—from its beginnings in Russia, and on to China, North Korea, Vietnam, Laos, Cambodia, Ethiopia, Cuba and Latin America—embraced violence as a means of enforcing its utopian vision. At one point nearly one third of earth's population was ruled by Communist regimes. Planned famines, torture, beatings, shootings, concentration camps, death by overwork, and burying people alive, were all methods used by communists to subdue those under their control. Any organization or person who opposed the communist ideology was considered an enemy or threat.

The highest proportion of deaths under a Communist regime—the Khmer Rouge led by Pol Pot—occurred in Cambodia, where about two million people were murdered and imprisoned. These deaths comprised about one third of the entire population! The Khmer Rouge sought to eliminate religion, money, and private property. Anyone considered to be an intellectual (those who wore glasses were often considered intellectuals) was murdered.

The Chinese version under Mao was by far the deadliest in terms of sheer numbers. From 1958 to 1962 China undertook what was called the Great Leap Forward. China's peasant way of life was forced into a comprehensive collective system which included agriculture and food production. The result was a monstrous human calamity. In the words of Jean-Louis Margolin, "Mao and the system that he created were directly responsible for what was, and, one hopes, will forever remain, the most murderous famine of all time, anywhere in the world."[40] Numerous

---

38. Jacobson, "Nations Authorizing Abortion," in *Abortion Worldwide Report*, 45

39. Affection for Joseph Stalin lingers on writes Douglass Murray in his article, "One Hundred Years of Evil." A June 2017 survey of the Russian people asking them to name "the top ten outstanding people of all time and all nations" considered Joseph Stalin #1—the greatest man in all of human history! Obviously an outstanding survey.

40. Margolin, "China: A Long March into Night," 487. Margolin in citing death

scholars, estimate that Chinese Communism is responsible for at least 65 million deaths. Its depredations continue. Mike Pompeo, Secretary of State in the Trump presidency, declared the People's Republic of China to be guilty of genocide of the Uighurs through forced abortions, sterilizations, and separation of the children from their families. The Biden administration has concurred in this decision.[41]

How many other lives were profoundly disrupted through the mind control, oppression and grief brought on by Communist brutality and tyranny is incalculable. The destruction of thousands of churches, monuments and works of art, the disruption of family life, and an untold amount of damage to the environment, are also part of Communism's vast "achievements." David Satter, in an op. ed. piece in the *Wall Street Journal*, marking the 100th birthday of the Communist Revolution, wrote that its 100 million victims "makes communism the greatest catastrophe in human history."[42] This number is astonishingly large, and yet it *excludes* the lives lost to abortion in Communist regimes.

It is important to note that the eugenics movement was a factor in Communism in two ways. It was introduced into Russia in the 1920s by A. S. Serebrovsky, a eugenicist, who thought that the central planning characteristic of Communist ideology would make the breeding of "desirable qualities" a possibility. Stalin, when he came to power, was not impressed by the idea that the qualities of men like Lenin could be biologically inherited by the population through eugenic methods, and this emphasis died out.[43] Eugenics in terms of the struggle of nations, however, characteristic of many German military leaders in World War I, flourished as Communist leaders throughout the world believed that

---

statistics states that China's invasion of Tibet (considered by many scholars as an instance of genocide) resulted in the death of 10–20% of Tibet's population, 463–64. See also Becker, *Hungry Ghosts,* and Jung Chang, *Mao,* chapter 40, "The Great Leap: "Half of China May Well Have to Die."

41. Kontorovich, "A Genocide Test Faces the West."

42. Satter, *100 Years of communism,* A17. As Zbigniew Brzezinski has pointed out, it is truly a moral outrage that no Soviet official, on any level, has ever been brought to trial for his role in the atrocities of the Stalinist regime. This is also true of the Communist regimes in China, Vietnam, and Cuba. The exception it would seem is that of Cambodia. In 1979 Cambodia was invaded by Vietnam (also a Communist regime). Pol Pot was denounced in a show trial in 1979, and died during house arrest a year later. Revelations about the mass killings led to a United National tribunal in 2009, during which three top Khmer Rouge officials were given prison sentences, the only convictions of men involved in the Cambodian genocide.

43. Gellately, *Lenin, Stalin, and Hitler. The Age of Social* Catastrophe, 331–32

the classless, socialist society they envisioned would eventually prove superior to all other societies globally. And it did so on a far larger scale, a superiority they were willing to establish with violence.

Stephen Courtois, author of the concluding essay of *The Black Book of Communism,* wrote that in Communism "there exists a sociopolitical eugenics," and Lenin, with his penchant for brutality was considered a "master of the knowledge of the evolution of social species." Assuming that the bourgeoisie belonged to an earlier "stage of humanity that had been surpassed, its liquidation as a class and the liquidation of the individuals who actually or supposedly belong to it could be justified."[44] Courtois added: "The real motivation of the terror . . . stemmed from Leninist ideology and the utopian will to apply to society a doctrine totally out of step with reality."[45] Part of that separation of ideology from reality embraced by the Communist movement was due to what Courtois has termed a

> deviant form of Darwinism, applied to social questions with the same catastrophic results that occur when such ideas are applied to racial issues. One thing is certain: Crimes against humanity are the product of an ideology that reduces people not to a universal but to a particular condition, to a lower form of humanity, be it biological, racial, or sociohistorical.[46]

Communism is truly a rogue ideology. It is a worldview in which the sanctity of human life has no place. Communism has often been lauded for its emphasis on egalitarianism. But its emphasis on equality, on building a classless society that strips the individual of dignity and responsibilities, is a utopian fantasy that requires the constant application of propaganda and violence to enforce.

NATIONAL SOCIALISM

Adolph Hitler was deeply influenced by the ideas of a number of German writers, among them Arthur Schopenhauer, and Friedrich Nietzsche. Their emphasis on the power of the will to overcome obstacles resonated deeply with Hitler, as did Nietzsche's rejection of Judeo-Christian

---

44. Courtois, "Conclusion: Why?," Black Book of Communism, 752.
45. Courtois, "Conclusion: Why?," Black Book of Communism, 737.
46. Courtois, "Conclusion: Why?," Black Book of Communism, 752–53.

morality.[47] Houston Stuart Chamberlain, a contemporary of Hitler's, and a racist and anti-Semite, contributed to Hitler's hatred of the Jews, a prejudice already deeply embedded in German religion and culture, but deepened in the nineteenth and twentieth centuries as prejudice against Christianity—and its Judaic roots—became more pronounced.[48] Many Germans, Hitler among them, also blamed the Jews for contributing to Germany's loss in World War I.

A third stream of ideas came from the work of Charles Darwin, whose ideas about evolution undermined the belief, widespread in Europe at the time, in the sacredness of human life. The dynamic intertwining of these ideas, promoted by scholars in philosophy,[49] science, law, politics, and popularized in Hitler's book *Mein Kampf*, culminated in an irrational, utopian, eugenicist, and racist ideology that led to World War II, the Jewish Holocaust, and ultimately the death of 55 million people, most of them non-combatants.[50]

Though violence was utilized by the Nazi Party before Adolph Hitler was elected chancellor, it increased greatly once he was in power. As noted in the section on eugenics, it began on a organized scale with the sterilizations of those thought to be "unworthy of life," who constituted a financial burden to the nation. It continued with the euthanasia program which lasted—much of the time in secret—to the end of the war. Their deaths were considered a form of "medical cleansing."[51]

With the outbreak of World War II the Nazi's murderous program expanded still further. In the newly occupied lands conquered by the German Army special police battalions, the Einsatzgruppen, murdered over a million men, women and children (mostly Jews). Jews, along with

47. Weikart. *Hitler's Religion*. See chapter two, "Who Influenced Hitler's Religion?" 15–37.

48. Weikart, chapter six, "Did Hitler derive His Anti-Semitism from Christianity?" 147–71. Weikart's earlier book, *From Darwin to Hitler*, provides an in-depth look at the complex interchange of ideas, personalities and events that led from Darwin and his followers to the rise of Hitler and the Third Reich.

49. Viktor Frankl in his important book, *Man's Search for Meaning*, was convinced that the death camps were first envisioned by philosophers.

50. According to Wikipedia, 50–56 million people died directly in the war, and perhaps another 20 million from war-caused famine and disease. See "World War II Casualties, at https://en.wikipedia.org/wiki/World_War_II_casualties."

51. Euphemisms were common. The killing of children was not murder, but a "putting-to-sleep." Friedlander, 51. The organization for euthanizing adults was called the "Reich Cooperative for State Hospitals and Nursing Homes." Friedlander, 73.

Roma, Poles, and Slavic peoples (all considered sub-human), were considered dispensable—a surplus population.

Michael Burleigh wrote that the atrocities carried out by the German army were in part motivated by factors such as the strangeness of Jewish and Eastern European culture and language. They were also deeply influenced by the *worldview* they carried with them. As Burleigh comments, " it was what these troops *had in their heads* from their time in the Hitler Youth or in the Reich Labor Service, that partly explains why they disregarded war's important moral aspect, namely not to squander whatever moral capital one's own side possesses through gratuitous violence."[52]

Over a period of several years over five million Jews were murdered, a million of them children, most of them in death camps constructed for that very purpose.[53] Five hundred thousand Gypsies (Sinta, Roma) were also murdered in these camps, as were huge numbers of Russian prisoners of war. Had the Germans succeeded in conquering Russia, there were plans (discovered after the war), to eliminate millions of Slavic peoples in order to provide living space for German people. All considered as sub-human.[54]

The Holocaust, the genocidal murder of five million Jews by the Nazis, is unique in terms of the actions taken. But at its core were ideas that stemmed from the theories of Charles Darwin, developed by sympathetic sociologists, philosophers, and scientists into what became the eugenics worldview and movement. Darwin opposed slavery, and yet he was a racist, and on the basis of his own ideas believed that races he considered superior (mostly European) would in time subdue peoples he considered inferior. It is quite probable that Darwin himself would have condemned the atrocities of the Nazis and Communists. Nonetheless, as Richard Weaver emphasized, ideas have consequences, among them the working out of the implications implicit in the core ideas. Included in the implications of Darwin's theory was the denial of the truth that all

---

52. Burleigh, *Moral Combat*, 121–22. (My emphasis)

53. The main killing centers were Sobibor, Treblinka, Auschwitz, Chelmo, and Belzec. Many thousands were killed in other centers referred to as "concentration camps." Tens of thousands of people, nearly all men, were murdered at Dachau, the first of these camps, though its primary purpose was training SS troops, and the incarceration of political prisoners. See Rubernstein and Roth, *Approaches to Auschwitz*, chapter 5.

54. Germany's "Master Plan for the East" included plans for the colonization of central and eastern Europe. Leading Nazi Heinrich Himmler predicted that human losses might be as high as 30 million people. See https://en.wikipedia.org/wiki/Generalplan_Ost. Accessed August 3, 2022.

people are made in the image of God and are, therefore, equal. Further, when God is ignored or denied as the creator of the human race, and as the source of moral truth—when, as Solzhenitsyn argued, people forget God—it opens the door for human beings to take on the role of master of their own destiny. This means in fact that some human beings, should they assume political power, can direct the lives of other human beings through making up the moral rules that will govern society. The eugenics movement encouraged this, particularly with the negative eugenicist approach which emphasized coercive and racist tactics involving immigration, sterilization, and euthanasia, all of which were employed by Nazi Germany. As Richard Weikert stated in his book on the connection of evolutionary-eugenics with Hitler's Germany:

> The evolutionary process became the arbiter of all morality. Whatever promoted the evolutionary progress of humanity was deemed good, and whatever hindered biological improvement was considered morally bad. Multitudes must perish in this Malthusian struggle anyway, they reasoned, so why not improve humanity by speeding up the destruction of the disabled and the inferior races? According to this logic the extermination of individuals and races deemed inferior and "unfit" was not only morally justified, but indeed, morally praiseworthy. Thus Hitler—and many other Germans—perpetrated one of the most evil programs the world has ever witnessed under the delusion that Darwinism could help us discover how to make the world better.[55]

Though the eugenics movement played an outsize role in Nazi Germany, another major factor contributing to their murderous activities was anti-Semitism. Richard Rubenstein and John Roth, in their book, *Approaches to Auschwitz*, argue that anti-Jewish sentiments began centuries before the rise of Hitler in the ancient world, where Jews, a uniquely religious people, were viewed and often resented as a strange people due to their religious rites, and perhaps especially their belief in one God. With the arrival of the Christian faith there was a time when believing Jews and Gentiles worshipped and worked together. St Paul had made explicit the fact that God, through Jesus Christ, had given his life to reconcile the world to God, and the Gentile and Jew to one another. As the centuries passed, however, there were theologians who began to view the Jews as responsible for the death of Jesus (ignoring the fact that the Romans, who

55. Weikart, *From Darwin to Hitler*, 227.

were Gentiles, were actively involved in his crucifixion). This view hardened, leading at times to the expulsion of Jews from certain locales, and at other times to violence. The Protestant Reformation, and Martin Luther's harsh response to the Jewish community's non-acceptance of the Gospel, added considerably to antisemitism, particularly in Germany. Prejudice toward Jews deepened further following World War I, as the National Socialist Party took shape, and found in the Jews a scapegoat for Germany's defeat. The incipient antisemitism of German society provided a fertile environment for Nazi propaganda.

The violence perpetuated by the Nazi regime was barbarous, brutal, and often impersonal, and yet it was a very human enterprise.[56] As scholar Wendy Lower, writing of the Nazi regime, described it, "Genocide as an idea and an act is a human phenomenon. Perpetration of genocide requires human cognitive abilities, *an ideology of hatred* with all its mythic and emotional power, and well-developed systems for organizing and implementing it. Humans are the only animals that commit genocide."[57]

It was also, especially with the Nazi regime, highly bureaucratic, given to layers of administrative functions, rules, policies (and efficient record keeping, which provided a good deal of evidence for the Nuremburg trials following the war). Lower refers to the individuals who worked in these offices—politicians, military personnel, aides, secretaries—as "desk murderers." Many desk murderers were women.[58] There were also

---

56. Much Nazi violence, as with so much modern mass killing, was impersonal, i.e., not motivated by a personal vendetta or personal connection. It must be acknowledged that the Allied forces in WW I and II included American forces which also inflicted a great deal of violence, also very impersonal, much of it from a distance, as in the bombings of the cities of Germany, Austria and Japan. Reflection by numerous scholars, while concluding that WWII in particular was a just war, also admit that much of the bombing carried by the Allied forces often targeted civilians in ways contrary to the Geneva Convention's rules of war. A retired U. S Army officer told me that the use of nuclear devices against the Japanese cities of Nagasaki and Hiroshima would today be very difficult to justify, and might very well be considered war crimes. War, though it may at times be necessary, is always a terrible reality. C. S. Lewis was one of few Christians who criticized the bombing of cities in Germany.

57. Lower, *Hitler's Furies*, 159. (My emphasis).

58. "This type of modern genocidaire assumes that the paper, like its administrator, remains clean and bloodless. The desk murderer does his official duty. He convinces himself as he orders the deaths of tens of thousands that he has remained decent, civilized, and even innocent of crime. What about the women who staffed those offices, the female assistants whose agile fingers pressed the keys on the typewriters, and whose clean hands distributed the orders to kill?" Lower, *Hitler's Furies*, 98–99.

a number of women who were directly involved in the killings, a fact sometimes overlooked in studies of Nazi evil.[59]

These statements are in line with my argument, that at the root of mass killings are ideas, a mindset, a worldview. Further, that worldviews and ideologies are embraced and sustained by the choices we make, even though we may not be fully aware of the initial decisions that opened the door to them. Daniel Goldhagen, in one of his books on the Holocaust, wrote: "The human beings who slaughtered the victims had views about what they were doing, and these views substantially informed their choices to act in the ways they did." Their basic motive: "race hatred."[60]

His books have been heavily criticized, but I find myself in agreement with his point that the idea of "collective guilt" makes light of the moral responsibility that belongs to each of us as individuals. He is convinced that individuals must assume responsibility for their own actions, whether—in the case of the Holocaust—a foot soldier, pastor, courier, typist, police officer, lawyer, judge or politician. He continues:

> At the center of this by now widespread rejection of the dominant paradigm of external coercion is a recognition of human agency, which necessitates the end of the caricature of Germans and others, whether perpetrators or bystanders, as unknowing, unthinking automatons or as herd-like, simply frightened people, option less people. This recent development is critical because only with this recognition is moral responsibility restored and genuine moral inquiry possible. The central premise underlying the reinvestigation of the Holocaust and the Nazi period that is finally underway has been the need to shift the

---

59. One account Lower provides is that of a woman named Erna Petri. She was the wife of an SS officer who was responsible for managing an estate after the invasion of Ukraine. On this occasion she discovered six Jewish children, realized they had escaped from a train headed for one of the death camps, lined them up, and killed them. Arrested after the war she was asked how, as a mother of two, she could do this, she replied: "I am unable to grasp at this time how in those days that I was in such a state as to conduct myself so brutally and reprehensibly—shooting Jewish children. However earlier [before arriving at the estate in Ukraine] I had been so conditioned to fascism and the racial laws, which established a view toward the Jewish people. As was told to me, I had to destroy the Jews. It was from *this mindset* that I came to commit such a brutal act." Lower, *Hitler's Furies*, 156. My emphasis.

60. Goldhagen also notes that "no German perpetrator was ever killed, sent to a concentration camp, or severely punished for refusing to kill Jews, and that though many of the perpetrators knew explicitly that they could exempt themselves from killing, only a few of them chose not to be willing executioners." Goldhagen, *Moral Reckoning*, 10, 11. *Hitler's Willing Executioners,*

focus of inquiry to the events' actors and to treat them as moral agents.⁶¹

RWANDA

In 1994 the nation of Rwanda, a land-locked nation in central eastern Africa, underwent a violent and devastating convulsion that ranks with the worst of twentieth century mass killings. Conflict between the Hutus and Tutsis, the country's two major ethnic groups, was not uncommon. This despite the fact that nearly all Rwandans were considered Christians. At the time well over 50 percent were Roman Catholic, with nearly 40 percent being Protestant. Tensions increased when Belgium colonized Rwanda in 1916, and made ethnicity an issue. Hutus, about 85 percent of the population were thought to be inferior to the Tutsis, who received better opportunities with regard to jobs and education. Even so there was a good deal of cooperation. Hutus and Tutsis share a common language and culture, there were may intermarriages, and business interactions were widespread.

For several decades prior to the great massacre, during which the Hutus assumed the reins of government following the departure of the Belgians in 1962, the Tutsis became victims of discrimination. There were riots resulting in the death of thousands in the 1950s, and in 1990 a group of Tutsis exiled in Uganda, in response to Hutu injustices, mounted an armed invasion against the Hutu rulers, and succeeded in gaining ground. A peace accord was signed in 1993, and though it brought an end to armed conflict unrest continued. Among the Hutus there was a growing concern that the Tutsis, should they ever become the ruling party, would prove vindictive.⁶² In the 1980s and early 1990s a hate campaign undertaken by the Hutus gained momentum. A Hutu manifesto, the "Ten Commandments of the Hutu," was published in which Tutsis were characterized as dishonest and untrustworthy. Any Hutu who married a Tutsi, or employed one would be considered a traitor. Government, military, and educational positions were to be filled with Hutus. The Tenth of these commandments emphasize the importance of their ideology:

---

61. Goldhagan, *Moral Reckoning*, 11.

62. BBC, "Rwanda: how the genocide happened," 5/17/11. See htpps://www/bbc.com/news-world-africa-13431485. Accessed August 20, 2022.

The Social Revolution of 1959, the Referendum of 1961, and the *Hutu Ideology*, must be taught to every Hutu at every level. Every Hutu must spread this ideology widely. Any Hutu who persecutes his brother Hutu for having read, spread and taught this ideology, is a traitor.[63]

Once the peace accords fell apart in 1993 fighting began again. It grew quickly in intensity following the death of President Juvenal Habyarimana in April 1994, when his plane was shot down. Although no one was found to be responsible the Tutsis were blamed. Hutus leaders called them "cockroaches," and said they were to be exterminated. The land was to be "cleansed" of Tutsis—and this meant all Tutsis including children. The killing began with modern weapons, and continued with machetes, spears and clubs. Samantha Powers writes, "The Rwandan genocide would prove to be the fastest, most efficient killing spree of the 20th century. In 100 days some 800,000 Tutsis and moderate Hutus were murdered. The United States did almost nothing to stop it."[64] There were thousands of UN soldiers in Rwanda at the time, but they were ordered not to become engaged. Political decision makers in the US and UN lacked the courage to act.[65]

Powers' account is well worth reading. She is wrong about one thing, however. While Rwanda may have been the fastest killing spree in history, it does not compare with abortion. Many Tutsis eventually escaped with their lives, but the victims of abortion very rarely do. They cannot speak, and they cannot defend themselves against their executioners. And those who plan their death are not members of another ethnic group but their own mothers and fathers!

ABORTION

Abortion has been practiced through the centuries, but was relatively rare given the danger to pregnant women, and the widespread belief in the sanctity of human life that prevailed in nations influenced by

---

63. Quoted in Power, *Problem From Hell*, 339.

64. Powers, *Problem From Hell*, 334.

65. Chapter 10 of Powers book, 'Rwanda: Mostly in a Listening Mode,' 329–90, is a fascinating account of the US and UN response to the Rwandan genocide. It is tragic and infuriating to realize that hundreds of thousands of men, women, and children could have been saved had political leaders acted with dispatch and courage.

Christianity.⁶⁶ The Church's position on abortion, clearly articulated by the early Church, was eventually incorporated into civil law first in Europe, and then later in America as new colonies were established. The prevailing view for several centuries among theologians and physicians, based on the medical evidence then available, was that life began with "quickening," the time when a mother first felt the movement of her unborn child. Protection for the unborn child in law tended to begin at this point in the pregnancy. Though abortion remained a dangerous procedure well into the nineteenth century, better medical training made it somewhat safer for the women who sought it.

Scholar Marvin Olasky, in his book, *Abortion Rites. A Social History of Abortion in America,* noted that during the seventeenth and eighteenth centuries, abortion, though not unknown, was limited not only by the lack of medical knowledge and skill, but by the social pressures of family and church. Social pressures carried more weight than the law. Most women, pregnant out of wedlock, were married by the time the baby arrived. Infanticide was actually more common, given the health risks associated with abortion.⁶⁷

Industrialization in the nineteenth century, along with the rapid growth of cities, also increased social mobility. This brought with it a notable rise in prostitution, and with it, a sharp increase in pregnancies and abortions.⁶⁸ In mid-century came the odd "Spiritism" movement, with its advocacy of free love, and its dismissal of biblical religion. This movement expressed its desire in ideas that were to surface again a hundred years later: individuals should be able to do what pleases them; hindering the sexual drive is a denial of what is natural; it is better that a child die in the womb than be unloved and unwanted after birth; it would be unfair for women to be saddled with maternal responsibilities which they had not chosen for themselves; individuals should decide for themselves what is true or false, right or wrong. As Olasky comments, "feelings" were paramount, and no obligation was to be accepted that restricted personal freedom.⁶⁹ Thousands of married women, many well-to-do, were caught up in this movement, became pregnant, and sought abortions.⁷⁰

66. Jacobson and Johnson, *Abortion Worldwide Report,* 33. Nations influenced by Islam also tend to oppose abortion.

67. Olasky, *Abortion Rites,* chapter 1, 20–26.

68. Olasky, *Abortion Rites,* chapter 2, 43–60.

69. Olasky, *Abortion Rites,* 70.

70. Olasky, *Abortion Rites,* chapter 3, 61–82.

Though accurate statistics are unavailable, Olasky, based on his studies of medical and historical records, estimates that there were at least 160,000 abortions annually during the 1860s—about 100,000 by prostitutes, and another 60,000 by women involved in the radical spiritism movement of the period. Though the number could have been less, Olasky doubts it was below 100,000 abortions a year.[71]

Between 1803 and 1918, as medical knowledge grew and established the fact that every human life began with conception, seventy nations moved to prohibit it. The effectiveness of these laws, which helped contain abortion to some extent, were strengthened by the moral values held by many people. More effective contraceptives, and the widespread availability of adoption and social services, perhaps especially in America, also contributed. As Olasky put it, abortion "was frequent but not common."[72]

Beginning in 1920—though the number of nations protecting preborn human beings grew at least temporarily to 86—a great reversal began, starting with the nations that formed the Soviet Union. A major factor powering this drive to authorize abortion, in the Soviet Union as elsewhere, was the eugenics movement. The widely shared desire for sexual freedom for women as well as men was another factor.

As noted earlier in this chapter, most eugenicist leaders held a secular worldview which—if it did not reject God outright—strongly de-emphasized religion, while emphasizing population control, and the effort to purify the human race of those considered inferior. In the West certain ethnic groups (e.g., Slavs, Africans, Asians, people of color) were considered by most eugenicists to be inferior, as were those with mental and physical handicaps.

The actual elimination of the unfit through abortion was widely debated by eugenicists in Europe and the United States at the dawn of the twentieth century. While sterilization and strict immigration policies were the methods of choice in curtailing the reproduction of unwanted people in the United States and several other countries, some, including Arthur Tregold in England, and Madison Grant in the US, openly advocated their elimination. As American physician, W. Duncan McKim so delicately put it, "The surest, the simplest, the kindest, and most humane means for preventing reproduction among those we deem unworthy of

---

71. Olasky, *Abortion Rites*, 289–92.
72. Olasky, *Abortion Rites*, 292.

this high privilege [reproduction], is a gentle, painless death."[73] That medical and scientific authorities, along with a host of political figures, could entertain such notions was strong evidence of the declining understanding and support for the sacredness of human life long before it became widely accepted.

A book that contributed to this more radical approach in Germany was *The Release and Destruction of Lives Devoid of Value*, by jurist Karl Binding and psychiatrist Alfred Hoche. Published in 1920, this book argued for the legality of euthanasia and abortion, for the killing of men, women and children considered unworthy of care and a financial burden to the state.[74] The German government, once Hitler became chancellor, prohibited abortion for Aryan women: Aryan children, as adults, would be needed to fulfill future plans for the expansion of the Third Reich. However, the children of a number of mentally and physically handicapped women were aborted, in keeping with the ideas of Binding and Hoche, and utilized in medical experimentation.[75] Compulsory abortion for Jewish women was imposed in Lithuania in 1942 following the German occupation, and also at the Theresienstadt concentration camp in 1943.[76] This was in line with the euthanasia program led by Dr. Karl Brandt that implemented some of the ideas in the book authored by Binding and Hoche.[77] Hitler, along with many other leaders of the Nazi government, shared these ideas, and encouraged their implementation.

73. Black, *War Against the Weak*, 249.

74. A number of recent scholars, Walter Wright, et. al, see similarities between the ideas of Alfred Hoche and Peter Singer, who now teaches at Princeton University. A growing number of European nations, along with seven American states, have legalized euthanasia in some form. Wright, "Peter Singer and the Lessons of the German Euthanasia Program," 27–43.

75. Friedlander, *Origins of Nazi Genocide*, 30.

76. Ofer and Weitzman, "Women in the Holocaust," In some camps imprisoned doctors aborted children to save their mothers from execution. Pregnant women and mothers with newborns were often a particular target. See Lifton, *Nazi Doctor*, 183.

77. Karl Brandt was a German physician and scientist who was introduced to these ideas in Alfred Hoche's medical school classes. Though Brandt found euthanasia agreeable, he was a scientist with an interest in medical experimentation, and performed numerous abortions on women considered mentally disordered. He did so in the expectation that their offspring would also be disordered, but subjects worthy of study. Brandt eventually became Adolph Hitler's personal physician, and a member of Hitler's inner circle at Berchtesgaden, in Bavaria. He was later appointed as the head of Germany's T-4 Euthanasia program. After the war he was tried and executed for helping put Hoche's and Binding's ideas into practice, which were considered crimes

As noted above, the Union of Soviet Socialist Republics, having embraced atheism as foundational to its worldview, became the first nation to legalize abortions. The decree noted that abortions, though illegal, were increasing in number. Because many women were harmed by unsafe abortions, and that punishing the women, physicians, and quacks involved was ineffective, the government therefore decreed that abortions would be made available in hospitals without charge. It was argued that this would reduce the number of abortions. In fact they increased. By 1932 abortions had surpassed one million. The number of abortions exceeded that of live births in numerous cities.[78] In 1936 the USSR restricted abortions, and then in 1955 re-authorized it, after which time it became the primary means of birth control.[79] Abortion remains widely used today as a method of birth control in a number of former Soviet republics.

Ten other nations, most of them in Europe and including Sweden, England and Germany, authorized abortions in the 1920s and 1930s, for reasons such as rape, the mother's health, or the possibility of physical or mental problems with the preborn child.[80] Today, one hundred years later, there are 136 nations which have authorized abortion in some measure.[81]

The authorization of abortion by Asian nations came later, as described by Mara Hvistendahl in her informative book, *Unnatural Selection*. She points out that a big first big step was taken in Japan after the conclusion of World War II, and the beginning of the American occupation. General William Draper, with General Douglass MacArthur, was given oversight of the occupation, noted the baby boom in Japan as thousands of soldiers returned home, and worried that a burgeoning population might lead to an increase in poverty. Further, Draper was concerned that were this to happen, Japan's economy would suffer and possibly undermine America's Asian foothold. Draper was further concerned that a stable Japan become a bulwark against the influence of Communism, growing ever more powerful in her neighbor, China. These concerns were shared by many leaders in the West who deemed population control to be of great importance, and thought that eugenicist abortion might be a solution. Certain upper-class Japanese were in

---

against humanity at the Nuremberg trials.

78. Jacobson and Johnson, *Abortion Worldwide Report*, 46.

79. Jacobson and Johnson, *Abortion Worldwide Report*, 61.

80. These included Sweden, England and Germany. See Jacobson and Johnson, 47.

81. Jacobson and Johnson, *Abortion Worldwide Report*. 33–45. Ireland and Columbia did so after publication of the AWR.

agreement, and in 1948 the Eugenic Protection Law was enacted which legalized both sterilization and abortion. The result was a population decline for Japan. By 1955 there were far more abortions than births. Meanwhile Japan's economy flourished. Draper, among others, was convinced that abortion provided the means to slow population growth, and thus increase economic growth.[82]

In 1952 John D. Rockefeller III convened a conference in Williamsburg to discuss population problems and the importance of family planning, particularly in Asian countries. The populations of India and China were of great concern. China at that time had the largest population in the world. The concerns raised at this conference generated a host of activities. Organizations were founded to focus on these concerns, and joined forces with the World Bank, the Ford Foundation, the United Nations Population Fund, and the International Planned Parenthood Federation to "sell Asian nations on population control, primarily by spreading the logic that lower birthrates lead to richer people."[83]

Hvistendahl points out that while abortion was first considered a successful population tool in Japan, it was in South Korea, following the Korean War, that abortion—with major American influence and funding—was further refined as a useful tool in establishing population control.[84] India fell in line with this policy in the early 1970s. About the same time China became another nation to embrace abortion as a means to population control. These nations derived considerable support for their efforts from the West, wherever fears of over-population increased dramatically—fears driven to a considerable degree through the work of an entomologist at Stanford University.

This scientist, Paul Ehrlich, was of the opinion that there were far too many people in the world—and *multiplying* all too rapidly. The result would be a human disaster. He expressed his fears in the book, *The Population Bomb*, which predicted that hundreds of millions of people would die of starvation. Though his predictions would eventually prove to be

---

82. Hvistendahl, *Unnatural Selection*, 123–25.

83. Hvistendahl, *Unnatural Selection*, 33. Though the Democratic Party has been strongly identified with support for legal abortion in recent decades, in the mid-twentieth century some prominent Republicans also gave it their support, among them George H. W. Bush and Henry Kissinger. Kissinger at one point signed on to a memo that stated that "No country has reduced its population growth without resorting to abortion." Hvistendahl, *Unnatural Selection*, 127.

84. Hvistendahl, *Unnatural Selection*, 129–34.

wildly inaccurate, his influence in the 1970s was notable. As Hvistendahl notes, "Ehrlich was ... a smart, passionate spokesman who disseminated *concepts* that had once been reserved for elites."[85] These concepts—these *ideas*—taken seriously by many others in academia, government and philanthropic foundations, propelled population control into a major movement. The idea of couples limiting themselves to two children became quite widely accepted in western societies, though Ehrlich thought American couples should limit themselves to one.[86]

China, with the world's largest population and a totalitarian government, despite the tens of millions of deaths caused by Mao's Great Leap Forward (1958–1962), took Ehrlich's idea seriously and made it *illegal* for couples to have more than one child. Quotas for the "One Child Policy," which were implemented nation-wide in 1980, were set for each locale. Women, after giving birth, were required to have an IUD inserted to prevent further pregnancies. Women found pregnant with a second child were often forced to have an abortion, even if late in the pregnancy.[87] On numerous occasions children who survived an abortion were killed by the abortionist, usually midwives trained by the government.[88] Women who did give birth to a second child were usually sterilized. As Elizabeth Gerhardt has pointed out, these practices were also aspects of gendercide, the disparagement and injury of women based on their gender.[89]

The efforts of politicians and family planners to augment the use of abortion in the nations of Asia were aided by the development of technologies such as sonograms and amniocentesis that enabled physicians to determine the sex of a child before birth. These eugenic birth control efforts were made easier by the fact that they coincided with certain

---

85. Hvistendahl, *Unnatural Selection*, 95–96.

86. When my wife, Carol became pregnant with our third child, John, it was somewhat difficult to ignore the fact that in the opinion of some people at the time, a third child was one too many.

87. According to Jacobson and Johnson 381,000,000 abortions were performed in China from 1956 to 2015, the most of any nation by far. Abortion Worldwide Report, 214.

88. Author Steven Mosher with Chi An, in their book, *A Mother's Ordeal*, tells the story of her life as a government abortionist, and the actions the Chinese government took to force women to have an abortion they fervently opposed to keep pace with government quotas. Disenchanted and heartsick with her work, she now lives in the United States.

89. As Gerhardt points out, gendercide is "an intentional effort to harm and injure women and girls based on their gender." *The Cross and Gendercide*, 20.

cultural factors, particularly in China and India, such as the preference of many couples for having a boy. Once this technology became widely available, again with a great deal of technological and financial aid supplied by the United States, the abortion of preborn girls increased rapidly. This process, which has seriously skewed the sex ratio in China, India, and a number of other nations, is described in detail by Hvistendahl's book in the section entitled "A Great Idea."[90]

The authorization of abortion in the West came somewhat later than that in Asia, and in terms of numbers has been smaller in scope. But the push had been underway for decades. In the United States newspapers such as the *New York Times*, which in the late nineteenth century had strongly favored anti-abortion laws, moved toward a less critical stance in the early twentieth century, and became openly favorable as the decades passed.[91] Within the medical community, which by and large supported the preborn child's right to life, new voices were heard which argued that abortion was occasionally necessary, even something that in certain instances could be considered morally correct.[92]

In the United States, as in Asian nations, Planned Parenthood proved to be a powerful force for promoting abortion. It is today the leading provider of abortion in the United States, even though it claims to be pro-woman. As Patrina Moseley has pointed out in a publication for the Family Research Council, this is far from the truth.

> Sadly, this organization has been caught repeatedly violating the law and violating women, from aiding and abetting sex traffickers, covering up child sexual abuse, and selling the remains of aborted baby parts to ignoring the disastrous effects that abortion has on women's physical and mental health. From its racist eugenic roots to the targeting of vulnerable communities today, their scandals continue to pile up.[93]

Mosley's article reminds readers that Planned Parenthood, founded by Margaret Sanger in 1926 as the American Birth Control League and renamed in 1942, was rooted in the American eugenics movement. As she puts it, "While its current leadership does not openly embrace the

---

90. Hivistendahl, Unnatural Selection, 77–155.

91. Olasky, *Abortion Rites*, 268–78. In the mid-twentieth century nearly every state allowed abortion if the mother's life was genuinely endangered.

92. Olasky, *Abortion Rites*, 261–63.

93. Mosley, "Planned Parenthood Is Not Pro-Woman," 1.

noxious view of its founder, the eugenic heart of Planned Parenthood still beats."[94]

In 1973 Nobel Laureate James Watson, in an interview with *Prism* magazine, said "If a child were not declared alive until three days after birth, then all parents could be allowed the choice only a few are given under the present system . . . I believe this view is the only rational, compassionate attitude to have."[95] Peter Singer, a bioethicist who teaches at Princeton University, and an atheist influenced by Marxism, agrees that killing a disabled child after birth is not wrong.[96] He has long supported abortion, and has repeatedly called for the legalization of infanticide and euthanasia. He does not believe that human life is sacred, and insists that animals are as valuable as human beings. Those who do not agree he labels a "speciesist."[97] Singer has called for those on the political left to take seriously the ideas of modern Darwinism, particularly the fact that human beings are merely sophisticated animals.[98] In 2012 Alberto Giubilin and Francesca Minerva authored an article in the *Journal of Medical Ethics* (March 2, 2012) entitled: "After-birth abortion: why should the baby live?" In answer to their own question they wrote,

> We argue that, when circumstances occur *after birth* such that they would have justified abortion, what we call *after-birth abortion* should be permissible. In spite of the oxymoron in the expression we propose to call this practice 'after-birth abortion', rather than 'infanticide', to emphasize that the moral status of the individual killed is comparable with that of a fetus (on which 'abortions' in the traditional sense are performed) rather than to that of a child. Therefore, we claim that killing a newborn could be ethically permissible in all the circumstances where abortion would be. Such circumstances include cases where the newborn

---

94. Mosely, "Planned Parenthood Is Not Pro-Woman." 21–22.

95. James Watson interview in *Prism* magazine, May 1973, cited by Schaeffer and Koop, in *Whatever Happened to the Human Race*, 73.

96. See "Singer on abortion, disability and replaceability," 10/31/2012. At htpps://peped.org/philosophicalinvestigatios/singer-3/.

97. See Weikart, *Death of Humanity*. 45. Also Singer, *Unsanctifying Human Life*, 202. Christians certainly agree with Singer that animals are to be respected and cared for, as part of God's good creation. And yet, not being made in God's own image, do not share the rights God has conferred upon human beings. See Dean Koontz, Introduction to Smith, *A Rat is a Pig is a Dog is a Boy*.

98. West, *Darwin Day in America*, xv.

has the potential to have an (at least) acceptable life, but the well-being of the family is at risk.⁹⁹

Taking things a step further is Eric Pianka, a biologist and evolutionary ecologist at the University of Texas. Multitudes would probably agree with his idea that human beings are often poor stewards of Mother Earth. However, at a speech at the Texas Academy of Science in 2006 he said things that caused a bit of an uproar, particularly his comment that earth would be better off with fewer people. An ebola virus that was 90 percent lethal would—in his view—greatly lessen the impact of humans on planet earth. To say the least.¹⁰⁰

Not surprisingly the ideas expressed by Watson, Guibilin, Minerva and Pianka have provoked comment. Guibilina and Francesca responded, rather disingenuously, by saying that their article was never meant to encourage a change in the law. Pianka has said he was misunderstood. Perhaps so, but these ideas do have consequences—ideas which legislators in various countries are pursuing even now.

The quest to authorize abortion, and keep it legal, has drawn strength from numerous sources. The eugenics movement and social Darwinism helped lay the groundwork by denigrating biblical religion, asserting that the purification of the race necessitated a distinction between higher and lower races, and worked to limit the reproduction of the latter. The population control movement contributed with the idea that abortion could help control population size. The modern feminist movement aided the trend with the idea that women had the right to control their bodies, which they insisted gave them the right to abort an unwanted child. Economists Steven Leavitt and Stephen Dubner have suggested that a higher incidence of abortion among low income women could save the country from some of the high costs of crime and mental health support that are often associated with the children born to these woman.¹⁰¹

---

99. Guibilina and Minerva, "After-birth abortion: why should the baby live?," The idea of a post-birth probationary period during which acceptance of the newborn as human persons would depend on their undergoing extensive testing to determine their fitness for inclusion. Such testing might well include psychological testing of the parents do determine their fitness and willingness to care for their child. (my emphasis)

100. Cited by Weikart, *The Death of Humanity.* 3–4. Also see Pianca's website: www.zo.utexas.edu/faculty/pianka/eric.html.

101. Leavitt with Dubner published their book, *Freakanomics,* in which they suggested (perhaps a bit tongue-in-cheek) that legal abortion may have contributed to

Ideologies Gone Rogue

The sketches of mass violence included in this chapter are due in considerable degree to ideas inherent in the secularization of western, and world culture. Neglect or denial of God has brought with it a radical change in the meaning of the concept of "freedom." In earlier centuries freedom carried with it the idea of an individual being able to make his or her own choices without coercion or interference of religion, culture or government. Freedom was also understood as being necessary to moral responsibility, the exercise of which should be in accordance with moral principles, and self-control. Today, however, for countless numbers of people East and West freedom has come to mean, essentially, the same thing as *license:* doing whatever one wants to do without restraint—whether with regard to sexual issues, marriage, or the killing of preborn babies.[102]

The other factor, of even greater importance, has been the loss of confidence in truth—truth in the sense of being rooted in physical and spiritual reality. Social Darwinists, eugenicists, Communists, Fascists, Feminists, and today's post-modernists have all in one way and another resisted the biblical story and worldview. Though the hard sciences have tended to resist the idea that all knowledge, including the understanding of the material world, is relative, the social sciences (e.g., sociology, psychology), along with history, literature, and philosophy, have embraced it to a considerable degree.

The biblical story often is ridiculed. Moral absolutes, even the possibility of determining objective facts, are denied. Everything in life is contingent, and related to one's personal circumstances. To argue for moral truth is to be labeled intolerant.

This trend has been ongoing for many decades. For many people today truth is relative, and means little more than a personal preference or way of looking at things. One's understanding of things, material or spiritual, is just a social or personal construct with little or no concern as to whether it corresponds to reality. Morality, as communists, fascists and secular humanists would say, is nothing more or less than what the adherents of these movements say it is. The law is what the legislative

---

the falling crime rates of recent decades, in that abortion is sought by large numbers of women with limited financial means, many under the poverty line, a demographic marked in part by a disproportionately greater number of children becoming involved in criminal activities. Pinker disputes this. See *Better Angels*, 119–21.

102. *Last Call for Liberty*, by Os Guinness, is a first-rated study of the threats to freedom today, including the efforts to change its fundamental meaning.

bodies and courts of society say it is, with precedent providing the determination of legal cases—too often with little regard for what is truly just and fair.[103]

The massive shedding of innocent blood of our modern era has typically involved the distortion of language and communication through lies, the repetitive use of terminology that dehumanizes targeted groups, and in creating euphemisms which put a positive spin on evil actions.[104] Language such as this, which is used to dehumanize others is called the "semantics of oppression" by sociologist William Brennan, and has been widely used by the perpetrators of violence.

Some early Americans in their effort to claim land from native Americans referred to Indian peoples as animals or vermin. American slave owners considered their slaves as an inferior class or an article of property. Leaders of the USSR often considered peasants as beasts of burden, the kulaks as parasites, and those they killed as "un-persons who had never existed." The Nazis in their hatred of the Jews referred to them as parasites, vermin, garbage and a form of disease.[105] The German medical community began its euthanasia program with the killing of children. Since that was unacceptable to many citizens, euphemisms were often employed to conceal their efforts. For example, the organization designed specifically for the killing of children was euphemistically dubbed the "Realm's Committee for Scientific Approach to Severe Illness Due to Heredity and Constitution."[106]

Those advocating abortion's legalization have also employed semantic manipulations. One candid example was provided in a *California Medicine* editorial in 1970. Editorial writer, Dr. Malcom Potts, asserted that the old Judeo-Christian ethic, which upheld the sanctity of every human life, provided the foundation for numerous laws and social policies, as well as the motivation for physicians to do what they

---

103. Modern law tends to shift with the times, and given the power of government to enforce laws, federal courts can make decisions which coerce compliance nationwide. So it has been with Roe v. Wade, Doe v. Bolton and Obergefell v. Hodges. These three Supreme Court decisions have radically changed American society, though the first two have done the most damage with regard to the sanctity of human life. See Jaffa, *Crisis of a House Divided* for a fascinating account of how the "historical" view of law championed by such men as Oliver Wendell Holmes, Carl Becker and John Dewey, removed the idea of objective or natural law as the foundation for law.

104. Schaeffer and Koop, *Whatever Happened to the Human Race*, 67.

105. Brennan, *Dehumanizing the Vulnerable*, 6–7.

106. Brennan, *Dehumanizing the Vulnerable*, 6–7.

could to protect and prolong the lives of their patients, was being eroded. Growing concerns over population, the possible lack of resources necessary to accommodate the kind of life many people wanted to live, and a growing concern for quality of life had led many people to consider abortion as a solution. However, since the acceptance of abortion was then socially repugnant, it was considered necessary to keep the ideas of abortion and killing separate. To do so necessitated a "considerable semantic gymnastics"—a "schizophrenic subterfuge"—to make this " new" ethic acceptable.[107]

In Brennan's book, *Dehumanizing the Vulnerable*, which was published after the Supreme Court's Roe decision in 1973, he provides a list of some of the rationalizations that Potts referred to as "schizophrenic subterfuges" that were actually used with regard to the unborn child. Of course, knowing that these subterfuges were given under "socially impeccable auspices" is wonderfully reassuring.

- "The fetus, at most, represents only the potentiality of life." (*U.S. Supreme Court decision, 1973*)
- "A fetus is not a human being." (*Rabbi Wolfe Kelman, 1984*)
- "Pregnancy when not wanted is a disease . . . in fact, a venereal disease." (*Professor Joseph Fletcher, 1979*)
- "People's body parts (embryos) are their personal property." (*Attorney Lori Andrews, 1986*)
- "An aborted baby is just garbage . . . just refuse." (*Dr. Martti Kekomaki, 1980*)
- "The word 'person,' as used in the 14th amendment, does not include the unborn." *U. S. Supreme Court decision, 1973*)[108]

Word games such as these journalist Gabriele Kuby refers to as the "political rape of language."[109]

> Language exists to express something about reality and to communicate it to others. We have not made the reality nor the linguistic vessels to hold it in. Does the speaker strive to bring both into accord, so that the vessel contains the truth? Or does the

---

107. Potts, "A new ethic for Medicine and Society, 67–68.

108. Brennan, *Dehumanizing the Vulnerable*, 6–7. Brennan supplies a number of tables which provide greater detail.

109. Kuby, *Global Sexual Revolution*, 108.

speaker deliberately use language to represent reality differently than it is? The latter of the two is called lying. And manipulation can be a refined form of lying. Let's say someone wants another person to change his thinking and behavior *without even noticing it*. Terms are turned into false labels that misrepresent the contents of the package. When political leaders do this, we call it propaganda.[110]

Separating the idea of abortion from that of killing, avoiding scientific evidence, utilizing semantic gymnastics to rationalize abortion as anything but taking a human life, and the use of schizophrenic subterfuge, is moral dishonesty. And yet it has proven to be quite effective. Millions of people in this, and other countries, have been taken in by such distortions. Kuby in her chapter on the rape of language provides an apt quote: "You need not have advanced very far in your learning in order to find good reasons for the most evil of things. All the evil deeds in this world since Adam and Eve have been justified with good reasons."[111] The words of Isaiah come to mind—"Woe to those who call evil good and good evil, who put darkness for light and light for darkness" (Isa 5.20).

What is it within the hearts and minds of some human beings that makes them willing to kill, to murder, to exterminate other human beings on a large scale? The basic answer as I have attempted to show in this chapter has to do with ideas, with ideologies, specifically those which deny or downplay religion and the sanctity of human life. A number of scholars who have studied modern violence, though they do not consider abortion, would I believe concur. Historian Paul Johnson, in his massive look at twentieth century history, held the view that the extraordinary violence of modern times was due to the loss of Judeo-Christian values, and the moral relativism that resulted from the misapprehension of Einstein's theory of relativity.[112]

Zbigniew Brzezinski, more recently, agreed with Johnson's emphasis on the collapse of moral standards, and believed that the decline of religion was an impediment to understanding the massive social and political changes of our modern world. As he put it, "Ultimately it is ideas that

---

110. Kuby, *Global Sexual Revolution*, 108–9. Her emphasis.

111. The Hegel quotation as cited by Kuby, *Global Sexual Revolution,* 109, was earlier cited by Josef Pieper, *Abuse of Language: Abuse of Power,* 15.

112. Johnson thought that the move toward moral relativism was also influenced by the work of Sigmund Freud, who considered religion a delusion. *Modern Times,* 5–11.

mobilize political action and thus shape the world."[113] Robert Conquest, author of several books on Soviet terror, in reflecting on the ravages of the twentieth century wrote that "humanity has been savaged and trampled by rogue ideologies."[114] These "ideas' or "ideologies" refer to what many today call a worldview—the " 'lens" through which people view life and the world, and which shapes their behavior.

As a Christian I am convinced that the root cause of the worldviews or ideologies responsible for so much twentieth century violence is sin— a turning away from God, and the human wickedness in all its varied manifestations that flow from this fact. To turn away from God is to turn away from truth, knowledge and wisdom, and toward thinking and doing evil, a point often noted in the Bible. The prophet Jeremiah puts it succinctly: "The heart is deceitful above all things, and desperately corrupt; who can understand it?" (Je 17.9).

Jesus concurred with this idea, and amplified it in a conversation with Jewish leaders. Responding to their criticism that he and his followers were ignoring certain Jewish traditions regarding the washing of hands, Jesus said, "Well did Isaiah prophesy of you hypocrites, as it is written, 'This people honors me with their lips, but their heart is far from me; in vain do they worship me, teaching as doctrines the precepts of men.'[115] You leave the commandment of God, and hold fast the tradition of men" (Mk 7.6–8). Speaking later, in response to questions of his disciples about this issue, Jesus amplified his thought with this generalization:

> Then are you also without understanding? Do you not see that whatever goes into a man from outside cannot defile him, since it enters, not his heart but his stomach, and so passes on?" (Thus he declared all foods clean.) And he said, "What comes out of a man is what defiles a man. For from within, out of the heart of man, come evil thoughts, fornications, theft, murder, adultery, coveting, wickedness, deceit, licentiousness, envy, slander,

---

113. Brzezinski, *Out of Control*, x.

114. See *Reflections on a Ravaged Century*, xi, xii.

115. The word "heart" in biblical thought refers to the center of a person's being— their thoughts, ideas, desires, the orientation of the will. To guard the heart, to be careful of one's thoughts and ideas, as stated in Prov 4.23, is to keep one's heart and mind centered upon God and his purposes and commands. It is in fact, to keep one's worldview in line with the teaching of God and his Word, the living Word, Jesus the Christ. To do so enables an individual to abide in the love of Christ. It enables an individual to bear good fruit, i.e., to live a life of love and service that is pleasing to God.

pride, foolishness. All these evil things come from within, and they defile a man (Mark 7.22–23)."[116]

These words of Jesus, though ancient, are an in-depth and succinct description of human motivation in every age. Alexander Solzhenitsyn provided a modern affirmation in writing of his experience in the Soviet Gulag: "Gradually it was disclosed to me that the line separating good and evil passes not through states, nor between classes, nor between political parties either—but right through every human heart—and through all human hearts."[117]

In saying that the evil and violence of the world is driven by the "evil thoughts" of the heart does not overlook the role of emotion. It is important, however, to note that emotions themselves are driven largely by cognitive activity, which includes thoughts, ideas, ideologies, memories and images.[118] As Conquest notes in his study of twentieth century rogue ideologies, "our problems have been due not to fallacious ideas in the abstract but to the extreme, uncontrolled, emotional charge they carry."[119] Richard Weaver, who famously wrote, "ideas have consequences," would have agreed that the *emotional* force of ideas are one aspect of the consequences that follow from them.[120]

116. We may not think of Jesus as a philosopher, but he was in his insistence that bad ideas and thoughts must be repented of, and replaced with an understanding of, and obedience to, his ideas about the love of God, love of neighbor, even the love of the stranger and the enemy. Jesus was also very practical, giving to disciples not only a worldview but the help of the Comforter, the Holy Spirit, who draws believers into fellowship while providing guidance, remembrance of Jesus and his teaching, and power, the inner power to develop the habit of thoughtful obedience. Dallas Willard, in words every Christian—indeed, every human being—should take to heart, said of Jesus: "We need to understand that Jesus is a *thinker,* that this is not a dirty word but an essential word, and that his other attributes do not preclude thought, but only ensure that he is certainly the greatest thinker of the human race: "the most intelligent person who ever lived on earth." He constantly uses the power of logical insight to enable people to come to the truth about themselves and about God from the inside of their own heart and mind. Quite certainly it also played a role in his own growth in "wisdom" (Luke 2.52)." Willard, *The Great Omission,* 189, (Willard's emphasis)

117. Solzhenitsyn, *Gulag Archipelago,* (Vol. 2), 615

118. The effectiveness of cognitive-behavioral therapy owes much to its emphasis on ascertaining and reprogramming the thoughts and ideas of clients, thereby changing and ameliorating their emotional consequences.

119. Conquest, *Reflections on a Ravaged Century,* xii.

120. See Weaver, *Ideas Have Consequences,* 2013. Weaver's book is helpful in tracing the shift in ideas in Western culture from pre-Reformation times into the twentieth century.

It is for this reason that the Bible throughout emphasizes the importance of guarding the heart (Prov 4.23) and seeking knowledge, insight and wisdom from God (Proverbs 2.1–6). To guard the heart is truly to guard the mind, that is, to discipline oneself with regard to what one reads, listens to, observes, remembers and thinks about. Many acts of violence result from memories harbored, and replayed over and over again. Each replay of a memory can, and very often does generate a new wave of emotion. The more negative the thought or memory, the more negative the emotion which is generated. And the more likely that this process will become habitual.

The historical record provides numerous examples of mass violence driven by ideas, whether eugenics, World War I, Communism, or the Holocaust. Ideas—ideologies, worldviews—were at the heart of Turkey's Armenian massacre, and Japan's brutal military adventures in Asia and the Pacific. So too were the crimes against humanity perpetrated by Communism and Nazism. The perpetrators of the Rwandan massacre, the civil wars of the Congo, the Vietnam War, the Iraq-Iran War, the genocide in Somalia and Sudan, and a host of other conflicts were likewise driven by ideas. This is also true of many of the murders which occur daily in so many countries.

Ideas are foundational, and are reinforced by custom, tradition, habits and laws built up within the culture of family, tribe and nation. During the twentieth century a number of cultures or societies—though quite different with regard to dominant religious values, political structure, and economics—embraced the idea that certain groups were a threat. To exploit and kill them in very large numbers was acceptable, and legal, once the perpetrators had the political power to change the law to suit them. Modern governments and their militaries have proved remarkably successful in implementing such ideas, in part through training that conditions and desensitizes soldiers to killing.[121]

Abortion, however, which has been authorized by dozens of nations, has proven to be even more effective. It is cheaper than war, doesn't damage public property or produce massive refugee movements, and serves

---

121. David Grossman, in his book, *On Killing*, relates how the U. S. military in Vietnam, utilizing a systematic process of desensitization, conditioning and training increased the individual firing rate from a World War II baseline of 15 to 20 percent of infantrymen to an all-time high of up to 95 percent. Grossman believes that a similar process of systematic desensitization, conditioning and vicarious learning is contributing to the unleashing of an epidemic of violence in America. When one considers the increase in mass shootings it seems a plausible scenario. *On Killing*, 304–8.

as a convenient way for men and women to avoid the responsibility of parenthood. And to do so privately, without the shame or embarrassment of public scrutiny. Abortion has also proved to be a highly profitable enterprise for its practitioners—and the institutions or organizations to which they belong (hospitals, medical practices, abortion facilities, including those run by Planned Parenthood).[122]

In saying all of this it is important to remember that maturity in thought and action is hindered, not only by one's culture, laws, habits and past, but by the spiritual malignancy Christians refer to as Satan—the Evil One. Of him Jesus said, "He was a murderer from the beginning, and has nothing to do with truth, because there is no truth in him. When he lies, he speaks according to his own nature, for he is a liar and the father of lies" (John 8.44b). Abortion, in particular, perpetuates the lie that the preborn child is unworthy of full protection by the law.

Another factor studied by a number of biblical scholars is the category of "rulers," "powers" and "authorities" of which St Paul wrote in Eph 6.10–18. They believe that Paul was referring not to demonic spirits as such, but to the earthly instrumentalities, structures, institutions, rulers, and laws which are opposed to God and his kingdom, and which—given the power and authority inherent in them—become instruments of evil.[123] It is certain that many earthly institutions, laws and authorities have served evil purposes. However, it falls well within the biblical understanding of reality to think that such "powers" may be influenced by actual demonic spirits of some kind.[124]

When an organization or government possesses (and is possessed by) ideas or a worldview that excludes God and denigrates and disparages others, violence often results. Worldviews which deny God almost invariably have a tendency to deny the human rights of those individuals and groups they consider inferior or a threat. To ponder the violence of our modern world and the worldviews associated with is to see that many of its proponents are, truly "in love with death" (Prov 8.31).

---

122. In the recent movie, *Goznell*, there is a trial scene where a female physician admits to having performing thirty thousand abortions. Thirty thousand abortions, say a profit of $50 for each one (and probably more), and she would be a millionaire.

123. See Stassen, *Authentic Transformation*, 211–22.

124. I was fascinated to read in William Shirer's monumental study of Nazi Germany that Houston Stewart Chamberlain, a man who greatly influenced Adolph Hitler, claimed to be driven by demons. Shirer, *Rise and Fall of the Third Reich*, 105.

COMMONALITIES

The twentieth century has witnessed countless acts of violence and mass killing. In this chapter I have attempted to describe several instances of such violence, and to set down some of the ideas and worldviews that I believe motivated the perpetrators. Proponents of Nazism, Communism, Hutu superiority, and abortion, do not hold identical views with regard to race, history, politics, economic systems, and philosophy, and yet are remarkably alike in their willingness and ability to dehumanize and kill large numbers of human beings they consider inferior and disposable as a means of "bettering" their society or nation. What follows are some of their commonalities:

1. Basic to these mass killings are ideas—a view of reality that distinguishes between the society, nation, or culture to which the perpetrators belong, and the group or groups that are considered as enemies or threats. These ideas or worldviews, in their original form, are usually promulgated by intellectuals, philosophers and journalists.

2. A primary commonality of some perpetrators of modern mass killings—the heart of their worldview—is a rejection of God—the biblical God, the Maker of heaven and earth, the God of truth, righteousness and justice. This would be true of Communist ideology and those on the political left who hold a form of scientific materialism which leaves no place for a deity.[125]

3. There are also religious views of reality in which the deity, as understood, lacks a universal appreciation of human worth. Many liberal

---

125. Alexander Solzhenitsyn in his address at Harvard University in 1979 (date?) related the view of his grandmother that the calamities associated with World War I and the rise of the Communist revolution had happened because men had forgotten God. In fact, many people who have expressed a belief in God have committed violence too. One can think of the Christian crusades, slavery, the religious wars in Europe, the burning of witches in New England, the liberal support for abortion, and the depredations of radical Islam. It is important to note, however, that Christians support for violence has often been at odds with the high view of life given to the world by Jesus Christ. Even in World War II, viewed by most scholars as a just war, and supported by most Christians whether liberal or conservative, there were serious moral lapses. The stance of the peace churches, of course, has been consistently opposed to all wars. Differing understandings of God, and the dignity and value of human beings, as I have tried to clarify in this study, have led liberal and conservative Christians to radically different views with regard to abortion and euthanasia.

Christians and Jews have watered down the biblical view of God on which human dignity and worth depend with regard to abortion, infanticide and euthanasia.

4. The rejection of God necessarily means a rejection of the biblical truth that every human being is made in the image of God. Of his creation, including humankind, God says that it is "very good." (Gen 1.31). Those responsible for mass killings do not agree. Both the progenitors and perpetrators of mass killings view their victims as subhuman, inferior, parasites, or as a threat of some kind.

5. Moral relativism is another commonality. In each instance those responsible for mass killings have denied or rejected an objective morality. Paul Johnson titled the first chapter of his book, *Modern Times*, "A Relativistic World." It is not that those responsible for these instances of mass violence lacked a moral code, but that the moral values that motivated them were whatever their political party, or nation, or organization determined them to be. As C. S. Lewis pointed out, a society that loses its belief and confidence in the objectivity of truth will eventually destroy itself.[126]

6. Deciding which worldview is or has been the most heinous of modern times may be debatable; many scholars consider Nazism to be a class by itself. But one thing common to all the savagery of the last century is that so many of the victims were deliberately targeted and killed. The means were often quite different: bombing, shooting, hanging, knifing, burning, famine, gassing, and the use of torture. Whatever the means, the goal was the death of individual persons—a woman, a man, a child. Some were young, even preborn, some were older, some very old. And now they are dead. Eliminated and disposed of. Countless hundreds of millions of other human beings—very probably more than a billion—have and do suffer physically and emotionally because of the violence they've witnessed, or with which they were treated.[127]

---

126. Lewis, "The Poison of Subjectivity," in *Christian Reflections*, 73.

127. It is probable that the most influential philosophy or worldview at present is that of scientific materialism, aka scientific naturalism. To a considerable degree it permeates cultures East and West—Communist and Capitalist, Asian, European, African and American. That this is so is due in large part because nations around the world are embracing modern science and technology. And to embrace modern science is to benefit not only from the industrial-technological advances built upon it, but the philosophical ideas—the atheism and moral relativism—so often connected with it.

7. The political perpetrators of modern violence for the most part have been coercive utopians. Convinced that their vision for the future of their nation or the world is best, they have employed the coercive power of government and the support of other cultural institutions (e.g., academia, the media) in their efforts to build a "better" society.[128]

8. The vision of the world held by these perpetrators includes the willingness not only to kill and destroy, but to do so in large numbers. Once in power they readily utilize the power, authority and weapons of the state to authorize or enact their deadly programs of mass killing.[129] While the police and military arms of government have been

---

John West in his book, *Darwin Day in America*, focuses on the public policy consequences in the United States that have followed from Charles Darwin and his philosophy of evolution. Darwin's work, though often criticized during his lifetime, gradually gained ground among scientists and philosophers, who over the decades refined and developed his ideas further. West presents a thoughtful critique of scientific materialism and its influence on criminal science, mental illness, race, sexuality, ecology, business and politics.

> According to Darwin's account, natural selection and the laws of heredity acting on the material world produced mind, morality, and civilization. Whether or not Darwin wished to call himself a materialist, his theory had the consequences of making a materialistic understanding of man and society finally credible. By describing in detail natural mechanisms that could produce the complexity of life as we know it, Darwin helped transform materialism from a fantastic tale told by a few thinkers on the fringe of society to a hallowed scientific principle enshrined at the heart of modern science. See West, *Darwin Day*, 41.

Though modern technology and industry have combined forces in making ever deadlier weapons, it must be noted that large scale violence can be, and often has been, very effective without sophisticated technology. Consider the murder of over a million eastern European Jews by Einsatzgruppe units using rifles, the Rwandan massacre where machetes and hoes as well as rifles killed nearly a million people, the massacre of the Armenians in World War 1, in which many died of starvation. This was also true in the Ukrainian famine in the 1930s carried out by the Soviet Union, and that of the Chinese Communist Party in the famine connected to the Great Leap Forward in the later 1950s and beyond, in which many millions of people perished.

128. In the United States and Europe university education, particularly in the humanities and social studies programs, has gone a long way toward inculcating political correctness in their student bodies. Though lip service is paid to free speech and an honest quest for truth, those who attempt it are often shouted down, or ignored. Numerous media outlets are often willing to comply.

129. Police and military force, as utilized by fascists, Nazis, and Communists, has—unsurprisingly—proved to be very effective in perpetrating mass killings. But the coercion applied politically through propaganda, changing laws, and taxation, has also proven to be highly effective in gaining the support of millions of people (some Christians among them) for regimes responsible for mass murder. Brzezinski

responsible for killing millions, many of the deaths resulting from slavery, euthanasia, and abortion were carried out legally by private citizens and medical personnel authorized to do so by a government.

9. A related commonality is the ability of the perpetrators of mass killings to persuade or pressure other individuals to carry out the actual killing. *Ordinary Men*, Christopher Browning's study of a German Police Battalion that murdered Jews in occupied Poland, documents the fact that these men, mostly middle-aged, went about their grisly task quite willingly. Men who chose not to take part were not punished. Nazi propaganda, military authority, and peer pressure, were motivation enough.[130]

10. In democratic societies public institutions—universities, media, professional organizations and associations—are targeted by the proponents of violence. The support of religious communities favorable to such goals is sought. Once a cultural shift takes place,

---

has noted the fact that both the Nazi and Communist regimes were highly effective in encouraging millions of citizens in the nations under their control to denounce one another—denunciation which in many instances led to the death of the individual who was denounced. Brzezinski writes, "In all the former Communist states once-secret archives which now have become available reveal that much of the dynamism for the mass arrests, and for many of the executions, was generated by a veritable orgy of denunciations. Such archives contain literally millions of written denunciations of neighbors by neighbors, even of relatives by relatives. This was very deliberately encouraged as part of the process of ideological conditioning . . . It was a system not only of mass murder—on a scale without precedent in human history—but of the deliberate demoralization of society and of the reckless devastation of the physical environment. In brief, both the soul and the body of society were its victims." See Brzezinski, *Out of Control*, 36–37.

130. Browning in the conclusion to this book writes,

I fear that we live in a world in which war and racism are ubiquitous, in which the powers of government mobilization and legitimization are powerful and increasing, in which a sense of personal responsibility is increasingly attenuated by specialization and bureaucratization, and in which the peer group exerts tremendous pressures on behavior and sets moral norms. In such a world, I fear, modern governments that wish to commit mass murder will seldom fail in their efforts for being able to induce "ordinary men" to become "willing executioners." *Ordinary Men*, 223.

It must be pointed out, however, that racism is not always necessary. The million and more Cambodians killed by Pol Pot's Communist regime were murdered by fellow Cambodians. The perpetrators of the many millions of Chinese killed by China's Communist government were also Chinese. The vast number of young human beings, of whatever ethnicity, who are aborted die at the hands of someone of the same ethnicity. And it is their parents who acquiesce is their death.

and the views of leaders of these institutions increasingly align with those seeking to perpetrate their violent ideologies (sterilization, abortion, euthanasia, etc), there is an increasing effort to encourage political, professional organizations, and cultural institutions such as universities, medical facilities, courts and state legislatures to authorize and implement their vision.[131] And further, to demonize their opponents.

11. A cultural shift in worldviews that provide opportunities for personal gain often is accompanied by greed. Slavery proved profitable for many slave owners in the Americas, and elsewhere. Hundreds of German companies benefited financially from the Jewish Holocaust. Abortion facilities, including those run by Planned Parenthood, and a great number of physicians and nurses have profited by performing abortions.[132]

12. In most instances of mass violence there is a concerted effort to euphemize, minimize or cover up the violence, and to silence or intimidate those who oppose the violence. With fascist and communist regimes this is not difficult as media outlets are controlled by the government. In the West the mainstream media—TV, newspapers, journals—do not provide extensive coverage of news related to abortion, and have been willing to consider the aborted fetus as a "product of conception," abortion as a "health procedure," the killing of the preborn child a mother's "right."

13. Another commonality of these various perpetrators is the remarkable effectiveness of their plans. Killing and injuring large numbers of people requires a great amount of planning and organizational effort with regard to procedures, weapons and instruments of violence, and cooperation and communication among the perpetrators. Modern businesses are often willing to provide needed materials,

---

131. War between democracies has become a thing of the past, an advance one can only hope will be sustained in the future. Legal violence toward certain individuals, however, as is the case with abortion and euthanasia, has not. Dozens of modern democracies have authorized abortion, and several have authorized euthanasia in some cases. Those who support abortion and euthanasia do not refer to such actions as forms of violence, but are euphemistically labeled as social benefits or civil rights.

132. See Nathanson with Ostling, chapter 9, "The Merchants of Abortion," in *Aborting America*. Clark, "Planned Parenthood Makes as Much as $23 Million Annually from Selling baby Body Parts."

whether weapons, drugs, or the instruments such as those used with sterilization or abortion.[133]

In chapter three we will look at a number of instances of large-scale violence that took place in areas where substantial numbers of Christians lived, but proved to be of little help in either preventing or reducing the violence. On some occasions they took part in the killing. It is my conviction that a major reason for this fact has been the failure of the Christian communities in these situations to effectively disciple their members in the worldview and lifestyle that Jesus taught.

---

133. See Black's book, *IBM and the Holocaust*, for an account of the Nazi use of technological help provided by IBM in identifying and locating Jews.

3

Lilies That Fester
The Scandal of Discipleship

Nevertheless, whether or not they approved of Hitler, they all did their duty, as workers, farmers, bureaucrats, taxpayers, bankers, clergy, police officials and warriors, and that is precisely what made the "Final Solution" possible.

—Richard L. Rubenstein[1]

[T]he current position of the church in our day may be better explained by *what liberals and conservatives have shared* than by how they differ. For different reasons, and with different emphases, they have agreed that discipleship to Christ is optional to membership in the Christian church.

—Dallas Willard[2]

Can Christians be ethical? . . . Can Christians be righteous? After the Holocaust, this question is worth asking.

—David Gushee[3]

---

1. "Waldheim, the Pope, and the Holocaust," 278.
2. Willard, *The Divine Omission*, 11. (His emphasis)
3. *The Righteous Gentiles of the Holocaust*, 147.

For sweetest things turn sourest by their deeds;
Lilies that fester smell far worse than weeds.

—William Shakespeare[4]

Justice is rebuffed and flouted
while righteousness stands aloof;
truth stumbles in the marketplace
and honesty is kept out of court,
so truth is lost to sight,
and whoever shuns evil is thought a madman.
The Lord saw, and in his eyes it was an evil thing,
that there was no justice.

—Isaiah 59.14–15 (NEB)

INTRODUCTION

THE FOCUS IN CHAPTER Two was on the ideas and ideologies (worldviews) which in several instances contributed greatly to the mass violence of the twentieth century, and did so in defiance of the traditional Western ethic which valued human life at every stage from conception to natural death.[5] In the situations noted here—primarily (but not exclusively) in Western nations and the USSR—there were sizable Christian populations. In some cases Christians have been supportive of violence, or became bystanders. Where protests were made, they were often muted or ambivalent. In other cases, such as Rwanda and legalized abortion, they have actually contributed to violent activity. What does this say about the way in which the Christian churches disciple their people?

---

4. "They that have the power to hurt and will do none." Sonnet 94. Available at https://www.45100/Sonnet-94-they-that-have-the-to-power-to-hurt-but-do-none. Accessed on September 16, 2022.

5. Other instances of mass killing and the Christian response worthy of consideration I left aside for reasons of space.

POINTED QUESTIONS

In November 1938, Germany underwent a spasm of violence organized by the Nazi government against the Jewish community in which hundreds of synagogues and businesses owned by Jews were destroyed, often by fire. To add insult to injury the Nazis charged the Jewish community with the cost of cleaning up the damage. Many people were hurt and killed. It was a moral outrage in a nation in which over half the population was considered to be Christian. Alice Eckhardt, a historian and professor at Lehigh University, in pondering the "Night of Broken Glass"—*Kristallnacht*, as it has become known—found herself as a Christian deeply troubled by this event.

> When we think about the events of *Kristallnacht* we are led to conclude that surely they must have roused Christians of Germany to an awareness of the true nature of their government and to an alarm on their own behalf in the future. For places of worship—houses of God—were despoiled and torched, scrolls of Torah—an intrinsic part of the Christian Bible—were foully desecrated and burned, and peaceful neighbors, orphans, old people, and hospital patients were forcibly removed from their homes and institutions of care. No one could avoid knowing what happened (unlike later more secretive events). So how could anyone not be shocked and angered, and especially the adherents of a faith that proclaimed God's love?[6]

It is an important question, one that is to be asked of the other events chronicled here. How can those who belong to the faith that proclaims the love of God for the world, not be shocked and angered by the evils to which they have been witness? And how is it that in some instances Christians have supported and participated in great evils? As David Gushee asks, "Can Christians be righteous?"[7]

EUGENICS

Among those who supported this new movement and its worldview in the United States, at least in part, were religious leaders—Protestant and Jewish for the most part—who embraced eugenic ideas quite wholeheartedly. That it would eventually lead to evils such as sterilization,

---

6. Eckardt, "The Pogrom of Kristallnacht," 57.
7. Gushee, *Righteous Gentiles*, 147.

euthanasia, and abortion seems to have been little understood or anticipated by them. Christine Rosen, in her insightful study, *Preaching Eugenics,* had this to say:

> Certain kinds of religious leaders gravitated toward eugenics in the early twentieth century, ministers anxious about the changing culture but also eager to find solutions to its diagnosable ills. Theirs was a practical spirituality better understood in terms of *worldviews* than theologies.[8]

This was made somewhat easier because, as Ronen points out, the founder of eugenics, Francis Galton, presented his goals with a quasi-religious tone. He thought of this movement as being "like a new religion," with "strong claims to become an orthodox religious tenet of the future." He even employed Jesus's Parable of the Talents in asserting that eugenicists were like the "good and faithful servant" who used their talents wisely, in this case by applying their insights to the future health and well-being of society.[9]

To develop further public support for their growing but fledgling movement eugenicists sought the help of clergymen, who still enjoyed widespread influence in American culture. Such ideas fit well with the efforts many religious leaders were making in the late nineteenth and early twentieth centuries with regard to the Social Gospel. This movement was for the most part led by Protestant clergy from a number of denominations, most of them with a liberal bent in theology.[10] Their concerns were many. The arrival of millions of immigrants, many settling in the larger cities, contributed to a growing concern about industrialization, jobs and labor practices, poverty, and social unrest, though their greatest worry was that they would affect America's gene pool negatively.[11] This at a time when the size of American families was declining, especially those of Anglo-Saxon descent. America, thought a number of social gospel leaders, was an Anglo-Saxon nation, the vigor of which was due to the

---

8. Rosen, *Preaching Eugenics,* 5. (my emphasis)

9. Rosen, *Preaching Eugenics,* 5–6.

10. Among the best known Social Gospel leaders were Josiah Strong, Walter Rauschenbusch, Washington Gladden and Harry F. Ward. See Dorrien. *Social Ethics in the Making,* 60–140. It is worth noting that the emphasis on social issues actually began with the evangelical revivalists of the mid-1850s and the Second Great Awakening, though the liberal wing of the churches tended to take over this emphasis as differences over theology and biblical criticism intensified. See Smith, *Revivalism,* 148–62.

11. Black, *War Against the Weak,* 185–87; Rosen, *Preaching Eugenics,* 96–109.

process of natural selection so well described by Charles Darwin. God's solution to the problems brought on by immigration "was the Anglo-Saxon Christianization of America and then the world."[12]

The Social Gospel movement, along with efforts to limit immigration, also sought to alleviate social problems through education, legislation to provide better wages and working conditions, and the development of a host of charitable ministries. There were those who thought that a combination of such efforts could bring about the eradication of poverty.[13]

The eugenicists and Social Gospelers shared certain assumptions. Salvation for Social Gospelers was a social matter; social redemption was as much a part of salvation as one's own personal redemption. In a similar vein, eugenicists argued that heredity should be a social matter, and they too supported intervention and reform to guarantee the preservation of the race. Both groups appealed to society's social conscience in the interest of reform.[14]

The American Eugenics Society, one of the foremost eugenic groups in the United States, established a committee on Cooperation with Clergymen in 1925. Its members included a number of prominent and well-known ministers, most of them of liberal theological persuasion. Among them was Charles Clayton Morrison, whose journal, the *Christian Century*, was perhaps the leading Christian publication of the time. The purpose of this committee was to heighten the public awareness of the eugenics movement, and to encourage eugenics teaching in churches. A sermon contest on the church's responsibility for improving the "human stock" was one method the committee utilized, and through which some of the basic ideas and themes of the clergy who supported eugenics emerged. Christine Rosen lists several of them.

- The social implications regarding the adverse effect of certain groups thought to be inferior were more important than the "scientific details."

12. Dorrien, *Social Ethics in the Making*, 74–75.

13. It is worth noting that the concern shown by the Social Gospel movement for many problems associated with industrialization and immigration (including poverty, labor, and health) was reasonable. The difficulty from a Christian worldview perspective was assuming that Darwin's natural selection process favored Anglo-Saxons, and that coercive utopian programs, e.g., limiting immigration to favored groups, sterilization, etc, could solve them.

14. Rosen, *Preaching Eugenics*, 16.

- It was assumed that science and religion were compatible; and being associated with the increasing success and power of science was attractive.
- Sermons could be utilized to help church members accept the findings of modern science, which many pastors thought they could do more effectively than scientists.
- Scripture could be creatively applied to the eugenicist ideology in sermons. Various Old Testament stories, such as the Flood, and Sodom and Gomorrah, were utilized to illustrate God's concern to purify the human race by eliminating those thought to have a corrupting influence.
- Charitable concerns were also to be emphasized for those worthy of them (most non-religious eugenicists opposed charity in the belief that such aid tended to support groups they considered inferior).[15]

As Rosen comments, the pastors and preachers who promoted these ideas were those "who embraced ideas first and adjusted their theologies later."[16] In the United States, as noted earlier, this support helped encourage the sterilization of many thousands of people, restrictive immigration, and in a number of southern states the continued prohibition of mixed-race marriages.[17]

Conservative Protestants in America were critical of eugenics, but their opposition was muted compared to their controversy with liberal Christians in the early decades of the twentieth century over concern for biblical authority and the fundamental doctrines of the Christian faith.[18] As Rosen points out, conservative Protestants "were not necessarily hostile to reform or science, but as the materialistic philosophy of evolutionary theory grew, they became more intransigent in their insistence on Biblical infallibility."[19] This intransigence did not, however, lead to serious public criticism. An early, and notable exception was that of

15. Rosen, *Preaching Eugenics*, 122–24.

16. Rosen, *Preaching Eugenics*, 124.

17. See Black, *War against the Weak*, especially chapter 9, "Mongrelization," which describes the actions of American eugenicists to prohibit race-mixing.

18. Conservative Protestants, however, were strongly opposed to the persecution of the Jews. Holocaust scholar David Rausch has asserted that the conservative-fundamentalist movement in America "has traditionally been a firm supporter of the Jewish people and has staunchly opposed anti-Semitism." Rausch, *Legacy of Hatred*, 103.

19. Rosen, Preaching Eugenics, 17.

Pennsylvania governor, Samuel Pennypacker, a Methodist, who vetoed a compulsory sterilization bill put forward by the Pennsylvania legislature in 1906.[20]

The Catholic Church in the United States was guardedly open in its initial response to eugenics, insofar as the efforts made by eugenicists proposed social reforms that were in line with Catholic social concerns. With time and study, however, Catholics tended to become much more critical of the eugenics movement, and deserve a good deal of credit for their opposition to some of its worst initiatives. Sterilization, which leading eugenicists promoted in the early decades of the twentieth century, was of particular concern, as was the efforts of eugenicists to use the power of government to coerce the public into accepting and paying for the legislative efforts they put forth. Rosen summarized the Catholic position in this way:

> Any history of the U. S. eugenics movement would be incomplete without reference to the sustained opposition it received from Catholics. Indeed, most historians of eugenics have noted how the organized efforts of Catholics led to the defeat of many eugenics legislative proposals in the 1910s and 1920s. Contrary to the secular worldview embraced by eugenicists, Catholics argued that natural, divine law—not the laws of biology—governed human behavior and protected, among other things, the indissolubility of marriage, the sanctity of procreation and human life (born and unborn), and the family. By interfering with these things, eugenicists violated natural law, and thus earned the censure of most Catholics.[21]

Religious support for eugenics programs was not unknown in Europe. Sweden in 1934 passed a sterilization law which sought to weed out social undesirables (the mentally handicapped, et al.), and prevent

20. The Pennsylvania legislature passed what would have been the eugenics movement's first state compulsory sterilization law, but Pennypacker, a Methodist Christian, vetoed it. As he wrote, "It is plain that the safest and most effective method of preventing procreation would be to cut the heads off the inmates, and such authority is given by the bill to this staff of scientific experts . . . Scientists like all men whose experiences have been limited to one pursuit . . . sometimes need to be restrained. Men of high scientific attainments are prone . . . to lose sight of broad principles outside of their domain . . . To permit such an operation would be to inflict cruelty upon a helpless class . . . which the state has undertaken to protect . . ." Black, *War Against the Weak*, 66.

21. Rosen, *Preaching Eugenics*, 139. G. K. Chesterton, the popular and widely-read Catholic journalist, was particularly adamant in his opposition to the use of state power in promoting eugenics. Despite the opposition, many states legalized sterilization.

them from reproducing. Approximately 63,000 individuals were sterilized, with close to 90 percent of them being women. Its authorization was promoted largely by the political left, along with generous support from the Lutheran Church—then the national church—of Sweden. (The Lutheran Church was disestablished in 2000.) Only in the late 1990s was this program brought to light. Reparations were made to some individuals, and apologies by the church and the government were issued.[22] The Lutheran Church was also accused of helping to cover up the forced sterilizations of the Sami (Lapp) people of Sweden, a minority once thought to be biologically inferior.[23] Norway also authorized sterilization; it is said that 41,000 sterilizations occurred there, and as with Sweden, was strongly supported by the Lutheran Church.[24]

Christian response to the eugenics movement in Germany, which went much further than other countries in authorizing euthanasia, was ambivalent. The initial response was fairly positive, quite similar to that of liberal Christians in the United States. Protests only began once the killings became public knowledge in 1940, and even then such protests were quite limited. As historian Henry Friedlander notes in his study of Nazi genocide,

> The Protestant church in Germany had long supported positive eugenics involving the expansion of healthy and desirable population groups and did not totally reject negative eugenic measures such as sterilization. Although it opposed coerced sterilization, once the sterilization law had been passed, it did support non-voluntary sterilization with some hesitation and a few limitations. The Catholic Church was on record in opposition to negative eugenics and particularly sterilization, and both the Vatican and German bishops denounced the sterilization law. But they compromised their position and offered only verbal opposition because they did not want to endanger the Concordat and because they wanted to protect Catholic institutions and Catholic jobs . . . But when sterilization changed into

---

22. Shaw & Korbegovic, "Sweden." Bates, "Sweden Pays for a Grim Past."

23. Hartley, "Sami desire for truth and reconciliation process," in Politico. See https://www/ed/article/sami-reconciliation-process-Sweden-minority-multiculturalism-human-rights-discriminaton/.

24. Black, *War against the Weak*, 244. Also, Larsen, "Norway's Lutherans Apologize to Gypsies." Denmark passed a castration law in 1929, and over 1000 men were castrated as a result. Forced sterilization also occurred, though exact numbers are unavailable. The same is true of Switzerland. See Herzog, *Sexuality in Europe*, 82–83.

euthanasia, that is, when exclusion through killing replaced exclusion through surgical birth control, the churches were forced into opposition. However, even then the response was not as effective as might have been expected.[25]

Among the few who acted in protest were Pastor Paul Braune, who led the Protestant Home Mission, and Pastor Friedrich von Bodelschwingh, director of the Bethel Hospital. These men, along with the Catholic Charity Association, attempted to delay the transfer of patients from their facilities to the killing centers (all of them located in German hospitals). A number of Protestant bishops also voiced their concerns, as did a number of Catholic bishops who had the backing of the Vatican. Perhaps the best known was Clemens August von Galen, the bishop of Munster, whose protest had considerable impact. On August 3, 1941, von Galen denounced the killings in a sermon in Munster, which was also read in churches throughout his diocese. He had been told that the killings were "openly talked about in the Reich Ministry of the Interior and in the office of Reich Physician Leader Dr. Conti." His sermon ended with this warning: "My brothers in Christ, I hope there is still time. But time is running out."[26]

Numerous church leaders supportive of eugenics in the United States and other countries eventually dropped their support in light of a growing understanding of genetics, the depredations of Nazi Germany regarding their euthanasia program, and the mass murder of Europe's Jewish population, as depicted in chapter two. Nonetheless, interest in eugenics never died out. There would be a resurgence of activity and support by scientists and politicians in the 1950s and 1960s. Concern for overpopulation and the liberalization of sexual conduct loomed large in that resurgence, and would contribute to a growing support for abortion as a means of responding to both concerns. Liberal Christians who followed in their wake would once again become supporters of the new eugenics movement, strengthened and abetted by the worldview of secular humanism, and its embrace of abortion, euthanasia and genetic engineering. While the Christians who supported these ideas over the decades were not responsible for the eugenics movement, they often encouraged it, and overall failed to oppose its worst elements.

25. Friedlander, *Origins of Nazi Genocide*, 112.
26. Freidlander, *The Origins of Nazi Genocide*, 115.

COMMUNISM

The Christian response in the Soviet Union was particularly difficult not only because of the pervasive use of Soviet force and propaganda once it came to power, but because the national church, the Russian Orthodox Church, was so closely aligned with the Tsarist government. The Russian Orthodox Church had been closely aligned with the Russian state for a thousand years, and was always the most powerful religious body in Russia. Corruption in the Church and the Tsarist government was widespread. Though small sects and cults, both Christian and Islamic, made serious proselytizing efforts, the lack of religious freedom made any progress very difficult.

In the late 1800s conflict broke out between the Orthodox Church and a number of small evangelical groups over issues such as religious freedom and biblical authority.[27] These issues, though theologically of great importance, did little to prepare serious Christians for the onslaught of the ideology of the Communists, which employed violence against both the Orthodox Church and the evangelical sects from the onset of the revolution in 1917.[28] Those who sought to resist, and early on many Orthodox, Catholic and Evangelical believers did so, were met with violence.

Two major attacks against religion were made in Russia, one from 1918 to 1922, and a second in 1929–1930. Active persecution of believers, restriction of religious activities, along with the persistent use of state resources to inculcate Communist ideology were some of the means used by authorities.[29] Combined with these efforts, of course, was the use of force, including mass murder.[30] A planned famine, for example, was undertaken by Stalin against the Ukrainians in 1932–33. Called the Holodomor, the Great Famine, it killed nearly 4 million Ukrainians, most of them Eastern Orthodox Christians. A major focus of Communist leaders,

---

27. Pulonov, "The problem of religious freedom," 161–67.

28. Sorokowsky, "The Russian Christianity and the Revolution: what happened?"

29. de Oliveira, "The Church and the Communist State: The Impossible Coexistence."

30. Hundreds of millions of people have lived under Communist regimes, in the former Soviet Union, in China, Vietnam, Cambodia, Africa and Cuba. The socialist worldview was, and is, powerfully coercive. Violence was involved from the very beginnings of the Communist/Socialist movement. See Courtois, "The Crimes of Communism," 4. Numerous churchmen in the West lauded China despite its Communist ideology.

along with the use of force, was "The eliminating of existing religions, and the prevention of future implanting of religious belief, with the goal of establishing state atheism."[31] Special attention was given to inculcating the Communist worldview with children.

The scope and power of Communist ideology and propaganda, with its emphasis on equality and a classless society, though always backed up with the threat and use of violence, was highly effective, especially with the young. Alexander A. Ushakov, about to be arrested for "anti-communist writings," managed to flee the USSR, and take up residence in the United States. In the memoir of his escape, which took place in 1984, he commented on the unrelenting nature of Soviet propaganda.

> Insight came on its own, not right away, but gradually, under the influence of my surroundings. That can be understood only if you have tried to experience the life of a Soviet citizen as an uninterrupted process. Imagine that from earliest childhood you are brought up in the communist spirit—that is, false symbols, concepts, and evidence banged into your immature consciousness *ad nauseam*. And despite your instinctive resistance, it all influences you.[32]

Wherever Soviet Communism took root, as in Eastern Europe at the end of World War II, its leaders sought to implement their ideology, and to co-opt existing institutions—including the churches. This approach had been undertaken in the 1920s against the Orthodox Church in Russia so successfully that by the 1930s it was largely under Communist control. According to documents from the Russian archives, now housed in the Library of Congress, by 1939 all seminaries had been closed, church publications of all kinds were prohibited, and of 50,000 Orthodox churches, only about 50 were still in operation.[33] Bishops and other church leaders who survived these operations were mostly appointed by the Communist leadership, thereby allowing the government to say they supported religious freedom while actually maintaining strict supervision of religious activities.

Scholar Anne Applebaum, in describing the Soviet occupation of Poland in the late 1940s, provides an example of the efforts that the Soviet

---

31. "Religion in the Soviet Union," Wikipedia.

32. Ushakov, *In the Gunsight of the KGB*, 61. (Author's emphasis)

33. Jewish religious services, as well as Protestant and Catholic churches, were also heavily persecuted. "Anti-Religious Campaign." *Revelations from the Russian Archives*. August 31, 2016. Available att loc.gov/exhibts/archives/anti.html.

secret police employed from the earliest days to recruit Christians and their leaders into their plans. She writes that they "wanted the clergy to function openly in the service of the regime, as an arm of the communist party." This was an explicitly Soviet idea. According to Josef Swiathlo, a senior Polish secret police officer who defected in 1953, General Ivan Serow, a senior figure in Soviet intelligence, proposed the subversion of the church, such that it became an instrument of Soviet political aims.[34] In many locations this policy succeeded.

Consider the following comment in a speech given by Joseph Stalin in which he laid out the Soviet plans (ideas) for Eastern Europe:

> It is necessary that we isolate the Catholic hierarchy and drive a wedge between the Vatican and its believers. Depending on our success in Czechoslovakia, we will build up Catholic activities in Poland, Hungary, and the other countries. We must also make full use of the question of the finances of the lower-level priests. Our measures will divide lower-level priests from the hierarchy. Governments should order priests to take the citizen's oath, communist parties should force priests to spread the ideas of Marx, Engels, and Lenin through religious classes and sermons, and whenever they have direct contacts with their believers. We have to fight a systematic war against the hierarchy; churches should be under our full control by 1949.[35]

Though attacks on religion never fully destroyed religious belief, the pressures of the Communist regime such as those described by Stalin destroyed the faith of millions. Many Christians in the Soviet Union eventually succumbed to the incessant drumbeat of the Soviet ideology, with its willingness to use violence, and embraced the Soviet system and worldview—at least superficially. Among them for a time, a young Alexander Solzhenitsyn. Those who succumbed to what Robert Conquest considered a "rogue worldview" included not a few church leaders, particularly of the Russian Orthodox Church, who became willing to cooperate with state authorities. In return they were allowed to maintain their churches and religious services. Men much like those of whom St Paul wrote, who were "holding the form of religion, but denying the power of it" (II Timothy 3.5).

---

34. Applebaum. *Iron Curtain*. 269. Ivan Serov was a Soviet army officer who became a senior figure in Soviet intelligence.

35. Quoted cited in Applebaum, *Iron Curtain*, 269.

And yet there were others who, on some level, continued in faith, resisting where they could. In 1974 several Christian dissidents, including Alexander Solzhenitsyn (by then a Christian), published *From Under the Rubble*, a series of essays in which they attacked the Soviet regime, strongly criticized the West, and called for a Christian renewal of society. In his essay Evgeny Barabanov, recalling the contributions of Christianity to Russia over the centuries, cited two priests who had courageously protested the connivance of church leaders with the Soviet government:

> After the dozens of years when martyrdom was passed over in silence, when hypocrisy and servility reigned, it was two valiant priests, Nikolai Eshilman and Gleb Yakunin, who first referred publicly to this crisis. In their "Open Letter" to Patriarch Alexius, sent in November 1965, they protested not only against the illegal actions of the leaders and officials of the Council for Religious Affairs—actions which grossly violated their own legislation—but also against the craven, hypocritical position adopted by the higher ecclesiastical administration. They showed convincingly how a significant part of the governing episcopate, with voluntary silence, or cunning connivance, had assisted the atheists to close churches, monasteries and religious schools, to liquidate religious communities, to establish the illegal practice of registering christenings, and had yielded to them control over the appointment and transfer of priests.[36]

Alexander Solzhenitsyn, for years a communist, later became a Christian during his time in a Soviet prison, and in a series of powerful books described the catastrophe of the Communist revolution.[37] In his

---

36. Barabanov, "The Schism Between the Church and the World," 174. In the 1980s there was a resurgence of religious thought and life—particularly in Poland and East Germany—which, aided by the economic and political efforts of President Ronald Reagan, Prime Minister Margaret Thatcher, and Pope John Paul II, contributed to the fall of the Soviet Empire. See O'Sullivan, *President, the Pope, and the Prime Minister*. Also Gengor, *Pope and a Presdent*. Adrian Pabst in an article for *The Guardian*, made this comment: "Without Christianity the cold war would not have ended peacefully. Across the East, churches and religious organizations brought together workers, students and intellectuals. Under totalitarian rule, church services and religious festivals often provided the last bastion of freedom and resistance." See Pabst, "Christianity ended the cold war peacefully."

37. Solzhenitsyn was a prisoner in one of the hundreds of Soviet prisons he referred to as the Gulag Archipelago. Following an operation for cancer while imprisoned he was visited by a physician, Dr. Boris Kornfield, who shared his conversion from Judaism to Christianity. Kornfield's timely witness (he was murdered later that very night), led Solzhenitsyn—along with his own reflections—back to faith in God. See Volume

lecture upon receiving the Templeton Prize (given for outstanding contributions to life's spiritual dimensions) he said, "If I were asked today to formulate as concisely as possible the main cause of the ruinous Revolution that swallowed up some sixty million of our people, I could not put it more accurately than to repeat: *Men have forgotten God; that's why all this has happened.*"[38]

NATIONAL SOCIALISM

Germany in the 1920s was undergoing difficult times economically. The ravages and costs of WWI, the severe reparations demanded by the Versailles Treaty, and worsened by the worldwide Depression at the end of the decade all contributed. Inflation had made German currency nearly worthless. Unemployment was high. Breadlines were common. And complicating everything was the volatile political situation. Street fights between Communist sympathizers and the National Socialist Party's brownshirts (storm troopers who acted as street thugs) were common, and often deadly. Life for the majority of Germany's citizens was frustrating and hard. In this setting Adolph Hitler's speeches of a revitalized Germany brought hope, and his words blaming the Jews for Germany's problems became somewhat easier to take. Antisemitism, after all, had a long history in Germany.[39]

Two, *Gulag Archipelago*, 612–15.

38. From Solzhenitsyn's Templeton Prize acceptance speech. Most modern scholars believe his estimate of 60 million dead to be somewhat too high. (my emphasis)

39. Germany's anti-Semitism stretched back to the Reformation and the late-in-life diatribes of Martin Luther. Over the centuries, however, Jews had assimilated deeply into German culture. Intermarriage, conversion to the Christian faith, liberalizing trends in education, and increased participation in science, medicine, business and the military all contributed to this process. During WWI thousands of Jews served in the military, many with distinction. Still, Germany had lost the war. Who was to blame? The National Socialists, seizing upon the latent anti-Semitism of Germany, asserted that the Jews had stabbed Germany in the back. They pointed to the leaders of the growing, and violent, Communist movement in Russia, many of whom were Jews, and took note of the fact that some of Germany's prominent business leaders were also Jews. As such, it was believed by those willing to overlook the truth, that the Jews had somehow benefited from, and contributed to, Germany's loss in the Great War. With such ideas Adolph Hitler fanned the flames. He was confident that the constant propaganda would win over his people regarding the Jews, and was equally confident about the coming demise of Christianity. See Shirer, *Rise and Fall of the Third Reich.*, 24–27; see also Grobman and Landes, *Critical Issues of the Holocaust*, 16–101.

For many millions of Germans, Catholic and Protestant, the advent of Hitler as Chancellor made everyday life better. In the first years of the Hitler regime, from 1933 to 1937, unemployment fell from a high of six million to under one million. Nearly everyone had a job, and there was food on the table. Germany was on the move, vibrant and prosperous. Though some personal freedoms were lost, and despite the fact that restrictive racial laws were making life difficult for the Jews, there was hope for many that the future of the country was assured.[40]

According to Germany's 1933 census, the year that Hitler came to power, 52 percent of Germans identified as Protestants and 33 percent as Catholic. Many of them, noting the rising standard of living, and the economic vibrancy of the new Germany, found it easy to overlook the Nazi treatment of Jews and the curtailment of their own personal freedoms. It was widely known that Hitler was a baptized Catholic, and millions of Christians (Protestant and Catholic) viewed Hitler as Germany's foremost Christian leader, an understanding he furthered through some of his speeches. In one such talk he said,

> Today's Christians . . . stand at the head of [Germany]. I pledge that I never will tie myself to parties that want to destroy Christians . . . We want to fill our culture again with the Christian spirit . . . We want to burn out all the recent immoral developments to literature, to the theatre and in the press. In short, we want to burn out the poison of immorality which has entered into our whole life and culture, as a result of liberal excess.[41]

A number of well-known Protestant theologians were openly supportive of Hitler and the Nazi regime, among them Gerhard Kittel, Paul Althaus, and Emanuel Hirsch.[42] These men, like so many, strongly identified with the German *Volk,* to the point of overlooking (or tolerating) the Nazi policies with regard to the eugenics program and the mistreatment of the Jews. They were not alone. One Protestant pastor, deeply impressed

---

40. Lloyd George, prime minister of England during WWI, after a visit with Hitler proclaimed him a great leader. The 1936 Olympics were held in Berlin, and the Nazis made the most of it. Visitors from around the world were impressed: "[A]pparently a happy, healthy, friendly people united under Hitler—a far different picture, they said, than they had got from reading newspaper dispatches from Berlin." Shirer, *Rise and Fall of the Third Reich,* 231–33.

41. Alpha history.com/nazi Germany/religion_in_nazi_germany.

42. See Erickson, *Theologians Under Hitler.* All three men held strongly nationalistic views which they thought compatible with the Christian faith.

with Hitler had this to say: "Christ has come to us through Hitler . . . through his honesty, his faith and his idealism, the Redeemer has found us . . . We know today the Savior has come . . . We have only one task, be German not Christian."[43] A sizable number of Protestant pastors, who, with their congregations, strongly favored the Nazis and their racial doctrines, formed the German Christians Faith Movement. The goal was to unite all of Germany's Protestant churches into a "National Reich Church." Bibles were not to be published, nor displayed on church altars. Hitler's book, *Mein Kampf*, was to be displayed instead, and the Christian Cross was to be removed from all churches and chapels. Though favored by the Nazi regime, the influence of the National Reich Church was relatively small; still, about one third of Germany's Protestant clergy joined it.[44]

Protestant pastors who did resist were centered in a group of Lutheran and Reformed congregations known as the Confessing Church. Pastor Martin Niemoeller, who had initially favored the Nazi movement, became disillusioned with its doctrines and practices once Hitler came to power, and became the leader of the Confessing Church, which at its height included several thousand pastors. Karl Barth, a Swiss theologian teaching in Germany, was part of this movement. On the day Hitler came to power Barth wrote, "I saw my dear German people beginning to worship a false God."[45] In 1934 the Confessing Church convened at Barmen, Germany, and with Barth as its primary author, produced what became known as *The Barmen Declaration*. The initial dissent was focused on theological differences. The identification of the Christian faith with Hitler and the German state was viewed as heretical. The Declaration stated that Jesus Christ was Lord of the Church, and as such it could not be considered an instrumentality of the State. It also denied the totalitarian nature of the Nazi regime, and opposed the antisemitism embraced by the "German Christians."[46]

43. Lutzer, *Hitler's Cross*, 101.
44. Shirer, *Rise and Fall of the Third Reich*, 240.
45. Rubenstein and Roth. *Approaches to Auschwitz*, 205.
46. Rubenstein and Roth. *Approaches to Auschwitz*, 204–5. Barth, interviewed after the war, expressed regret that the Declaration had not made the Jewish question central. Many Christians in Germany (and elsewhere), though not anti-Semitic in modern terms, were anti-Jewish in the sense that the Jewish community had collaborated with the Romans in the crucifixion of Jesus. That they could hold to this view in the light of the parable of the Good Samaritan, or Paul's teaching in Ephesians 2.11–22, is shameful.

Dietrich Bonhoeffer was also a part of this movement, and one of the first Christian leaders to speak out against the anti-Semitic practices of the Nazis. Bonhoeffer remained a steadfast opponent of the Nazi regime, and encouraged many pastors to do the same through his work with an illegal Confessing Church seminary in Finkenwalde, a city northeast of Berlin that is now part of Poland. Bonhoeffer's book, *The Cost of Discipleship*, described the problem with the churches of Germany as being one of cheapening God's grace, such that one might believe in Christ without paying the cost of obedience to his teaching. Bonhoeffer became part of the resistance to Hitler, including the plot to assassinate him in 1944. The plot failed; Hitler survived the bomb blast meant to kill him with minor injuries. The conspirators, Bonhoeffer among them, were discovered, and many were executed. Bonhoeffer was hanged on April 9, 1945, just a month before the end of the war.[47] Despite the courageous stand of the Confessing Church and its leaders, its overall effectiveness was limited. From 1934 till the end of the decade the Nazi government arrested and imprisoned well over a thousand Confessing Church pastors, including Niemoeller.[48] At war's end Niemoeller said in a sermon that had there been—early on—a stronger, more principled response by Christian leaders and their congregations, the outcome might have been different.[49] The majority of Protestant pastors, however, like most Germans, were submissive.[50] Hitler's true feelings about Christianity and the effectiveness of its leaders were given in another talk: "Do you really believe

---

47. Bonhoeffer, *Cost of Discipleship*. For a splendid account of Bonhoeffer's life see Eric Metaxas, *Bonhoeffer. Pastor, Martyr, Prophet, Spy*.

48. It is interesting to note that Albert Einstein, exiled from the Third Reich for being a Jew, though very critical of Germany's universities, newspaper editors, and other intellectuals for their failure to defend freedom, said of the Church—"Only the Church stood squarely across the path of Hitler campaign for suppressing the truth. I never had any special interest in the Church before, but now I feel a great affection and admiration for it because the Church alone has had the courage and persistence to stand for intellectual truth and moral freedom." Quoted in *Time* magazine, December 23, 1940, 38, and cited by Lutzer, *When a Nation Forgets God*, 89–90. One can acknowledge Einstein's endorsement, and yet, overall, the churches of Germany did not do well.

49. '[I]f at the beginning of the Jewish persecutions we had seen that it was the Lord Jesus Christ who was being persecuted, struck down and slain in "the least of these our brethren," if we had been loyal to Him and confessed Him, for all I know God would have stood by us, and then the whole sequence of events would have taken a different course.' A quote from Martin Niemoeller's sermon, cited in David A. Rausch, *A Legacy of Hatred*, 169.

50. Shirer, *Rise and Fall of the Third Reich*, 237–39.

the masses will be Christian again? Nonsense! Never again. That tale is finished. No one will listen to it again. But we can hasten matters. The parsons will dig their own graves. They will betray their God to us. They will betray anything for the sake of their miserable jobs and incomes."[51] On another occasion Hitler expressed his contempt for Protestants, saying, "You can do anything you want with them—they will submit—they are insignificant little people, submissive as dogs, and they sweat with embarrassment when you talk to them."[52]

The use of terror and violence against opponents, including Christians, was utilized from the very beginning of the Nazi regime, and intimidated many.[53] The response to Kristallnacht by Christians, which was a particularly vicious pogrom against the Jewish community, is a case in point. Despite whatever shock and anger there may have been, within Germany and Austria criticism to Kristallnacht was very limited.[54] Fearing the violence unleashed against the Jews, few spoke out. Julius von Jan, a Protestant pastor, in a sermon asked—and answered—his own question:

> Where is the man who, in the name of God and justice, will cry like Jeremiah, "Maintain righteousness, rescue those deprived of their rights out of the hands of the transgressors? Do not oppress the stranger, the orphan and the widow. Do no one violence, shed not innocent blood." Such men as God has sent us are in a concentration camp or reduced to silence . . . Our bishops have not recognized their duty to stand shoulder to shoulder with those who have spoken the Lord's Word.[55]

---

51. Waite, *Adolf Hitler: The Psychopathic God*, 17. Quoted in Lutzer, *Hitler's Cross*, 104.

52. Shirer, *Rise and Fall of the Third Reich*, 238; quoted in Lutzer, *Hitler's Cross*, 117.

53. On June 30, 1934, several hundred of Hitler's early supporters including Ernst Rohm, the head of the thuggish Brownshirts, and thought by Hitler to be plotting against him were murdered in what is known as "the Night of the Long Knives." Shirer, *Rise and Fall of the Third Reich*, 219–24; Andrew Roberts, *The Storm of War*, 1.

54. Karl Barth, though living in Switzerland—having been forced out of Germany in 1934, did protest *Kiristallnacht,* saying that "anyone who is in principle hostile to the Jews must also be seen as in principle the enemy of Jesus Christ. Antisemitism is a sin against the Holy Spirit." Rubenstein and Roth, *Approaches to Auschwitz*, 206.

55. Eckardt, "Pogram of *Kristallnacht* in Christian Context," 58. Coverage of Kristallnacht, and the unfolding euthanasia program in Germany, was not unknown in the United States, but the response of the churches was limited and moderate. One of the few who spoke out vigorously was Reinhold Niebuhr. As early as 1933, the year the Nazi regime came to power, Niebuhr had concluded, "They are bent upon the extermination of the Jews." Niebuhr was also on record as saying that the triumph of

Resistance to the Nazi regime by Catholics was also limited, though concern over Hitler's rise to power led the Papacy to seek an agreement with Germany that was called the Munich Concordat. It was designed to protect Catholic ministries and properties in Germany, and was signed with the German Government in 1933. Even so, the Nazi worldview raised a number of concerns for Vatican scholars. Among them: the alleged superiority of Aryan blood, the prohibition of inter-racial marriage, the subjugation of the individual to the state, the legalization of sterilization (later, abortion and euthanasia for Jews), and the denial of the virtues of tolerance, compassion and truth so valued by the Christian faith.

In 1937 Pope Pius XI produced the encyclical, *With Burning Sorrow*, in response to these concerns, the actions taken against the Jews, and a growing worry about the possibility of war. Though the Nazi movement was not mentioned by name, the encyclical was understood as a sharp rebuke to Hitler and the Nazis. The German government responded with anger, and sought to prevent its dissemination through shutting down the printing presses involved, arresting anyone caught reading or disseminating it, and accused the pope of arousing anti-German sentiment.[56]

In 1939, following the death of Pius XI, Eugene Pacelli became pope—Pius XII. Opinion is divided on his actions during the war. Some argue that he failed to exercise his moral authority effectively in speaking out against the murder of the Jews and Gypsies. Journalist John Cornwell in his book, *Hitler's Pope*, excoriated Pius XII, not as a monster, but as a complex man whose life before and during his papacy was "not a portrait of evil but of fatal moral dislocation—a separation of authority from Christian love."[57]

Nazism would mean the death of Christianity. Relatively few American Christians, liberal or conservative, joined him. Franklin H. Littell. "Reinhold Niebuhr's Christian Leadership in a Time of Testing," 97. Niebuhr's quotation was taken from an article in *The Nation,* February 21, 1933.

56. See Burleigh, *Sacred Causes*, 192–93. Another encyclical was written by Jesuit John LaFarge in 1938. LaFarge, an American priest who had worked and written extensively about racial problems in the United States, while visiting Rome was asked by Pius XI to write an encyclical which would address the problems with Germany and Italy and their anti-Semitic plans forthrightly. He did so, with the support of several other Catholic scholars, but it was never published. It is thought that Vladimir Ledochowski, then superior general of the Jesuits, and known as the "Black Pope," had offered to help LaFarge with the encyclical, and being critical of Pius XI's growing antipathy toward Nazi Germany, managed to sideline the manuscript. See Eisner, *Pope's Last Crusade,* 134–38.

57. Cornwall, *Hitler's Pope,* ix.

There are, on the other hand, scholars who claim that Cornwell's view of the Pius XII is evidence of anti-Catholic bigotry. Princeton scholar Robert George, in an afterword to Ronald Rychlak's book defending the pope, acknowledges that many Catholic Christians during the Holocaust failed to do what they could and should have done to help Jewish people. But Pope Pius XII was not one of them. Indeed, asserts George, "it is almost certainly true that Pius XII saved the lives of more Jewish, and non-Jewish victims, of Hitler's madness than any other human being. In the estimate of Israeli diplomat Pinchas Lapide, the Vatican and other Catholic institutions, acting at the Pope's express direction, saved the lives of more than 800,000 European Jews."[58]

Despite these concerns, opposition by most Catholics to Nazism was limited. In Poland a number of bishops openly espoused anti-Semitism. In Slovakia, and especially in Croatia—countries with large Catholic populations—not a few priests actively cooperated with the persecution of the Jews following Germany's invasion.[59] Millions of lay Catholics throughout Europe cooperated with the Nazi regime through their involvement with politics, the military and industry. Thousands of priests and seminarians were conscripted (this was also true of Protestant pastors), and could not opt out as a conscientious objector. Most served, not as chaplains, but as support staff in one capacity or another. Those who were chaplains were caught between serving their men spiritually, while knowing that they were serving in an army bent on annihilation. Relatively few protested.[60]

---

58. George, "Afterword," in Rychlak, *Hitler, the War, and the Pope*, 310–11. Pope Pius XII speaking to church leaders at the war's end, in June 1945, described the Nazi movement, as it had revealed itself in the preceding years, as an "arrogant apostasy from Jesus Christ, the denial of his doctrine and of his work of redemption, the cult of violence, the idolatry of race and blood, the overthrow of human liberty and dignity." Shirer, *Rise and Fall of the Third Reich*, 234. It is also to be noted that the Vatican after the war organized over 900 trains to carry food, medicine and clothing to the people suffering in Germany. German Protestants also helped in by aiding in the distribution of over 60 million tons of food to the German people and refugees who fled to the West to escape the predations of the Soviet armies occupying eastern Germany and Poland. Burleigh, *Sacred Causes*, 303.

59. See Posner, *God's Bankers*, 86–92.

60. Rossi, in her book, *Wehrmacht Priests*, 252, notes that most German priests who became chaplains did so willingly, largely out of concern for the men they served. A number thought the war unjust, but very few protested. The one priest who refused to be conscripted, Franz Reinisch, was executed. In Poland, by way of contrast, one-fifth of the Catholic priests died. See Burleigh, *Sacred Causes*, 216.

Opposition to Germany's eugenicist euthanasia program by Christians, as noted in the section on "Eugenics" above, was genuine, but like other forms of protest, quite limited. The fact that the euthanasia murders became public knowledge only after war with Russia began, coupled with the years-long experience of the Nazi intimidation of Christians and other opponents prior to the outbreak of war, no doubt contributed to the reluctance of many Christians to speak out.

Taking note of the failure of so many Christians—Protestant and Catholic—to resist the Nazi regime, authors Richard Rubenstein and John Roth in their book on the Holocaust had this to say:

> Yet today the consensus is that apostasy was rife among baptized Christians in Germany and elsewhere during the Nazi era. For example, anti-Jewish legislation, *Kristallnacht*, and the methodical *Einsatzgruppen*, not to mention Treblinka and Auschwitz, demonstrated that in Germany Christian obedience to the state usually transcended loyalty to God, faith in Hitler commonly superseded dedication to Jesus, and true worship typically lost out to unrepentant idolatry as masses turned to the false gods of pure blood, race, and culture. Not only in Germany, but elsewhere millions of Christians did too little to thwart and too much to support a regime that would have sent Peter, Paul, Mary, and even Jesus to the gas chambers. Whether through failure to take Christian identity seriously, zealous commitment to a religion identified as Christian but fundamentally antithetical to Jesus' teachings, or some disposition in between, apostasy abounded in Christian civilization from 1933 to 1945.[61]

This is another way of saying that there was a widespread failure of Christian churches—Catholic, Lutheran and Reformed—to disciple their people as Jesus commanded. Dietrich Von Hildebrand, a Catholic Christian philosopher who fled Germany for Austria in response to death threats, would have agreed. In an article for *Der Christliche Standestaat*, the journal von Hildebrand and a friend founded in Vienna to combat National Socialism, he expressed his concern that fellow Christians not become morally blunted to the evils of Nazism, and offers an incisive comment on the power of an evil worldview, over time, to reshape the

---

61. Rubenstein and Roth, *Approaches to Auschwitz*, 200–201. (My emphasis) Though resistance to the Nazi regime in Poland was not all that it could, or should, have been, it is worth noting that the Polish people paid heavily. Poles died proportionately in much higher numbers than any other nation—220 war deaths for every thousand in the population, 216.

habits, the worldview and lifestyle of Christians. His concern remains relevant for Christians today, and is worth quoting at length.

> Habit is a sort of beneficial adaptability in human beings that can make their lives more bearable, yet it is also a force that can diminish spiritual alertness in a person, which is the foundation of moral and spiritual life. Under certain circumstances, it can even eliminate this alertness entirely... Whoever habitually consorts with persons who are morally perverted in their basic outlook will, as a result of putting up with their attitude, slowly become poisoned himself, even if he had initially rejected it with indignation and had never given it his approval in any way. If he does not "break" with the others, his initial indignation will soon subside and turn into a mere regret; he will become more and more desensitized by getting used to the base moral atmosphere they inhabit.[62]

In a reflective moment who of us would not admit to being tempted or drawn to some of the baser elements of our culture, thereby putting ourselves in danger of gradually being co-opted by it? Perhaps not unlike the proverbial frog which failed to exit a pot of water soon to boil.

The power of the state becomes ever more powerful when its philosophy is shared and reinforced by the courts, the academy, and the media. In the United States, for example, the authorization of abortion by the courts has been strongly reinforced by the media's unwillingness to provide in-depth news coverage of the pro-life community. In such cases, asserts von Hildebrand, moral degradation results.

> But if a state slowly descends—in its official statements, in its legislation, and its day-to-day conduct of affairs—ever more deeply into immorality and barbarism, then there is a tremendous risk that the populace will gradually become accustomed to its ethical level, that their initial indignation will subside, and that they will imperceptibly lower their own ethical criteria

---

62. Von Hildebrand, *My Battle Against Hitler*, 258, 260. Hildebrand may have had in mind a conference he attended in 1932 in western Germany where he met several theologians who were working to find common ground with the National Socialist movement. One of them, Fr Thaddeus Soiron, gave a talk that Von Hildebrand found deeply upsetting. His comment gives insight into the importance of worldviews and discipleship: "Soiron's talk was completely infected by the poison of collectivism and showed that, under the intoxicating influence of the Zeitgeist, he was completely blinded. He overemphasized the notion of community at the expense of the individual. His talk was not only philosophically false but also heretical and politically dangerous, particularly at that moment." Von Hildebrand, *My Battle Against Hitler*, 39.

when they see that all the crimes committed by the state go unpunished as it continues to exist with the dignity of its own inherent authority and the formal recognition of other states. At the time, the laws passed by the National Socialist regime in the year 1933 provoked great indignation everywhere in the world. Since then, however, so many even more terrible things have happened that the events of 1933 no longer make much of an impression on most people. They have gotten used to the Third Reich by means of an imperceptible process of acclimatization that has led to its increasing acceptance. *Their own moral sensitivity has suffered harm.*[63]

This is indeed what happened in Germany. As Richard Rubenstein noted: 'Nevertheless, whether or not they approved of Hitler, they all did their duty, as workers, farmers, bureaucrats, taxpayers, bankers, *clergy,* police officials and warriors, and that is precisely what made the "Final Solution" possible.'[64]

Joseph Ratzinger (later Pope Benedict XVI) recorded a conversation that took place in 1927 involving physicists Paul Dirac, Max Planck, Wolfgang Pauli and Werner Heisenberg (reported by him in his book, *Physics and Beyond: Encounters and Conversations, 1971)* in which the parents of Max Planck and Werner Heisenberg stated their view that Christianity and science represented two value systems, Christianity a subjective one, and science the objective one, a division that Heisenberg thought "unhappy." Pauli agreed: "The complete division between knowledge and faith is surely just a stopgap measure. In Western society and culture we could, for instance, in the not-too-distant future, come to the point at which the parables and images that religion has used up to now are no longer convincing, even for simple folk; and then, I fear, traditional morality will also very rapidly break down, and things will happen that are more frightful than anything we can yet imagine."[65] Particularly when, as in Germany, the Nazi government and many in the science community shared a worldview which denigrated Christianity and its moral values.

Ratzinger's sad summation of that moment was this:

At that time, in 1927, those taking part in the conversation could have at most a vague suspicion that soon afterward the unholy twelve years would begin, in the course of which things did

63. Von Hildebrand, *My Battle with Hitler,* 261. (My emphasis)
64. Rubenstein, "Waldheim, the Pope, and the Holocaust," 278 (My emphasis)
65. Quoted in Ratzinger, *Truth and Tolerance,* 138–39.

happen that were "more frightful" than could previously have been thought possible. There were of course a good number of Christians . . . who opposed the demonic forces with the power of their Christian conscience.[66] 'But on the whole the power of temptation was stronger; those who just went along with things left a clear path for evil.'[67]

This is similar to the thought of von Hildebrand, that immersion in a culture which is inimical to life and truth will, for most Christians—that is, Christians who are poorly discipled—lead to submission to that culture. But a submission that is often dressed in Christian clothing. In every time and place Christian churches need leaders who are capable of discerning the difference between Christian appeasement to the negative and harmful influences of the surrounding culture, and Christian obedience to the truth of the Gospel of Jesus Christ, and the ability to express this difference with clarity and power. The challenge that accompanies the clear teaching of Christian teachers and writers is helping pastors

---

66. Among the better known were some students in Munich. Aroused by the letters and testimony of Willi Graf, a young German soldier appalled by the atrocities committed by the *Einsatzgruppen* (police battalions) against the Jews in the Poland, they decided to act. Hans and Sophie Scholl, Alex Schmorell, Christoph Probst, Willi Graf, theologian Carl Muth, with philosophy professor, Karl Huber, formed a resistance cell they called "The White Rose." They published and distributed thousands of leaflets mostly on college campuses describing their concerns, and calling for resistance against the regime. Sophie and Hans were arrested while distributing their leaflets at the University of Munich, and with Christoph Probst were put on trial four days after their arrest, and found guilty. Eight hours later, with typical German efficiency, they were beheaded. As Sophie Scholl said at her trial, "'Somebody, after all, had to make a start." Rubenstein and Roth, *Approaches to Auschwitz*, 221–24; quote from Hanser, *A Noble Treason*, 274. See also Garber, *Fabric of Faithfulness*, 176–85. Here and there throughout Germany, and the nations occupied by the German armed forces, there were other instances of resistance, of faith and courageous action. The Holocaust Museum has given much time and effort to identifying what they call the "righteous Gentiles of the Holocaust." On a wall of remembrance at the Holocaust Museum in Washington, DC, there are listed several thousand names of men and women, a great many of them Christians, who opposed the Nazi regime by saving the lives of their Jewish neighbors. Often at considerable cost to themselves—emotionally, relationally, financially, at the cost of their very lives and families. It is worth making the effort to read from the growing body of literature that describes the actions of these heroic individuals and families. While these individuals deserve much credit, the sad truth is that millions of Christians throughout Europe—though baptized and confirmed, many of them church-goers—did little or nothing to help. They were bystanders. See Hilberg, *Perpetrators, Victims, Bystanders*, chapter 24, "The Churches."

67. Ratzinger, *Truth and Tolerance*, 139–34-.

and parents instill this understanding—and the discipline and courage to uphold it—in the everyday lives of their fellow Christians.

BYSTANDERS

Raul Hilberg, in his monumental book, *The Destruction of the European Jews,* helped make the world aware of the enormity and brutality of the Jewish Holocaust during World War II. In a follow-up book Hilberg provided considerable insight into those who observed the mass killings of the Nazi regime—but did little or nothing to help.[68] They were bystanders. It included neutral countries like Switzerland, Sweden, Turkey, Portugal and Spain, which valued their neutrality more than a moral obligation to fight an evil tyranny. Though thousands of Jews managed to escape into these countries, their governments were firmly opposed to providing refuge on any formal basis. Great Britain and the United States, though allies in fighting Germany, also severely limited immigration.[69]

There were organizations and businesses in many countries willing to do business with the German regime. Companies in Switzerland and Sweden cooperated with the German government by providing war materials. It must be noted, however, that the Swedes gave refuge to nearly all of Denmark's Jews, and perhaps half of those in Norway. Nearly all of Germany's industries became part of the Nazi war effort, and enriched thousands of businessmen. A number of these industries also made use of Jewish slave labor.[70]

The bystanders also included a great number of Germans who had Jews for neighbors. As racial laws and regulations forced large numbers of Jews out of work, and out of their homes, sizable numbers of Germans were willing to take advantage of their plight by snapping up their businesses, properties, and personal valuables at little or no cost.[71] There were other millions of men and women throughout Europe, and *outside* of Germany, who, although they hated Hitler, also disliked Jews. And because of prejudice and fear did nothing to help them. *Among them were millions who considered themselves Christians, but whose compassion did not extend to strangers.* David Gushee cites a conversation involving

---

68. *Perpetrators, Victims, Bystanders.*
69. Hilberg, *Perpetrators, Victims, Bystanders,* 256–59.
70. Hilberg, *Perpetrators, Victims, Bystanders,* 212–16.
71. Hilberg, *Perpetrators, Victims, Bystanders,* 196–97, 214.

Pieter Miedema (P), a Dutch Reformed pastor involved in rescue work, and his father-in-law (FL). It is taken from the book, *Quiet Heroes*, and illustrates the point.

> FL: You have a child now, you owe all your responsibility to her and to her mother. You can't get involved with the lives of every little Jew. What are those people to us anyway? Why should I risk my peace and tranquility for someone who means nothing to me?
>
> P: What if Christ himself came knocking on your door, father? Would you send him away too?
>
> FL: Of course not. How can you compare the two? One is our Savior, the other is just a nobody. I don't see the connection at all. You are a minister, you should be the first one to know that, Pieter.
>
> P: And you, father, as a Christian and an elder in our church, you should be more familiar with the words of Jesus Christ: "The things you do to the least of my friends, you do to me." Do you recall that Jesus was nothing more than a little Jew?
>
> FL: It's still different. I will risk nothing for a stranger.[72]

There have been, of course, bystanders in every instance of the mass killings of the twentieth century, including the massive, on-going violence directed toward unborn children. That so many Christians remained bystanders in such instances is, for me, an indication of poor discipleship.

RWANDA

The Rwandan genocide, along with the continuation of authorized abortion in dozens of countries, is a fairly recent instance of mass violence. As noted in chapter two it is a country in Eastern/Central Africa, populated largely by two ethnic groups, the Tutsis and the Hutus, the latter making up about 85% of the population Christianity was introduced in 1900 by Catholic missionaries, with Protestants—mostly Anglicans and Seventh Day Adventists—gaining ground in the 1930s. A 2012 census

---

72. From Stein, *Quiet Heroes*, 65, cited by Gushee, *Righteous Gentiles of the Holocaust*, 139.

revealed that 46 percent of Rwandas are Catholic, and about 45 percent Protestant.[73]

It has long been considered the most "Christian" country in Africa. Though there had been periods of conflict between these groups from time to time, cooperation and inter-marriage were quite common. Despite a common language and a common faith, ethnic tensions—exacerbated by "The Ten Commandments of the Hutu," which denigrated Tutsis—exploded following the death of President Juvenal Habyarimana. Though the world was appalled, no country—nor UN forces in the region—intervened. In a period of about 100 days as many as 800,000 Rwandans, mostly Tutsi Christians, were murdered by their Hutu Christian neighbors. Many with low-tech weapons such as machetes. It is estimated that nearly 200,000 Hutus took part in the massacre. As many as 250,000 women were raped, resulting in nearly 20,000 babies.[74] Nearly two million Rwandans became refugees.[75]

Though mob violence was the rule, studies of the genocide found later that both Catholic and Protestant churches helped stoke the violence. A Catholic priest, Fr Athanase Seromba, to take one example, was accused of genocide for allowing a church holding 2000 people to be crushed by bulldozers. Charges were later dropped. Another priest was lauded for saving nearly 2000 people at the St Paul church center in Kilgali, the nation's capital.[76]

Lee Camp, professor at Lipscomb University in Tennessee, was working with his wife Laura at a Christian school in April 1994, in Nairobi, Kenya, when they heard a radio broadcast describing an outbreak of violence in Rwanda, just several hundred miles away. Camp's comment on this act of genocide, and the fact that many of those involved were considered to be Christian, is yet another instance of mass violence that raises serious questions about the effectiveness of Christian discipleship.

73. "Religion Beliefs in Rwanda," see https://www.worldatlas.com/articles/religious-beliefs-in-rwanda/html#. Accessed 9/13/22.

74. Paquelle, Danielle, "Thousands of women were raped during Rwanda's genocide. Now their children are coming of age." 6/16/17. Available at https"//news.independent.co.uk/news/long-read=thousands-of-women-raped-now-their-children-are-coming-of-age. Accessed August 18, 2022.

75. "Rwandan genocide of 1994," See https://www, Britannica.com/event/Rwanda_genocide_of_1994. Accessed August 18, 2022.

76. "Rwandan priest tried for genocide." Available at news.bbc/1/world/Africa/3671464.stm. Accessed August 18, 2022.

Much of the subsequent attention focused on the breakdown of U. N. "peacekeeping forces" to restrain violence effectively or to protect the weak. But the breakdown of Rwandan Christianity, unable to stem the tide of mass murder, is all the more puzzling. Rwanda had often been cited as a case study for the success of "Christian missions," after the so-called *Tornade* in the 1930s swept the Tutsi aristocracy into the folds of the Catholic Church. Following the conversions of the leaders of Rwanda, the country was dubbed a "Christian Kingdom." But the genocide demonstrated—in a graphic and horrible way—that the Western Christianity imported into the heart of Africa apparently failed to create communities of *disciples*. In actuality the "triumph of Christian missions" preceded the triumph of ethnic hatred. When push came to shove, the Jesus who taught his disciples to "love your neighbor" was missing when young men were hacking old men, women and children to death, simply because these neighbors were of a different ethnic background. Numerous Christian martyrs of both Hutu and Tutsi ethnic identity died because of their resistance to the massacres. But that these faithful martyrs were a minority among the fold of Christians has led critics to suggest that the "gospel" imported into Rwanda failed to ever challenge the ethnic identities of its "converts"— they "became Christian," but many remained first and foremost either Hutu or Tutsi.[77]

ABORTION

At the beginning of the nineteenth century medical knowledge of conception and pregnancy was limited. Laws regarding abortion were few and unclear. That abortion was wrong was widely accepted. Christian churches, both Catholic and Protestant, held to the view that the unborn child was made in the image of God. Abortion was a sin. There were abortions, but they were usually dangerous, and sometimes deadly for woman and child. As medical understanding of conception as the beginning of a new life increased, many doctors, and a smaller number of pastors (both groups largely Protestant), encouraged the passage of laws protecting the lives of the unborn in the United States.[78]

---

77. Camp, *Mere Discipleship*, 15–16. (My emphasis)

78. Leadership in opposing slavery in the eighteenth century owed a great deal to the Society of Friends, the Quakers.

By mid-century it had become widely understood that the conception of an individual human began with the fertilization of the egg by the sperm. This fact convinced a number of physicians to work for a change in the laws that would protect this nascent life. This crusade against abortion, if it can be called that, was led primarily by physicians, and not clergy or politicians.[79] Physicians who did oppose abortion were also deeply concerned for the health of pregnant women. Though some abortions were done by trained physicians, a goodly number were carried out in unsanitary conditions by men and women who lacked both medical knowledge and skill. Many women suffered from infections and complications that were poorly treated, and death was not terribly uncommon. Even so, not all physicians were convinced. For some doctors abortion was highly profitable, and relatively few doctors who performed abortions faced criminal charges. Public knowledge of such things was limited and response was mixed.

Many women—perhaps most—who became pregnant out of wedlock married the father. Both parties to the pregnancy were encouraged to do so by families, churches, and the larger community, all of whom strongly supported marriage and family. Abortion was never considered a legitimate or legal response, and the women who sought an abortion—usually those without family or financial support—usually did so as a last resort.[80]

Newspapers, and in time, a number of religious periodicals, proved of considerable help in supporting the efforts of the medical community. *The New York Times* and the *National Police Gazette* deserve special mention for the efforts they made in arousing public concern over abortion, as well its negative impact on the health of women. As Robin Fox commented,

> These two newspapers joined the anti-abortion crusade by publishing editorials and news stories which emphasized concern for women and the unborn while viewing abortion as a form of oppression. Sensational headlines of grisly deeds and death were accompanied by editorials and other stories which revealed the

---

79. Fox, "Historical Perspectives on Abortion," 22. See also books by Brennan, *The Abortion Holocaust,* Mohr, *Abortion in America,* and Jacobson and Johnston, *Abortion Worldwide Report,* for further information on the history of this movement to outlaw abortion in the United States.

80. Olasky, *Abortion Rites,* 40.

affluent lives of abortionists in contrast to the destitution of women obtaining their services.⁸¹

The combined efforts of physicians, newspapers, lawyers, and a relatively small number of Christian churches and organizations, gradually led to growing restrictions on the practice of abortion in the closing decades of the nineteenth century. Though a number of Christian pastors and lay people worked to restrict abortion, and help those wounded by this practice, Marvin Olasky notes that the only denomination to actually condemn abortion in the nineteenth century was the Presbyterian Church in the USA, which did so in 1869.⁸² All in all, seventy nations and territories restricted abortion in some measure by 1918.⁸³

However, beginning in 1920 with Russia's authorization of abortion, the tide began to change. This was especially the case after 1950, when dozens of nations (many under communist control), began authorizing abortions, causing the number of abortions to increase dramatically. As of 2015, according to the data compiled in the *Abortion Worldwide Report*, 738 million abortions have been performed in communist nations, primarily China and the Soviet Union.⁸⁴ This is an astounding figure, and yet not surprising given their ideological embrace of violence, and the other mass killings of men, women and children noted above.

Nations with majority faiths, whether Islamic, Hindu, or Buddhist, have accounted for another 148 million abortions. In countries (most of them in Europe and the United States) in which the majority of their citizens were at least nominally Christian, there have been 131.2 million abortions.⁸⁵ This despite the fact that the faith which these Christians claimed to be adherents has historically been life-affirming. What happened in these countries, and among so many of their "Christians," to bring about this extraordinary reversal?

These changes did not occur overnight. A profound shift in worldviews regarding abortion in academia, medical communities, government, and the media, had been gathering momentum in numerous

---

81. Fox, "Historical Perspectives on Abortion," 22–23. Ironically, the *New York Times* is today one of the leading media voices in support of abortion.

82. Olasky, *Abortion Rites*, 163

83. Jacobson and Johnston, *Abortion Worldwide Report*, 43. Jacobson and Johnston also note that by 1910 every state in America had passed laws prohibiting abortion.

84. Jacobson and Johnston, *Abortion Worldwide Report*, xi

85. Jacobson and Johnston, *Abortion Worldwide Report*, xi.

Western nations for several decades. A revealing overview of those changes was provided in the California medical journal editorial referred to above. The author of that editorial, Dr. Malcom Potts, was quite candid with regard to the semantic gymnastics necessary to separating the idea of killing from that of abortion, especially when articulated by those with "impeccable" credentials. He was equally candid with regard to the fact that legalized abortion would have a major impact on Western society, and Western ethics and medicine, to the point that the traditional ethic upholding the sanctity of life might very well be abandoned altogether. Though social resistance was expected, Potts believed that the process of creating a new ethic was already well along, and particularly evident with regard to the issue of abortion.

> Its defiance of the long held Western ethic of intrinsic and equal value for every human life regardless of its stage, condition, or status, abortion is becoming accepted by society as moral, right, and even necessary.[86]

Today, the erosion of the traditional ethic is well along, and the "defiance" of the Western ethic increasingly includes the acceptance not only of abortion, but infanticide and euthanasia. The confluence of the eugenics movement with that of a growing secularization in the late nineteenth century, and which accelerated in the twentieth, contributed greatly to the erosion of this ethic and worldview. Though this movement developed first in the West, in Europe and the Americas, it proved to be of service in Asian nations when the rapid growth of the world's population in those countries aroused the concern of western foundations and institutions imbued with the eugenicist worldview. The financial and political support these organizations were able to share with China and India in particular—much of it from the United States—proved to be extraordinarily successful in eliminating hundreds of millions of lives through abortion. This success was aided significantly through the development of the technology capable of determining the sex of a preborn child, which in Asian countries, led to the targeting of female fetuses. This practice has seriously skewed the sex ratios of these nations.[87]

Liberal Christians in western countries—many of whom were and are open to a eugenicist point of view—have helped provide religious support for this secularization process, and the support for abortion that

---

86. Potts, "A New Ethic for Medicine and Society," 67–68.
87. See Hvistendahl, *Unnatural Selection*.

is commonly associated wish it. Momentum for this picked up considerably in the 1960s and 1970s.[88]

It might have been different. With victory in World War II assured, Allied governments put together plans for punishing the Nazi regime for war crimes. The Nuremburg trials, as they were called, tried Nazi leaders both for "crimes against humanity," which referred to the murder of the Jews, other civilians and prisoners of war, and "crimes against peace," which referred to the invasion of other countries. As it happened the Nazi defendants were convicted on crimes against humanity and crimes against peace only *after* the invasion of Poland. Incredibly, the atrocities committed *before* the invasion of Poland, such as the eugenic murders of the handicapped, were not considered as crimes. As Samantha Powers points out, "By inference, if the Nazis had exterminated the entire German Jewish population but never invaded Poland, they would not have been liable at Nuremburg."[89]

One man deeply concerned with these issues was Raphael Lemkin, a Polish Jew and a legal scholar. Nearly fifty members of his family were murdered by the Germans. Outraged and grieving he made it his life's work to introduce the concept of "genocide"—a word he coined—into international law. Lemkin was motivated in part by his realization that Germany's atrocities were legal under German law, and was convinced, as Power put it, that a "set of universal, higher norms, was needed as a backdrop to national law."[90] His relentless efforts eventually led the newly formed United Nations at its Convention on Genocide (held in France) to define and enact a law banning genocide on December 9, 1948.[91] The law included this definition of genocide:

"Any of the following acts committed with intent to destroy, in whole or in part, a national, ethnical, racial, or religious group, as such:

---

88. Following are the European nations with the year they authorized abortion since 1960: Norway (1960); United Kingdom (1967); Austria, Cyprus (1974); France, Italy (1975); Albania (1977); Luxembourg (1978); Netherlands, Portugal (1984); Spain (1985); Liechtenstein, (1987); Belgium (1990; Monaco (2009); San Marina (2016), Ireland (2018). Ireland, a nation with a large Catholic population, voted in May 2018 to repeal the ban on abortion stated in the eighth amendment to their constitution. See Kimiko Freytas-Tamura, "Ireland Votes to End Abortion in Rebuke to Catholic Conservatism."

89. Power, *Problem From Hell*, 49.

90. Power, *Problem From Hell*, 48.

91. Power, *Problem From Hell*, Chapter 4, "Lemkin's Law," 47–60.

A. Killing members of a group;

B. Causing bodily or mental harm to members of the group;

C. Deliberately inflicting on the group the conditions of life calculated to bring about its physical destruction in whole or in part;

D. *Imposing measures intended to prevent births within the group*;

E. Forcibly transferring children of the group to another group."[92]

On the very next day, December 10, the United Nations published its *Universal Declaration of Human Rights.* The *law* on genocide owed much to the dedicated efforts of Raphael Lemkin; the *passage* of the *Universal Declaration* owed much to the work of Christian leader Charles Malik, who guided the many discussions on the fundamental question of the day: What is the nature of man?[93] The answer, expressed in Article 3, was simple and direct: "Everyone has the right to life, liberty and security of person." Forty-eight nations signed the declaration, with eight abstaining, including the USSR.[94]

Earlier that same year, in September 1948, the World Medical Association published its *WMA Declaration of Geneva,* which included "The Physician's Pledge." The pledge contained a statement that reflected the respect for human life (including life before birth) prevalent at the time: "I will maintain the utmost respect for life from the time of conception until death."[95] Today, however, the latest version of the WMA Declaration *omits* the phrase "from conception until death."[96]

---

92. Power, *Problem From Hell,* 57. (My emphasis) It is this phrase (D) which some prolife leaders apply to the practice of abortion, particularly with regard to Planned Parenthood. It is alleged that by locating abortion facilities in low-income neighborhoods, PP has been targeting minority populations, e.g., blacks.

93. Historians give credit to Malik for not only guiding the discussion on the declaration, but for his work in obtaining the support of 48 nations. Despite the abstention of the USSR and its satellites, no nation voted against it. See Johnston, "Charles Malik, the UN, and Human Rights."

94. *Universal Declaration of Human Rights,* Article 3. In the next decade the civil rights movement in the United States, led by Martin Luther King and the Southern Christian Leadership Conference—and widely supported by moderate and liberal Christians—began to gain momentum.

95. See: "The Physician's Pledge." *WMA Declaration of Geneva.*

96. See WMA Declaration of Geneva for "The Physician's Pledge." The Hippocratic Oath, which stated that a physician would not give drugs to a pregnant woman to procure an abortion, was considered an important principle of medical ethics that reflected the Judeo-Christian worldview. Many medical schools no longer use it. See

These documents, in their original version, owed much to the Judeo-Christian sanctity of life ethic that prevailed in the West following the end of World War II, and the Nuremberg Trials in particular. Given the widespread support for these remarkable documents which upheld the right to life, and the universal sense of revulsion over the Jewish Holocaust, one might think that the erosion of the Judeo-Christian sanctity of life ethic asserted by Dr. Malcom Potts would have been forestalled. But it was not.

The promotion of human rights set forth in the Convention on Genocide, the *Universal Declaration of Human Rights,* and the *WMA's Declaration of Geneva*, was a noble ideal, and yet it failed to protect "the right to life" of preborn children in ensuing decades. Well over nine hundred million abortions would take place in the second half of the twentieth century, well over two hundred million occurring in nations which had voted *in favor* of the law on genocide and the *Universal Declaration of Human Rights.* Included among them were nations with substantial Christian populations which already had laws on their books prohibiting abortion.[97]

The root cause of the erosion and decline of the Judeo-Christian ethic, though it took place over several decades, both before and after World War II, was largely due to the fact—as Charles Malik and others would point out—that many people had "lost (their) hold on God," and no longer believed that the rights of human beings were inherent and inalienable.[98] The loss was pervasive. As Potts noted, "this shift in public attitude has affected the churches, the laws and public policy rather than the reverse."[99]

Among those responsible for this shift with regard to law and public policy was the American Law Institute (ALI). This prestigious organization began working on a Model Penal Code in 1951 as a guide for state legal codes. It downplayed the humanity and worth of the fetus, and recommended among other things that laws pertaining to abortion be liberalized. Rape, incest, physical abnormality, and the physical or mental health of the mother were to be permitted as acceptable reasons

---

Jones, "The Hippocratic Oath II," for his account concerning later revisions to the pledge.

97. Fifty-five nations voted in favor of the UN genocide law. Power, *Problem From Hell,* 59.

98. Charles Malik, cited in Jacobson & Johnston, *Abortion Worldwide Report,* 18.

99. Potts, "A New Ethic for Medicine and Society," 68.

for abortion. Its final version was published in 1962, and proved to be the first call for legalizing abortion by a national authoritative body. It had a major effect on public opinion, including that of numerous church leaders.[100]

Several men whose collaboration had an impact on Christian (and Jewish) attitudes toward abortion were Howard Moody, Lawrence Lader, and Bernard Nathanson. Moody, the pastor of Judson Memorial Church in New York City, was an early crusader for overturning American abortion laws. In 1967 he founded the Clergy Consultation Service on Abortion. This organization at its height included 1200 clergymen, both Christian and Jewish, who would refer women seeking abortions to a network of physicians willing to perform them.[101]

Disgusted by back-street abortions, Nathanson, a gynecologist, started sending women to a physician in Puerto Rico who performed abortions in the 1960s. Nathanson and Lader, a social activist, met at a dinner party in 1967, and found that they shared an interest in liberalizing abortion laws. Lader had recently published a book on abortion, and wanted to start an organization to combat the abortion laws in New York State. In 1968 he chaired a national meeting in Chicago for people interested in repealing abortion laws. Together Lader and Nathanson, with a few other like-minded individuals, founded the National Association for Repeal of Abortion Laws (N.A.R.A.L.) in 1969.[102] A year later New York, in a decision that delighted and yet surprised many proponents with the speed of its passage, legalized abortion. Nathanson then began to perform abortions himself, and eventually headed an abortion clinic

---

100. In the late 1960s, Colorado, California and New York made use of this code in revising their abortion laws. The work of the American Law Institute would also influence the Supreme Court's Roe v Wade decision in 1973. Another factor that affected public opinion, aside from public and legal challenges, was the thalidomide tragedy that erupted in the early 1960s. The wide usage of this drug (though blocked in the United States by the United States Food and Drug Administration) caused thousands of birth defects. Learning of these possibilities aroused a great deal of sympathy and led a number of women, including some in the Unites States, to seek a therapeutic abortion in Europe.

101. In 1971 or 1972, living in Vermont, I was approached by a fellow pastor in the United Church of Christ, who asked me if I wanted to join this consultation service. Though I had not at that point given serious thought to abortion, I found the invitation unappealing and turned it down.

102. N.A.R.A.L. was later to be renamed as the National Abortion Rights League.

founded by Howard Moody. Some 70,000 abortions were performed in the years that he led it.[103]

As Nathanson admitted, joining the abortion legalization effort was not difficult. A comment in his book, *Aborting America*, written after his conversion to a pro-life stance, reflects his mindset at the time he joined forces with Lader—a mindset shared by a fair number of (mostly liberal) Christians. As Nathanson wrote, "I was a willing recruit. I was not mesmerized, brainwashed, or deceived, and Lader never misrepresented his radical purpose: total abolition of abortion restrictions.[104]

As part of N.A.R.A.L.'s push for the legalization of abortion, Protestant and Jewish clergy were recruited to encourage its acceptance through their sermons (as eugenicists had encouraged clergy to support the eugenics movement decades before). The clergymen who favored this approach, notes Nathanson, were referred to as "our" clergy.[105]

The Feminist and the sexual liberation movements also gained momentum in the 1960s. Their contribution to the public sphere, and to studies and discussions in churches and seminaries, was not insignificant. Though Potts did not mention the feminist movement, it is certain that the feminists played a role in moving public opinion toward acceptance of abortion. Great numbers of women across the American landscape—many of whom were members of a church or synagogue—were seeking better pay, better work and educational opportunities, and the freedom to enjoy sex as men did. Central to sexual freedom was the idea that women should be able to choose their partners, and if they became pregnant, should be free to keep the baby or abort it.[106]

Another individual who exercised a considerable influence with regard to the issues of euthanasia, abortion and sexual liberation in the churches, was Joseph Fletcher, an Episcopal priest who taught for years in an Episcopal seminary, and who belonged to the Euthanasia Society of

---

103. Nathanson and Ostling, *Aborting America*, chapters 4, 5, 6.

104. Nathanson, *Aborting America*, 31. As Nathanson's book makes clear, he would in time, due in part to advances in fetology, become a vigorous opponent to abortion. Towards the end of his life Nathanson became a Christian.

105. Nathanson, *Aborting America*, 60.

106. One of the better-known feminists was Betty Friedan, an early supporter of Lawrence Lader and N.A.R.A.L, in the effort to seek legal abortion for women. Many early feminists, however, such as Elizabeth Cady Stanton and Susan B. Anthony, were opposed to abortion.

America.[107] Fletcher acknowledged that he became a priest, "not because he was convinced of the truths of Christianity, but because he wanted an outlet for his social activism."[108] In his books, *Morals and Medicine* and *Situation Ethics,* Fletcher set forth his pragmatic and eugenicist ideas, which he claimed owed nothing to Christian ethics. Central to his thought was the idea that to be a "person" certain traits were necessary: a certain level of intelligence, self-awareness, self-consciousness, and the capability of making moral decisions. An individual lacking these traits (in his book, *Morals and Medicine,* he listed 15 such traits in all) lacked moral worth. Preborn babies were among those who lacked these traits. Having a human body was not enough.[109] These ideas about what constituted personhood would be echoed often in the writings of other influential proponents of euthanasia and abortion, such as philosopher Peter Singer.

Other voices contributing to the intellectual climate that led to an acceptance of abortion in liberal Christian circles were those of feminists Mary Daly, Rosemary Radford Ruether, Elizabeth Schussler, and Beverly Harrison. Daly, Ruether and Schussler were Roman Catholic scholars whose many writings strongly advocated a feminist approach to the Bible, theology, and the rights of women. Harrison, a Protestant, who taught social ethics at Union Theological Seminary, was an outspoken feminist whose views of women in the church, and abortion, would have considerable influence in mainline denominations.[110]

Harrison considered the moral status of the preborn child to be of value, and yet uncertain—definitely of less value that a women's right to bodily integrity. As Harrison put it, "The fact of women's biological fertility and capacity for childbearing in no way overrides our moral claim to the 'right' of bodily integrity, because this moral claim is inherent to

---

107. There were, of course, numerous individuals in the twentieth century, though not members of Christian communities, whose worldview or activities promoted one or more of these issues of abortion, euthanasia and sexual liberation. Among them Margaret Sanger, Sigmund Freud, Alfred Kinsey, Simone de Beauvoir. Various institutions and governmental departments in Europe and the United States were also supportive.

108. Weikart, *The Death of Humanity,* 230.

109. Weikart, *The Death of Humanity,* 231–33.

110. See Dorrien, Social Ethics in the Making, 411–47.

human well-being. No society that coerces women at the level of reproduction may lay claim to moral adequacy."[111]

That most women who become pregnant, whether single or married, have a choice with regard to engaging in sexual activity, and the use of contraceptives, is often overlooked. Most women are not coerced. That this is so would seem to fall under the right of bodily integrity. If a women does not want a child, the responsible time for making choices is before she engages in sexual activity.

Liberal Christians, though many deserve credit for their support of the civil rights movement led by Martin Luther King Jr, have allowed their flexible approach to biblical interpretation, a lingering support for eugenics, strong support for the Feminist movement, and their openness to some of the ideas and practices of the sexual revolution of the 1960s, to overcome the historical Christian emphasis on the sacredness of human life and its defense of preborn life.[112] In so doing they have contributed to the erosion of the pro-life ethic that has been for centuries rooted in the biblical Christian worldview.

Several statements illustrate the stance of liberal Christians with regard to abortion in both the Catholic Church, and the mainline Protestant denominations:[113]

- The issue of abortion is not mentioned in the Bible.[114]

---

111. From Harrison, *Our Right to Choose*, 198–99, cited in Dorrien, *Social Ethics in the Making*, 427.

112. Most of the mainline denominations accept premarital sexual activity, homosexuality (even for ordained pastors), and support homosexual marriage. Richard John Neuhaus, a Lutheran pastor during his involvement with the civil rights movement (he entered the Catholic Church in 1990 and was ordained a Catholic priest a year later), was surprised and disturbed to find that most of his liberal Christian friends, valiant for the civil rights of black Americans, were not that concerned for the rights of the preborn.

113. Dennis DiMauro provides an overview of the controversies that erupted in numerous denominations in the sixties as the abortion issue became the focus of debate. *A Love for Life*, chapter 6. The mainline churches are these: American Baptist Churches USA, Christian Church—Disciples of Christ, Episcopal Church USA, Evangelical Lutheran Church of America, Presbyterian Church USA, United Methodist Church, United Church of Christ. All seven denominations accept legal abortion in some form. Common to each of these ideas is the idea that an unborn child lacks the value necessary to secure his or her protection by law.

114. Position of Frances Kissling, onetime director of Catholics for a Free Choice. In Hendershot, *The Politics of Abortion.*, cited by DiMauro, *A Love for Life*, 40.

- "[T]here is a period during gestation when, although there may be *embryo* life in the fetus, there is no living *child* upon whom the crime of murder can be committed."[115]
- Conservative Christians who oppose abortion "substitute religious authority for moral reasoning . . . [and evade] the moral inadequacies reflected in scripture."[116]
- The United Church of Christ at General Synod 16 stated that the UCC "upholds the right of men and women to have access to adequately funded family planning services, and to safe, legal abortions as one option among others."[117]
- "Because the pregnancy is hers, the decision to continue the pregnancy is uniquely hers. Like the Creator, she reflects upon what is good for the creation of which she is agent."[118]
- "For those who know their religious history, the deification of the conceptus is as heretical an idolatry as any pagan practice whereby a human was sacrificed for the sake of some idolized animal, stone or tree . . ."[119]
- "To criminalize a right [to abortion] that is grounded in the world's major religions is criminal itself. It is also a form of religious persecution."[120]

---

115. From the statement of purpose of the New York Clergymen's Consultation Service on Abortion (CCS), a liberal pro-abortion organization, cited by Mehan, "Saving Lives Through the Churches," 12. Emphasis of CCS.

116. Beverly Harrison, *Our Right to Choose*, 70.

117. Minutes of the United Church of Christ General Synod 16, 1987, 83

118. Paul Simmons, "Some Biblical References to Personhood," in *Prayerfully Pro-Choice: Resources for Worship*, 117. Cited by DiMauro, *Love for Life*, 42.

119. Howard Moody, *Prayerfully Pro-Choice: Resources for Worship*, a publication in 2000 of the Religious Coalition for Abortion Rights (later Religious Coalition for Reproductive Choice), 8. Cited in Gorman and Brooks, *Holy Abortion? A Theological Critique*, 21.

120. Daniel Maguire, a Roman Catholic scholar, from the Introduction to the book edited by him: *Sacred Rights: The Case for Contraception and Abortion in World Religions*, cited by Gardiner, "The Ecumenical Molech: The Latest Assault on the Unborn in the Name of the World's Religions," 58.

- "You are to claim your godlike, God-given role in creation by saying yes or no, secure in the knowledge that whatever you decide, after having honestly sought what is right, God will bless . . ."[121]

Intellectual support for abortion by Christians, reversing centuries of support for the sanctity of life, is deeply troubling.[122] More troubling still is the fact that in the United States, since the 1973 *Roe v Wade* decision, a majority of abortions are obtained by women who claim to be Christian.[123] *Life News,* a Christian website, cited a survey done by the Guttmacher Institute that noted the religious affiliation of women seeking abortions that covered the period from 2008 to 2014.

- 54 percent of the women surveyed identified with a Christian community.
- 24 percent as Roman Catholic.
- 17 percent identified as mainline Protestant.
- 13 percent as evangelical Protestant.
- 8 percent identified with another religion.
- 38 percent claimed no religious identity.[124]
- 43 percent of post-abortive women said that they attended church at least monthly at the time of their abortion.[125]

121. Episcopalian priest George Luthringer, in his book, *Considering Abortion,* 6. Cited in DiMauro, *Love for Life,* 43.

122. According to a January 2021 NBC report 45 percent of all Christians think abortion should be illegal in all or most circumstances. Mainline Christians 59 percent; Black Protestants 56 percent, and Roman Catholics 52 percent. The number for women of all faiths is 62 percent. See Ayubi, Peters, Raucher, "Religious woman have abortions, too. And many faiths affirm abortion rights." See https://nbcnews.com/Think/opinion/religious-women-have-abortions-too.many-faiths-affirm-abortion-rights-ncna1287846, accessed August 4, 2022.

123. A Care Net survey done in 2015 revealed that 70 percent of women obtaining an abortion identified as a Christian, with 16 percent identifying as Evangelical. This was very close to the results of a similar Pew Research Study. Though this report is somewhat higher than the Guttmacher report, it is in agreement with the claim that a majority of women in the USA who obtain abortions identify as Christians. See Earls, Aaron, "7 in 10 Women who Have an Abortion Identify as a Christian," December 2, 2021. See https://ResearchLifeway.com/2021/12/03/7-n-10-women-who-have-had-an-abortion-identify-as-a-christian/.

124. Bilger, "Shocking report shows that 54 percent of women getting abortions are Christians."

125. Bilger, "Shocking report shows that 54 percent of women getting abortions

These are several reasons that help explain these incredible results. The first reason I believe has to do with the ideas and events in western culture—including those of churches and religious organizations—that contributed to the erosion of the sanctity of life ethic, and eventuated in the authorization of abortion. For many people an activity that is considered to be legal is thought to be morally acceptable. This is especially the case when churches and religious organizations speak with an uncertain voice. The sexual revolution which evolved in the turbulent 1960s—often approved of in liberal Christian churches (and condoned in conservative churches)—has also been a factor. Another significant factor has been the change to the meaning of freedom, from the understanding that it entailed moral responsibility, and doing what is right, to following the desires of one's heart without restraint.

A second reason is that abortion is fairly inexpensive, and fairly safe—at least for the mother. Many abortion facilities in the states that permit abortion are within driving distance. In response to the Supreme Court's *Dobbs* decision, a number of companies have promised to provide transportation for women who live in pro-life states, and who would need to cross state lines to obtain an abortion.

A third reason according to many women who were surveyed about abortion thought that churches tend to be judgmental, and provide poor support for pregnant women, particularly those who are unmarried.

- 65 percent said that single women who are pregnant are judged by church members
- 54 percent were of the opinion that churches oversimplified the decisions pregnant women make
- Less than half, 41 percent, thought churches were prepared to help women with an unplanned pregnancy with her decision
- Only 33 percent thought that churches provided accurate information about pregnancy options[126]

---

are Christians."

126. Green, "New Survey: Women Go Silently From Church to Abortion Clinic." There is some truth in these assertions about the care given by churches, but it is fair to add that thousands of congregations in America today provide a variety of service, either directly, or through support for pregnancy care centers located nearby. These services include counseling, medical referrals, financial and material support (clothing, diapers, cribs, etc). The church I served as pastor has for many years provided support through congregational services, counseling and financial aid, as well as through

The fourth reason is that *discipleship*, which is the responsibility of the churches, has been ineffective, even among Catholics and Evangelicals. The secularization of the West, manifested in the scientific materialist worldview, is a view of life and reality that has infiltrated liberal Christian theology to a considerable degree. But many conservative Catholic and evangelical pastors have also been affected by this worldview, and have not done well in preparing their young people to counter it with a deep understanding of the Christian worldview and the sacredness of human life. As Dallas Willard wrote, "[T]he current position of the church in our day may be better explained by *what liberals and conservatives have shared* than by how they differ. For different reasons, and with different emphases, they have agreed that discipleship to Christ is optional to membership in the Christian church."[127]

THE SCANDAL OF DISCIPLESHIP

The accounts of the Christian response to instances of massive violence given in this chapter, though brief, are accurate. Insofar as they represent the overall thrust of the Christian response, with due recognition to the many thousands of Christians who did respond with courage and compassion, it is fair to ask: how could these things happen? How could Christians not be outraged by the violence done to their Jewish neighbors during Kristallnacht, the Night of Broken Glass? How is it that Hutu Christians could murder nearly a million of their Tutsi Christian neighbors? How can it be that Christian women abort their own children, and in this country represent the majority of those who do so?

The question Professor David Gushee asked with regard to the Christian response to the Holocaust applies to every instance of mass violence where Christians have been involved. Can Christians be righteous? Are these instances representative of what philosopher Dallas Willard called the "great omission" of discipleship? The answer I am convinced is yes.

---

providing support to a local pregnancy care center. There are more crisis pregnancy centers in America than there are abortion facilities, nearly all of which are operated and financed through the support of religious communities and organizations, and private individuals. Care-Net is one of the largest providers of crisis pregnancy centers, with over 1100 facilities nationwide. Birthright, which was founded in Canada, has over 300 chapters. As of 2013 there were over 2500 CPCs of some kind. A growing number provide limited medical services, such as sonograms.

127. Willard, *Divine Omission*, 11. (His emphasis).

We are witnessing the scandal of discipleship. Discipleship that is weak and inadequate, and damages the credibility of the Gospel.

The instances of mass violence dealt with—including abortion—have occurred where there were sizable Christian communities. I think it reasonable to assume that in each situation there occurred in some way what theologian Lesslie Newbigin has referred to as a secularization of the gospel.[128]

While the mass killings may have differed in extent, or with regard to the motivation and historical circumstances of the perpetrators, it is apparent that there has been an accommodation of the gospel to the pressures of the culture in which the violence took place. Following his return to England after decades of service as a missionary in India Newbigin was struck by the changes that had occurred among the Christian communities in his homeland, indeed, in much of the West, during his absence. He concluded that a major factor was a loss of confidence in the truth of the Gospel as a reflection of reality. In his insightful book, *The Gospel in a Pluralist Society*, Newbigin laid out his response to this state of affairs. He points out that the Christian faith began with extraordinary events—historical facts—associated with Jesus: that in and through his life, teaching, death and resurrection God had initiated a radical new approach in his plan to bring redemption to the whole world. For centuries that view of history and reality, of a truth good for all people everywhere, and for all times and places, prevailed in Christian churches. In recent centuries, however, a different view gained ascendancy, in which the claims of the gospel (or any other religion) came to be understood as being of limited factual value. The ideas of the Enlightenment, those connected to the rise of modern science and the theory of evolution, led many liberal and moderate Christians to a more limited view of truth, a diminished confidence in the authority of the Bible, and a growing acceptance of secularism. Religious ideas and values came to be seen as personal and subjective beliefs, as something one chooses to believe, but which have little bearing on the nature of reality. This worldview—the worldview of modern secularism with a dose of spirituality—in which modern science is the primary driving force, composes a structure of thought and life in which religion, and Christianity in particular, plays a limited role. The result of this secularizing process, embraced by many leaders in the mainstream churches (and not a few evangelical and Catholic leaders),

---

128. See Newbigin, *The Gospel in a Pluralist Society*, chapter 17, "The Myth of the Secular Society," 211–21.

was disturbing. As Newbigin summarized things, "We have learned, I think, that what has come into being is not a secular society but a pagan society, not a society devoid of public images but a society which worships gods which are not God."[129] The attraction of this worldview, and its distortion of the Gospel, remains powerful. The result has been that, for multitudes of modern people, Christianity, and its worldview, are no longer plausible. If this account of things is true, writes Newbigin,

> If it is a "fact" that human life is the accidental result of the ruthless suppression of the weak by the strong, and it is not a fact that "Man's chief end is to glorify God and enjoy him forever," then "values" have no factual basis. They can only be the expression of what some people choose, and—inevitably—it will be the views of the strong who prevail. The language of "values" is simply the will to power wrapped up in cotton wool. And we cannot use the language of right and wrong because it has no basis in the "facts" as we understand them.[130]

For those who accept this account of reality, there is no reason to believe that human life is sacred, and therefore no moral basis for opposing abortion, euthanasia or infanticide.[131] The Roman Catholic Church, at least in its official teaching, has steadfastly resisted this view of reality, and its ready acceptance of eugenicist ideas which promote, among other things, the acceptance of abortion. Given its understanding of abortion as a violation of the natural law, understood to be common to all people, the Catholic Church has had no hesitancy in speaking to the issue of abortion in the public domain, with state governments and with the United Nations.[132] This understanding is one that I believe the Protestant de-

---

129. Newbigin, *The Gospel in a Pluralist Society*, 220. Newbigin's book, though published in 1989, remains essential reading for Christian leaders, pastors and parents today. Geoffrey Wainwright's biography of Newbigin, chapter 20, "The Christian Apologist," is most insightful. See *Lesslie Newbigin, A Theological Life*.

130. Newbigin. *The Gospel in a Pluralist Society*, 17.

131. The Catholic Church in its official catechism sets forth three points with regard to the immorality of abortion. See Di Mauro, *Love for Life*, 62–63.

Abortion is a grave offense against both divine and natural law, harms the unborn, parents and society. Procuring an abortion is grounds for excommunication.

Abortion is a violation of the preborn child's human rights, and being unalienable cannot be taken away by the state. Abortion is also an offense against the command of Christ to love our neighbor.

As human rights are natural rights common to all people of all nations, preborn children should be protected by the state, with due penalty

132. Natural law is referred to in Romans 2.14–15: "When Gentiles who have not

nominations would do well to take more seriously. The Catholic Church has also strongly supported compassionate care for pregnant women and their children, as well as providing counsel and support for post-abortive women. And yet, as we will see, millions of women who have obtained abortions consider themselves to be Catholics.

Conservative Evangelical denominations, nearly all of which have held to the traditional understanding of life's sacredness, are the natural allies of the Catholic Church with regard to abortion and the other life issues, though for much of the twentieth century they remained on the theological sidelines.[133] Marvin Olasky and Herbert Schlossberg (both evangelical scholars) point out that during the twentieth century many conservative Christians focused on the growing secularization of American society and American schools, and what they perceived as the heresy of the mainline denominations: their denial of biblical authority, their neglect of personal holiness and evangelism. And they did so with an emphasis that was largely pietistic.[134] Olasky and Schlossberg in their

---

the law do by nature what the law requires, they are a law to themselves, even though they do not have the law. They show that what the law requires is written on their hearts..." As noted earlier, though some Protestants take note of the Natural law, as it is called, most Protestant communions do not place much emphasis on it. Protestant theologian Abraham Kuyper did so, as did C. S. Lewis, who argued that the loss of the Natural law, which was held to be objective and common to all peoples, would contribute to the destruction of modern civilization. See his book, *Abolition of Man*.

133. Major evangelical denominations include the Assemblies of God, Presbyterian Church of America, Orthodox Presbyterian Church, Church of the Nazarene, Evangelical Congregational Church, Free Methodist Church, Conservative Congregational Christian Conference, and the Lutheran Church-Missouri Synod. The Southern Baptist Church, the largest evangelical Protestant denomination with over 15 million members was initially supportive of the Roe v Wade Supreme Court decision, but in 1979 reversed this stance when a wave of more conservative theologians and pastors assumed leadership of the denomination.

134. Ranald Macaulay makes the point well: "When Evangelicalism most needed to present a vigorous refutation of man-made ideas she drew attention to herself, in fact, by her impressive silence. As the culture experienced its ever-increasing crisis during the first decades of the 20th century a prophetic response from the Evangelical Churches of the west was completely absent. Pietism had prevailed ... The point is this: one of the principal characteristics of Classical Pietism evidently still characterizes evangelicalism today despite sustained efforts to the contrary. To depreciate the mind earlier was serious; to depreciate the mind today is lethal. Classical Pietism's reaction occurred with a culture where, if anything, reason was overemphasized, but at least it was respected. Today the opposite is the case; we find ourselves in a culture virtually submerged by irrationalism ... The issue is the objective truth of Christianity. If Christianity is objectively true it necessarily involves the mind." Ranald Macaulay,

book, *Turning Point*, argue that this approach isolated the Evangelical community from the rest of the culture, and weakened the contributions they could have made in defending the Christian faith and the sacredness of human life in the face of the assaults of our secular age.[135]

The consequences of the pietistic approach have been serious indeed, as evangelical scholar Mark Noll points out in his 1994 book, *The Scandal of the Evangelical Mind*. He cited Charles Malik, the prominent Lebanese Christian who helped put together the United Nations Declaration of Human Rights. Malik was a lay theologian deeply concerned about the importance of ideas. Speaking at Wheaton College's Billy Graham Center, Malik said—in words every Christian leader, educator, pastor and parent should take to heart, "The problem is not only to save souls but to save minds. If you win the whole world and lose the mind of the world, you will soon discover you have not won the world. Indeed, it may turn out that you have actually lost the world."[136]

Mark Noll also quotes the well-known public intellectual, Os Guinness, who makes a similar point about taking the mind seriously. He added that when the use of the mind is depreciated, repentance is necessary. In his words, "It has always been a sin not to love the Lord our God

---

"The Pietistic Roots of Evangelicalism Today," 2–8.

135. Olasky and Schlossberg, *Turning Point*, Chapter two, "Piety vs. Pietism." Pietism was a religious movement that arose in the Lutheran Church in seventeenth century Germany in response to the scholasticism (intellectualism) of the time. Pietists stressed the importance of the Bible, in worship and in small group study of the Bible. In contrast to the religious formalism then prevalent, personal spiritual experience was strongly encouraged. It was important to know the will of God, and to do it. Missions and social concerns were also important concerns. The work of Pietists contributed to the revitalization of many Christians and many congregations. John Wesley and the Methodist Church which he founded, to take one example, were profoundly changed by pietism, and contributed a great deal to social efforts in support of education, founding a variety of programs to help the poor, and fighting the slave trade. However, in later generations the emphasis became more focused on personal piety.

136. Noll, *Scandal of the Evangelical Mind*, 27. Charles Malik, an Eastern Orthodox Christian from Lebanon, was President of the United Nations General Assembly following World War Two, and as noted helped write the UN Declaration of Human Rights. Malik worked across confessional lines, and was well known and respected by Catholics and Evangelicals. He was convinced that the most important thing in civilization was the human person, and the possibility of his "encounter with the person of Jesus Christ." Malik was deeply concerned about human rights, and the ability of Christian educational institutions to prepare their students for the intellectual and moral challenges of our modern age. See www.un.org/ga/55/president/bio13.htm; https://en.wikipedia.org/wiki/Charles_Malik. See also Malik's books, *Christ and Crisis*, and *A Christian Critique of the University*.

with our minds as well as our hearts and souls . . . We have excused this with a degree of pietism and pretend[ing] that this is something other than what it is—that is, sin . . . Evangelicals need to repent of their refusal to think Christianly and to develop the mind of Christ."[137]

Bringing the worldview of the gospel to the modern battle of ideas is of paramount importance, and should be a primary concern of every theological faculty that takes the historic Christian faith seriously. But it must be accompanied by a commitment to the task of *discipleship*—to helping Christians, lay and clergy, *put into practice* the ideas and worldview of Jesus. Much of modern theological education—evangelical as well as liberal—is largely academic in nature. A knowledge of biblical history, biblical languages, systematic theology, church history, ethics, and counseling are all vitally important in gaining an understanding of the Gospel and the Christian worldview. Such studies must of course include attention to social issues that call for a theological and moral response. But these studies must be accompanied with teaching and modeling the in-depth spirituality necessary for discipleship by professors who practice what they teach. This is necessary in order that their students—future teachers, pastors and church leaders—become disciples of Jesus, and learn how to disciple those they will work with.

Certainly there are large numbers of Christians who are taking seriously the challenge of living out their faith in their families, in their work, and in their communities. According to various studies, conservative Christians do more to live out their faith than do liberal or moderate Christians. But it is also true that a great many of them fail to do so. Seminary professor, Ron Sider, wrote a book which complements that of Mark Noll: *The Scandal of the Evangelical Conscience*. The subtitle of his book raises the question: "*Why are Christians living just like the rest of the world?*" When it comes to sexuality, easy divorce, materialism, or abortion, why are so many evangelical Christians so much like their nonbelieving neighbors? Sider's answer:

> Justification and sanctification are *both* central parts of the biblical teaching on the gospel and salvation. To overstate the importance of the one is to run the danger of neglecting the other. And that is certainly what popular evangelicalism has done. Whether emphasizing simplistic slogans such as "once-in-grace-always-in-grace" or focusing on seeker-friendly strategies that neglect

---

137. From "An Interview with Dr. Os Guinness." Quoted in Noll, *Scandal of the Evangelical Mind*, 23.

costly discipleship, we have propagated the heretical notion that people can receive forgiveness without sanctification, heaven without holiness. Notions of cheap grace are at the core of today's scandalous evangelical disobedience.[138]

The failure of millions of Christians to pursue an understanding of the big picture about reality and history their faith provides, and their failure to practice their faith—keeping justification and sanctification together in a thoughtful way—is what I call the scandal of Christian discipleship. When Christians fail to practice what they believe the Gospel is shortchanged. Those in need of spiritual and material help are bereft, and unbelievers, observing the failure of believers to practice what they preach, have the right to ask whether what they preach is really true. It is a sad and noxious situation. Shakespeare as so often put it well, "For sweetest things turn sourest by their deeds; Lilies that fester smell far worse than weeds."[139]

I believe it fair to say that these failures are common among Christians of every tradition the world over. There have been hundreds of millions of Roman Catholic, Protestant (liberal and evangelical), and Orthodox Christians who could recite the Lord's prayer, the great Creeds, publish books, construct and maintain extraordinary buildings, while remaining bystanders (and sometimes perpetrators) to the greatest mass killings in all of human history.[140] Chief among them, the atrocity of abortion.

---

138. Sider, *Scandal of the Evangelical Conscience*, 59. (His emphasis.) Thankfully, in the decades since the Roe V Wade decision the evangelical community has become more vocal, and more active. Many evangelical pastors, recognizing the importance of the life issues and standing firmly on the official stance of their communions, have become outspoken on the issue of abortion. The congregations they serve provide a variety of services in support of women who face unplanned abortions, as well as helping their children. Evangelical institutions such as the Family Research Council and Focus on the Family, with their state affiliations, help provide leadership with political developments, from developing voting guides to working with politicians in fashioning legislation that will uphold the sacredness of human life in the public arena.

139. "They that the power to do harm but will do none." Sonnet 94. Available at https://www.poetryfoundation.org/45100/sonnet-94-they-that-have-the-power-to-harm-but=do-none. Accesses September 16. 2022.

140. Orthodox Churches are officially pro-life. Rev. John Breck of the Orthodox Church in America has stated that "The Orthodox stance on the issue of abortion has never been in doubt. From biblical times to the present, abortion has been regarded as the morally condemnable act of destroying an innocent life." See DiMauro, *A Love of Life*, 91. Of the Roman Catholic Church I know somewhat more, from my reading and association with many Catholic friends. It's intellectual and spiritual legacy is deep and strong. Unquestionably, the Catholic Church in the United States is the strongest

Brian Fisher, pondering the Christian response to abortion, asks: "Why do Christians, many of whom profess to honor the sanctity of life, still abort their children? Why do they promote a pro-life worldview publicly but, when facing an unplanned pregnancy themselves, lose their convictions and take the life of their child?" Fisher answers his own questions by saying that "abortion is, at its core, a spiritual issue. Thus, the reason Christians abort their children is their lack of understanding and acceptance of the gospel of the kingdom." The problem, writes Fisher, is a lack of discipleship.[141]

> Too many Christians do not preach, and practice, the fullness of the gospel . . . Yet the gospel, in its fullness, is the remedy to abortion. We must therefore affirm and live out the gospel in its fullness. Praying the prayer of salvation is a wonderful, monumental moment. It is not generally the cure for abortion. *Discipleship is.* The Great Commission does not command us to go into the world and make converts. It commands us to make disciples. By its very definition, discipleship requires time, energy, commitment, knowledge, patience and skill. It requires love, compassion, kindness and candor . . . Why are Christians aborting their children? They don't fully understand and accept the gospel. And they aren't being disciples. They know Jesus and accept him as their Savior but do not know or understand His lordship. They do not know the radical, transformative, awe-inspiring impact of being a disciple.[142]

Lee Camp, a professor present in Africa at the time of Rwandan genocide, has made a similar point about discipleship. Camp's comment on this act of genocide in which nearly a million Rwandan Christians were murdered, a quarter of a million women were raped, and the fact

---

prolife voice in the country, from which many resources of the pro-life community in terms of financial support, education and ministry, flow. And yet my impression is that while discipleship is important, it is not as effective as it could, and should, be. I think of the thousands of priests and bishops caught up in sex abuse scandals. This has been costly in terms of the energy, time and financial resources given to dealing with them. But even more so with regard to the effect such immoral conduct has had on the image of the Church. It is true that sexual scandal is not limited to the Catholic Church; many Protestant and Orthodox clergy have also been guilty of sexual abuse. Still, there is reason to believe that these scandals have been disproportionately present among Catholic priests and religious orders.

141. Both quotations in this paragraph are from Fisher, "Why do so many Christians have abortions?"

142. Fisher, "Why do so many Christians have abortions?" (My emphasis)

that many of the murderers and rapists were considered to be Christian, is worth pondering deeply.

> In fact, the Rwanda genocide highlights a recurrent failure of much historic Christianity. The proclamation of the "gospel" has often failed to emphasize a fundamental element of the teaching of Jesus, and indeed, of orthodox Christian doctrine. "Jesus is Lord" is a radical claim, one that is ultimately rooted in questions of allegiance, of ultimate authority, of the ultimate norm and standard for human life. Instead, Christianity has often sought to ally itself comfortably with allegiance to other authorities, be they political, economic, cultural, or ethnic. Could it be that "Jesus is Lord" has become one of the most widespread Christian lies? Have Christians claimed the lordship of Jesus, but systematically set aside the call to obedience to this Lord? At least in Rwanda, with "Christian Hutus" slaughtering "Christian Tutsis" (and vice versa), "Christian" apparently served as a faith brand name—a "spirituality," or a "religion"—but not a commitment to a common Lord.[143]

These insights and questions regarding discipleship, particularly with regard to the situation in the United States, are confirmed by the work of Christian Smith, a sociologist at the University of Notre Dame, who led the National Study of Youth and Religion on the spiritual and religious lives of teenagers. This research study was carried out at the University of North Carolina from 2001 to 2005 through thousands of phone calls, and later hundreds of personal interviews from among those earlier contacted by phone. It involved adolescents and a number of parents from 45 states. The purpose was to gather information about the state of religion in America. Participants were asked about their religious activities—church attendance, youth groups, prayer, Bible reading—as well as interactions with their families about religious and spiritual matters. There were also questions about the truth of religions, and the relationship between different religions. The findings provided information about many different subjects, not least the consequences that result when worldviews and discipleship are neglected.

Large numbers of U. S. teenagers, reports Smith, from all kinds of backgrounds, say that "religion is very valuable, important and influential in their lives."[144] This affirmation made a good initial impression, but

---

143. Camp, *Mere Discipleship*, 15–16.
144. Smith and Denton, *Soul Searching*, 154.

that impression faded once those being interviewed spelled out what they meant by this. Smith's explanation calls for caution:

> [O]bservers should know that the religion to which most of them appear to be referring seems significantly different in character from versions of the same faith in centuries past. The religion that many U. S. teens acclaim today is not commendable for youth because, for example, it is revealed in truth by holy and almighty God who calls for all to a turning from self and a serving of God in gratitude, humility and righteousness. Nor is it commendable, alternatively, because it inducts them into a community of people embodying a historically rooted tradition of identity, practices and ethics that define their selfhood, loyalties, and commitments. Rather, the religion that many U. S. teenagers acclaim today is for them commendable because it helps people make good life choices and helps them feel happy. What legitimates the religion of most youth today is not that it is the life-transformative, transcendent truth, but that it instrumentally provides mental, psychological, emotional and social benefits that teens find useful and valuable.[145]

Smith refers to this dominant view of religion among U. S. teenagers, most of whom consider themselves as Christians, as "Moralistic Therapeutic Deism."[146] That religion should help people make wise decisions about their lives is not a bad thing; but it is far from the discipleship that Jesus Christ commands of those who would follow him. It is far from inculcating the wisdom and courage necessary for young people to withstand the currents of a culture of death and become builders of a culture of life that is good for all people—including preborn human beings.

Smith notes in the conclusion to this study that parents are very important to the developing faith of their children. The strongest social

---

145. Smith and Denton, *Soul Searching*, 154.

146. Smith and Denton, *Soul Searching*, 162. The "creed" of this religion, which is particularly dominant among Catholic and mainline Protestant youth, but also evident among Jewish, and evangelical youth, Smith depicts as follows: "A God exists who created and orders the world and watches over life on earth:

God wants people to be good, nice, and fair to each other, as taught in the Bible and most world religions.

The central goal of life is to be happy and to feel good about oneself

God does not need to be particularly involved in one's life except when God is needed to resolve a problem.

Good people go to heaven when they die." Smith and Denton, *Soul Searching*, 162–63.

predictor of "what the religious and spiritual lives of youth will look like is what the religious and spiritual lives of their parents *do* look like."[147] However, as this study makes clear, many parents—though religious themselves—are failing to truly disciple their children in the transforming truth of the Christian faith.

In a follow-up study, *Souls in Transition*, designed to track teenagers as they become emerging adults, ages 18–23, Christian Smith, with Patricia Snell, pointed out that over half of those interviewed continued in the path begun as teenagers. Highly religious teenagers remained highly religious, moderately religious teens remained moderate in their views, and those not very religious remained aloof from religion. For most emerging adults, however, the dominating outlook is indifference to religion.

> [A]mong emerging adults religious beliefs do not seem to be important, action-driving commitments, but rather mental assents to ideas that have few obvious consequences. What actually does have the power and authority to drive life instead are the feelings and inclinations of the emerging adults themselves. They as individuals can determine what is right, worthy, and important. So they themselves can pick and choose from religion to take or leave what they want.[148]

Smith and Snell note that one significant factor in understanding emerging adults is "the contemporary crisis of knowledge and value." They have grown up in a time when moral values have become relative and truth has become culturally and historically conditioned. There is no such thing as objective truth, or moral absolutes. Though some moral beliefs may feel right, emerging adults, by and large, lack the intellectual and moral skills necessary to make thoughtful judgments. Therefore, no one idea or moral belief can be taken as truly right. To claim something as true would be considered rude or intolerant. While this may seem to encourage humility it also encourages acquiescence to whatever intellectual or moral currents are fashionable. The glut of information available on the internet adds to the confusion. Many "lack larger visions of what is true and real and good, in both the private and the public realms."[149]

"Moralistic therapeutic deism," and the easy-going tolerance characteristic of millions of American youth and their parents—a fruit of

---

147. Smith and Denton, *Soul Searching*, 261.
148. Smith and Snell, *Souls in Transition*, 286–87.
149. Smith and Snell, *Souls in Transition*, 292–94.

the domesticated Gospel of which Lesslie Newbigin has written—bears little resemblance to the discipleship that Jesus Christ commanded. Becoming a disciple takes faith, commitment, discipline and courage. And time. It is my conviction that this understanding has often been missing from the efforts of churches (and parents) to disciple their young. We need, as Glen Stassen has argued, a "thicker Jesus," a discipleship that is "incarnational."[150] A discipleship that takes the Lordship of Jesus seriously.

Undiscipled or poorly discipled Christians fail to grasp what David Gushee, in his book, *The Righteous Gentiles of the Holocaust*, calls "the boundaries of moral responsibility."[151] For many Christians the boundaries of moral responsibility have been limited to their friends, their family, their ethnic group, their fellow Christians, their country. Tragically, for far too many Christians the understanding of the boundaries of moral responsibility do not include those who are being knit together in their mother's womb, but are yet unborn.

There are several things to be noted. *First* is to acknowledge that in numerous ways I too have failed to speak and to act as a disciple of Jesus. I have no good excuses, and I am profoundly grateful for the fact that we are saved by God's grace. Still, when I ask for forgiveness as I often must do, I must also remember to pray for the faith, the discipline, courage and compassion to become a better disciple, a more mature disciple—and with the help of the Holy Spirit to do the good works for which he has saved me. This is a prayer I that I also offer for my brothers and sisters in Christ.

Second, it must be emphasized that there have been many, many Christians who have demonstrated genuine discipleship, often at great cost to themselves. I am honored to know some of these individuals personally, many far more mature than I am. The reader is also encouraged to learn the names of those who are disciples in the best sense, whose words and actions truly glorify God, who stand firm in defense of the sacredness of every human life.[152]

Third, it is possible to change. As noted, many evangelical Christian churches were caught off guard by the ideas and events which led to the Supreme Court's decision to legalize abortion. Initially they did

---

150. See Stassen, *A Thicker Jesus*.

151 Gushee, *Righteous Gentiles*, 5–6.

152. One must be thankful for the leadership of the Catholic Church, and the millions of American Christians who are in some way part of the prolife movement. Their many and varied efforts constitutes the largest social action movement in the history of the United States.

relatively little to help their members understand the ideas and worldviews involved, and provided relatively little support for women facing an unexpected pregnancy or an abortion. Thankfully, since that time numerous Evangelical churches have strengthened their stand on abortion, and have become more outspoken and more active on the life issues. Moreover, thousands of churches now provide, or support, services for women struggling with pregnancy or abortion.[153]

Much remains to be done if the scandal of Christian discipleship is to be overcome. As Christians we must engage the ideas—including the wrong worldviews at the root of what Pope John Paul II called the culture of death. We must also give serious attention to rooting out the distorted understandings and lifestyles so prevalent in the household of God. We must seek understanding of the process of spiritual formation that enables believers to become disciples. We must become obedient, to the point of putting our very lives on line in defense of the most vulnerable amongst us.

And if not? As Lesslie Newbigin wrote, the Church must be vigilant in upholding the truth of the Gospel. God, the maker and sustainer of reality, meaning and truth, has become present in history through the life, teaching, death and resurrection of Jesus, in such a way that the power of sin has been broken, "and has created a space and a time in which we who are unholy can nevertheless live with God who is holy."[154] This story must be understood as *fact*, as reflecting reality, and a way of life Christians must live out seriously. This means the willingness to speak out and advocate for this truth, this understanding, in the public square—in the schools, in the media, in industry and politics, throughout the culture where Christians live and work. It was his hope, as it is mine, that this would be done with excellence, and with humility, in such a way that the

---

153. The Southern Baptist Convention, for example, the nation's largest evangelical denomination, was initially supportive of the Roe v Wade decision, but to their credit came out strongly with a pro-life resolution in 1982. This commitment was further strengthened by a resolution passed at their convention in 2003, which included a concern over euthanasia, the harvesting of human embryos, and a confession of the denomination's initial blindness to the cost of abortion. "RESOLVED, That we humbly confess that the initial blindness of many in our convention to the enormity of Roe v. Wade should serve as a warning to contemporary Southern Baptists of the subtlety of the spirit of the age in obscuring a biblical worldview . . ." From "Resolution #8: On Thirty Years of Roe. V. Wade," adopted at the SBC, June 2003, quoted in Di Mauro, *A Love of Life*, 142.

154. Wainwright, *Lesslie Newbigin*, 387.

Christian way of life can be seen as a distinctive and wholesome way of life, "a new social order," as the salt and light that Jesus said his people were to be.[155]

In a speech at a world conference on mission and evangelism in Brazil, Newbigin recalled a dockside service that had been held by the conference two days earlier, to provide an opportunity for those attending the conference to express repentance for the slave trade. In cooperating with the slave trade Portuguese Christians had "domesticated the Gospel and so acted in ways that turned it into bad news . . ." Standing there he remembered the thoughts that came to mind.

> [W]hen we stood in the old slave market on Saturday morning, on the stones which had felt the weight of the bare and bruised and shackled feet of countless of our fellow human beings, when we stood in that place so heavy with human sin and human suffering and were told to spend two minutes in silence waiting for what the Spirit might say to us, I thought first how unbelievable that Christians could have connived in that inhuman trade. And then there came to my mind the question: Will it not be the case that our great-grandchildren will be equally astonished at the way in which we in our generation, in our so-called modern, Western, rich, developed culture, connive at the wholesale slaughter of unborn children in the name of the central idol of our culture: freedom of choice?[156]

---

155. Wainwright, *Lesslie Newbigin*, 380–87.
156. Wainwright, *Lesslie Newbigin*, 388–89.

4

Jesus, Discipleship, and Worldviews

It is easy to get caught up in the latest controversy or breaking news story. But current events are merely surface effects, like waves on the ocean. The real action happens below the surface, at the level of worldviews.

—Nancy Pearcey[1]

False ideas are the greatest obstacle to the reception of the Gospel. We may preach with all the fervor of a reformer and yet succeed only in winning a straggler here and there, if we permit the whole collective thought of the nation to be controlled by ideas which prevent Christianity from being regarded as anything more than a harmless delusion. What is today a matter of academic speculation begins to-morrow to move armies and pull down empires. In that second stage, it has gone too far to be combated; the time to stop it was when it was still a matter of impassionate debate. So as Christians we should try to mold the thought of the world in such a way as to make the acceptance of Christianity something more than a logical absurdity.

—J. Gresham Machen[2]

---

1. *Love Thy Body.* 9.
2. Cited by William Lane Craig, 17.

Every individual bases his thoughts, decisions and actions on a worldview. A person may not be able to identify his worldview, and it may lack consistency, but his most basic assumptions about the origin of life, purpose, and the future, guarantee adherence to some system of thought.

—David Noebel[3]

We do indeed give the primacy of that spiritual truth revealed in the Bible and incarnate in Christ. That does not mean, however, that those aspects of truth discoverable in the realm of mathematics, chemistry, or geography are any whit less than the truth as it is in Christ . . . But all the time there is the unity of truth under God, and that unity we deny in education at the peril of habituating ourselves to a fragmentary kind of learning found on some avowedly Christian campuses today.

—Frank E. Gaebelein[4]

If I light an electric torch at night out of doors, I don't judge its power by looking at the bulb, but by seeing how many objects it lights up. The brightness of a source of light is appreciated by the illumination it projects upon non-luminous objects. The value of a religious, or, more generally, a spiritual way of life is appreciated by the amount of illumination thrown upon the things of this world.

—Simone Weil[5]

SPIRITUAL TONE DEAFNESS

Years ago I heard Professor Franklin Littell, an authority on the Jewish Holocaust, give an installation sermon for a former student at a little church in northern Vermont.[6] He began by reading by reading a few

    3. *Understanding the Times*, 1.
    4. Quoted in Lockerbie, *Christian Paideia*, flyleaf.
    5. *First and Last Notebooks*, 147.
    6. Franklin Littell is considered the father of Holocaust studies. He questioned how Christians in the heart of "Christian Europe could have killed or ignored the killing of six million Jews. A big part of the answer, as he found it, was that Christians from the time of Jesus on had shown systematic contempt for Jews and their beliefs." Martin,

lines from a newspaper, which stated: "Increasing noise levels in American society are contributing to the loss of hearing in our children. As a result of this increasing noise they are becoming more and more tone deaf. More and more of our children, as they grow older, are unable to distinguish clearly between one tone and another."[7] Far more serious said Littell, was the fact that millions of children were growing up *spiritually* tone deaf, unable to tell the difference between right and wrong, good and evil, truth and falsehood.

Littell's point was that the Christian churches were not discipling their children effectively. Sociologist Christian Smith's research with young people referred to above—most of whom considered themselves Christians—has done much to lend credence to Littell's claim. The dominant view of religion among the youth Smith surveyed was "Moralistic Therapeutic Deism," not the outcome Jesus had in mind when he gave the apostles the commission to make disciples. If the scandal of discipleship is to be overcome, and Christians are to achieve the unity that restores respect for the credibility of the Gospel (John 17.13–26), then we must deepen our commitment to the prayers and teaching of Jesus—Savior, Lord, and Master Discipler.

JESUS, THE WORLDVIEW DISCIPLER

Following a time of spiritual testing in the wilderness, Jesus called twelve men to be with him and to learn what it meant to be a disciple.

Learning was gained in part by observing and pondering Jesus's life and teaching. They learned to pray by observing him pray. His prayerfulness taught them the importance of trusting in God, and emphasized the seriousness with which he took his relationship to God his Father. His parables and questions encouraged thoughtfulness and critical thinking. His regular attendance at the synagogue taught the importance of community and discipline. When he took the part of a servant at the Last Supper and washed the feet of the disciples, he was teaching them the value of humble service.

Jesus, as the incarnation of God—the Word made flesh—lived what he taught. And what he taught and lived was rooted in the Old Testament (the Hebrew Bible) teachings about creation, the fall of man, the

---

"Franklin Littell, Scholar of the Holocaust, dies at 91."

7. Quotation from my notes taken at the time of Littell's sermon.

law and the prophets, and redemption. The stories he told often included quotations from, and allusions to, the Old Testament. He attributed great authority to this written Word, but he also amplified and deepened its meaning with his own teaching. His teaching and the miracles he performed amazed those who observed, and demonstrated the authority he had been given by God.

On some occasions he assumed this authority, but in the Sermon on the Mount he stated it plainly with words that echoed the sayings attributed only to God in the Old Testament: "Think not that I have come to abolish the law and the prophets; I have come not abolish them but to fulfil them. For truly, I say to you, till heaven and earth pass away, not an iota, not a dot, will pass from the law until all is accomplished" (Matt 5.17-18).[8] In speaking of divorce and anger he made reference to an Old Testament passage, and amended it with a comment that deepened and sharpened the point.[9] The authority with which he spoke and acted astonished those who listened (Matt 7.28), but also aroused opposition, e.g., when he performed a healing on the Sabbath, and his claim to be one with God the Father (John 5.1–18).

Jesus was the embodiment of God's grace and goodness, demonstrated in his acts of compassion. He healed the sick, delivered many from evil spirits, treated women with respect, and enjoyed the presence of children. His compassion was present when he was alone with the apostles, with those in mourning, in his responses to those with questions, in the small and thoughtful courtesies and kindnesses given to whomever needed them.[10] When Jesus was with people, he was truly "present." Jesus was a servant, a way of life and love he wanted his disciples to emulate (John 13.1–20).

Philosopher Elton Trueblood, in his book, *The Humor of Jesus*, argues that Jesus enjoyed a sense of humor, a fact few scholars have noticed. There is the story of the Canaanite woman who came to Jesus seeking deliverance for her daughter, saying: "She is severely possessed by a demon.

---

8. In Matthew 28.18-19, Jesus further clarified this in saying, "All authority in heaven and earth has been given to me; therefore go, and make disciples of all nations . . ." (NIV).

9. Matthew 5.21–48 includes five instances in which Jesus contrasts a statement from the Old Testament with a deepening clarification of his own, introduced each time with the words, "You have heard that it was said . . . but I say unto you . . ."

10. I think of the child Jesus healed. "She has died," her parents said. "No," he said, "she is asleep," And when he had awakened her to new life he said, "Give her something to eat" (Mark 5.35-43).

Have mercy on me, O Lord." He refuses to help, saying that he had been sent to the lost sheep of Israel. The woman then kneels before him and says, "Lord, help me." Jesus answered, "It isn't fair to take the children's bread and throw it to the dogs." Harsh? Or was there humor? The woman persists, "Yes, Lord, yet even the dogs eat the crumbs that fall from their master's table." And Jesus answered—I like to think with admiration for her witty reply and the love and faith which motivated her, "O woman, great is your faith! May it be done for you as you desire" (Matt 15.21–28). And her daughter was healed.

Jesus was a "friend of sinners," whether prostitutes, corrupt tax collectors, or hypocrites. The account of the woman taken in adultery, as reported in John's gospel, is a case in point. According to the law, she was to be put to death.[11] Jesus' response—which among other things illustrated his authority to amend the law—was to say to her accusers, "Let him who is without sin among you be the first to throw a stone at her." One by one her accusers went away. When alone with the woman, Jesus said, "'Woman, where are they? Has no one condemned you?" She said, "No one, Lord." And Jesus said, "Neither do I condemn you; go, and do not sin again."[12] The mercy and grace of God that he expressed to this woman gave her the possibility of a new beginning.

Grace was present in the shrewdness and wisdom Jesus demonstrated with those who opposed him, as it was in the courage and perseverance with which he faced rejection, torture and death. In saying to those who crucified him, "Father, forgive them; for they know not what they do" (Luke 23.34), it was apparent that the grace of God included those responsible.

The words of Jesus made clear that the redemption God's love made possible was meant for all people: Jews, Samaritans, and Gentiles. The Gospel of God's kingdom was to be universal. That Jesus enacted these words, that he suffered and gave his life as an atonement, an "expiation . . . for the sins of the whole world" (I John 2.2), demonstrated as words alone could not, the value that the living God places on human beings.[13]

Anticipating that Jesus would bring liberation to Israel, the apostles were slow to realize the universal significance of Jesus' death. That realization began with the resurrection of Jesus, and deepened greatly

---

11. Lev 20.10 states that both adulterer and adulteress should be put to death.

12. Quotes are all from John 8.1–11.

13. There are numerous New Testament passages which say this, two of the most explicit being found in Ephesians 2.11–22 and John 3.16.

with the baptism of the Holy Spirit at Pentecost. The resurrection had astounded them, and awakened in them "a living hope."[14] A living hope undergirded by the Spirit-led understanding that the grace of God given through Jesus was costly, and called for a disciplined and fruitful faith in response. Undoubtedly the Spirit reminded the apostles often of Jesus' teachings, as when he stated, "he who does not take his cross and follow me is not worthy of me. He who finds his life will lose it; and he who loses his life for my sake will find it" (Matt 10.38–39).

The apostles were open to the Holy Spirit reminders of Jesus's teaching because he had lived with them. They knew from personal experience that he loved them, and following the resurrection realized that he was alive, in a transformed but very real body. When they fully grasped the truth of his resurrection, they knew he had conquered death. Still, there was no overnight maturity for the apostles, for they were often slow to learn. As N. T. Wright points out, the crucifixion of Jesus did not easily fit their idea of what the Messiah would be like. As he put it: "When Jesus was crucified every single disciple knew what it meant: We backed the wrong horse."[15] The resurrection, therefore, also caught them by surprise. For just as they did not expect the Messiah to die, there was no expectation that he would rise again to new life, despite the fact that Jesus had pointedly told them that he would. In Mark 8.31–32 Jesus "began to teach them that the Son of man must suffer many things, and be rejected by the elders and the chief priests and the scribes, and be killed, and after three days rise again. And he said this plainly." This slowness to understand what Jesus's death and resurrection meant was not for lack of intelligence, but because the learning Jesus desired required a radical change in their worldview—a deeper insight into the nature of ultimate reality, and God's plans for the world. But also because this new understanding would require a change in their *behavior*. Jesus in commanding his followers to make disciples wanted them to embrace a worldview rooted in the biblical story that would lead to fruitful *action*. A renewal that would require their openness to the Holy Spirit—the Spirit of truth.

Eventually, through the renewal of mind brought about through the work of the Holy Spirit, the disciples became convinced that he not only

---

14. All four Gospels note that the apostles were slow to believe in the resurrection. The first witnesses in each case were women, a most unusual detail given the subordinate status of women at the time. Even so, it took a special revelation for Peter to grasp the universal implications of the Good News. The quote phrase is from I Peter 1.3.

15. Wright, *Surprised by Hope*, 38.

was Savior but the LORD.[16] He was the promised Messiah foretold in the Old Testament. He was Emmanuel—God with us. (Matt 1.23–24). As the apostle John understood, Jesus was God incarnate, the "Word who was with God, who was God . . . through whom all things were made." The Word was "the true light which enlightens every man, . . . the Word [that] became flesh and dwelt among us, full of grace and truth." For though the Law came through Moses, "grace and truth came through Jesus Christ."[17] Paul sounded a similar note when he wrote that "in him all things hold together," that Jesus was "head of the church, . . . For in him all the fullness of God was pleased to dwell, and through him to reconcile all things, whether on earth or in heaven, making peace by the blood of the cross."[18] The supremacy of Jesus Christ is cosmic.

These understandings, rooted in his very being as the Son of the living God, formed a way of life in which Jesus sought to ground the apostles. A way of life in which he would accompany them through the presence of the Holy Spirit, the Spirit of truth, the Spirit of loving power. Taken together they provided a coherent framework through which all aspects of life and reality were to be understood as being meaningful, purposeful, and hopeful because Christ had defeated death. This extraordinary truth, illuminated and energized by the Holy Spirit, galvanized the early Christian community into sharing the Good News of God's kingdom boldly with the world around them—and practicing the command to love one another substantially enough to make the good news they shared credible to others.

The teaching of God's love, grace and truth that Jesus lived and taught with such power, though not systematic in any modern sense, was coherent.[19] Coherent in the sense that what he lived and taught fit into, and made sense of, the biblical story as a whole. A story that "is a unified and progressively unfolding drama of God's action in history for the

---

16. Philippians 2.8–11.
17. John 1.1b, 3, 5, 9. 14, 17.
18. Col 1.17, 18, 29.
19. His Sermon on the Mount in Matthew 5–7 (and the version given in Luke 6) provide his most extensive and straightforward teaching. Much of what Jesus taught was made evident through his lifestyle—his stories, his compassionate interactions with people, his response to questions and criticisms, and the courage with which he faced his trial and execution, all as an corroboration, extension and fulfilment of the story as given in the Old Testament.

salvation of the whole world."[20] And it is the foundation for a dynamic worldview in which the foundational truths, through the guidance of the Spirit of truth, remain fresh and unchanging, but also adaptable to new circumstances. In the Great Commission Jesus said, "All authority in heaven and on earth has been given to me. Go therefore and make disciples of all nations, baptizing them in the name of the Father and of the Son and of the Holy Spirit, teaching them to observe all that I have commanded you, and lo, I am with you always, to the close of the age."[21] In saying this Jesus was commanding the disciples to embrace the reality of the biblical story, to make it their own with the empowerment of the Holy Spirit, and to teach others to do the same.

In the history of the early church set down in the Acts of the Apostles it is readily apparent that the apostles, though imperfect, took the commission to make disciples very seriously. Having received the power of the Holy Spirit at Pentecost, there was an ongoing emphasis on fellowship, worship and teaching. Many signs and wonders were done, accompanied by the teaching necessary to explain the meaning of events with regard to the inauguration of God's kingdom through Jesus and to help new believers find their place in this great biblical drama, to make the biblical story their own.

The first disciples of Jesus, and those who came after them, were continually challenged by the culture around them to ponder ever more deeply the reality of God as he had revealed himself through historical events, the scriptures, and especially in the life of Jesus. Through the Spirit-led study, worship, and discussions of the following centuries there emerged among thoughtful Christians a growing conviction that the source of reality on every level, including the glimmers of truth and understanding found in mathematics, science, philosophy, and art, was to be found in God.[22] But while truth can be expressed in limited measure through symbols, propositions and images, they realized that Jesus,

20. Bartholomew and Goheen, *Drama of Scripture*, 14.

21. Mt 28.18–20. (My emphasis)

22. Frank Gaebelein, headmaster of the Stony Brook School on Long Island, noted: "We do indeed give the primacy of that spiritual truth revealed in the Bible and incarnate in Christ. That does not mean, however, that those aspects of truth discoverable in the realm of mathematics, chemistry, or geography are any whit less than the truth as it is in Christ . . . But all the time there is the unity of truth under God, and that unity we deny in education at the peril of habituating ourselves to a fragmentary kind of learning found on some avowedly Christian campuses today." Quoted in Lockerbie, *A Christian Paideia*, on the flyleaf.

in living a fully human life, revealed that the ultimate source of truth is *personal*. Further, in revealing that God is triune, he made clear the fact that truth is *relational*.[23] In revealing that God is love, he revealed that love—*agape*, the love that is rooted in God's very nature—is to be the hallmark of human relationships, the means to knowing God more deeply, and the impetus to share the Jesus way of life with others.

As Paul wrote in his letter to the Colossians, "Him we proclaim, warning every man and teaching every man in all wisdom, that we may present every man mature in Christ . . . in whom are hid all the treasures of wisdom and knowledge For this I toil, striving with all the energy which he mightily inspires within me" (Col 1.28, 3.2).

THE DRAMA OF SCRIPTURE

The Bible as a whole, both Old and New Testaments, is organized according to genre—such as historical chronicle, wisdom literature, poetry, prophecy, letters, or the more biographical approach of the gospels. No book-length outline, no final summary, and no overarching chronology of biblical events is to be found. The result for many Christians is something of a jumble, in which the Bible is seen as catchall of ideas and stories that are good for the devotional life, but which provide little help in seeing the big picture, or in interacting wisely and fruitfully with the culture in which they live. A big picture view, therefore, can be very helpful.

Craig Bartholomew and Michael Goheen are convinced that the Christian worldview, and the shape of our very lives, must be rooted in the story of Jesus and the Bible. As they explain in their book, *The Drama of Scripture*, the Bible presents us with a unified story beginning with God's creation of the universe, and his redemptive work in establishing his Kingdom, the choosing of Israel, the coming of Christ the Redeemer King, the Mission of the Church, and the completion of redemption through the return of Christ the King and the creation of a

---

23. The doctrine of the Trinity has been a stumbling block for many, but as Alister McGrath notes, it has enjoyed a resurgence in the past century. "Many reasons might be given; perhaps the simplest is that it safeguards a distinctly Christian vision of God by refusing to allow what the human mind simply cannot comprehend on account of its vastness to be reduced to what is rationally manageable. The doctrine of the Trinity is the outcome of the Christian community's principled stand against reducing God to the level of what we feel comfortable with at the *intellectual level. It aims to tell the truth about God, no matter how difficult we find it to take this in.*" McGrath, *Enriching our Vision of Reality*, 130. (His emphasis).

new heaven and earth. "This comprehensive scope of creation, sin, and redemption is evident throughout the biblical story and is central to a faithful biblical worldview."[24]

To see the Bible as a *unified story* as opposed to a mosaic of passages about theology, history, morality and devotion—which is the way many people read it—is of great importance.

> If we allow the Bible to become fragmented, it is in danger of being absorbed into whatever *other* story is shaping our culture, and it will thus cease to shape our lives as it should. Idolatry has twisted the dominant cultural story of the secular Western world. If as believers we allow this story (rather than the Bible) to become the foundation of our thoughts and actions, then our lives will not manifest the truths of Scripture but the lies of an idolatrous culture. Hence, the unity of Scripture is no minor matter: a fragmented Bible may actually produce theologically orthodox, morally upright, warmly pious idol worshippers! If our lives are to be shaped by the story of Scripture, we need to understand two things well: the biblical story is a compelling unity on which we may depend, and each of us has a place within that story.[25]

It is my conviction that the extraordinary and horrific violence of the modern world derives, in part at least, from the fact that many believers, perhaps the majority of believers, have in fact allowed the worldviews of "the secular Western world" to dominate them such that Christian discipleship in so many communities is nothing short of a scandal. The following paragraphs provide a brief description of the biblical story.

CREATION

The Biblical story begins with the God's creation of heaven and earth, and the understanding that there is a radical distinction between God and all that he has brought into being. On planet earth, ordered and fine-tuned for life, God brought forth myriad forms of plant and animal life, including human beings. Human beings, male and female, though they share a physical nature with animals, are unique in that they are made in the image of God, with the desire and capability for relationship with God their creator, and with one another, while being caretakers of the earth.

24. Bartholomew and Goheen, *Drama of Scripture*, 14.
25. Bartholomew and Goheen, *Drama of Scripture*, 14. (Authors' emphasis)

The whole vast, dynamic, panoply was a display of intelligent design with which the Creator was well pleased: "And God saw everything that he had made, and behold, it was very good" (Genesis 1.31a). It is just here, in the statement that human beings, male and female, are made in the image of God, that the understanding of the sacred worth of all human beings—the preborn included—is rooted.

FALL

Though made for fellowship with God, in a world created for the flourishing of human life, the first human beings turned away from him, and sin with all its ugly manifestations entered the world.[26] In the words of Goheen and Bartholomew: "Although sin is first and foremost an offense against God, it is an offense also against the creation, against human life, *shalom,* health, prosperity, wholeness and human flourishing."[27] Sin perverts, corrupts and destroys everything it touches. With regard to this essay it is striking to note that sin, early on, led to violence, told vividly in the story of two brothers, Cain and Abel. Cain, angry that his offering to God is not accepted, is counseled by God to master the sin of anger, but failing to do so, murders Abel. In time this early human society became so filled with corruption and violence, that God brought judgment upon them: 'Now the earth was corrupt in God's sight, and the earth was filled with violence . . . And God said to Noah, "I have determined to make an end of all flesh; for the earth is filled with violence through them; behold I will destroy them from the earth."' (Gen 6.11–13) And judgment came.

That God judges human sin and violence serves to highlight his concern for justice and righteousness, a concern that is expressed throughout the Old Testament, notably in the prophets. God is a moral God, but he is also a God of love and grace. It is important to keep in mind that God's concern for justice and righteousness is rooted in his redemptive love for the world and the human race.

---

26. Though Adam and Eve were influenced by the "serpent," they were held responsible for their choices.

27. Bartholomew and Goheen. *Living at the Crossroads,* 47–48.

REDEMPTION BEGINS

In pronouncing judgement on the serpent and Adam and Eve there was also given a word of hope, understood by biblical theologians as the promise of a Redeemer: To the serpent God said, "I will put enmity between you and the woman, and between your seed and her seed; he shall bruise your head, and you shall bruise his heel" (Gen 3.15).

After the time of judgment came the beginnings of God's great drama of redemption, and the long journey leading to the fulfillment of his promise of a Redeemer, and ultimately the restoration of all things. With Abraham God made a covenant, promising him descendants as numberless as the stars. From him came the nation of Israel. Though enslaved for a time in Egypt, God liberated them. To them, though given to rebellion and idolatry, God gave the moral law (the Ten Commandments) and consecrated the covenant earlier made with Abraham.

These commands, in contrast to the ethical rules of other ancient religions, made it clear that God—not human beings—is the source of moral authority. The first reads, "You shall have no other gods before me" (Exod 20.3). The other nine commands which follow show that obedience to God means that human beings are to treat one another ethically—with respect, decency and fairness.

Then followed their entrance into the land God had promised them long before. Prior to occupying the land God commanded them to drive out and destroy the cities and people living there, with the particular emphasis of destroying their religion. This command has been troubling for modern minds—among them, many Christians—to whom it suggests genocide and ethnic cleansings. There is good reason to think, however, that the violence which followed was considerably more limited than the literal words would suggest. This conclusion is based on knowledge of the hyperbole common to mid-Eastern peoples, and to the archaeological evidence which indicates that the actual destruction of cities such as Jericho was quite limited.[28]

---

28. The violence accompanying the occupation of Israel is an important issue, and raises moral and theological questions that deserve serious attention. Numerous scholars have done so. Some, like Tremper Longman III, argue that the best way to view these instances of Old Testament violence is in seeing that God is a Warrior, even in his incarnation in Jesus, and that except for God's grace, all people deserve death. See Cowles, et al, *Show Them No Mercy*. Paul Copan in his book, *Is God a Moral Monster?*, provides an excellent study of the hard texts of the Old Testament, and concludes that while the Canaanites were indeed a wicked people whom God judged,

In any event, despite their covenant with God, and the many blessings bestowed upon them, the Jews time and again fell prey to surrounding idolatries. God responded by sending a series of prophets, who in calling their people time and again to repentance and faith, deepened and clarified the meaning of God's mercy, love, and justice.

REDEMPTION ACCOMPLISHED

In the fullness of time, out of this nation came Jesus. Through his miracles, teaching, death and resurrection, he was eventually recognized as the Redeemer promised long before—God's only begotten Son, the Lord of all the earth. As John the apostle would put it, Jesus was in fact God incarnate—the Word of God, the Logos, made flesh.

Though Jesus brought division in the sense that the radical nature of his life and teaching provoked a decision for or against him, his mission as the Redeemer King was to continue the journey of redemption through living a life of service and compassion, a life which embodied God's love and grace, and the life of service which he intended for his disciples once they were baptized with the power of his Spirit. His life culminated with his atoning death, as the Lamb of God who takes away the sin of the world. His death on a Roman cross brought reconciliation between God and humankind, and made clear that reconciliation was his will for all human beings.[29] The fact of Jesus' resurrection from the dead became the basis for the powerful hope that he had conquered death.

---

the emphasis was the destruction of their religion rather than the total annihilation of their people. The Canaanites were, in fact, not eliminated, but, along with other tribal groups, gradually assimilated. With the coming of Jesus, it became clear that God's salvation was meant for all nations, including the Canaanites, Jebusites, etc. See Copan, particularly chapters 15–20.

29. The ministry of reconciliation, which assumes the sacredness of *all* human beings, is a crucial point often neglected by Christians. The history of warfare, including the massive violence of modern times, is that of one man or party or nation seeking to dominate another—whether for treasure, property, vengeance, or establishing hegemony over a region or organization. Too often Christianity, considered as a state religion, has been co-opted by the rampant nationalism of a given nation. Furthermore, Christians have not always sought to counter the worldviews we've pondered Communism, Nazism, and Secular Humanism—whose adherents not only sought to dominate other group or nations, but deliberately murdered many of the individuals of the targeted population. Preparation for such efforts inevitably includes the determination to de-humanize the intended victims. These potential victims are labeled as inferior, sub-human, parasites, threats, enemies, or trash—and therefore disposable. It

As Paul was to write of him, "[I]n Christ God was reconciling the world to himself, not counting their trespasses against them, and entrusting to us the message of reconciliation" (2 Cor 5.19). This redemptive mission of the Church, empowered at Pentecost by the same Spirit who raised Jesus from the dead, was to continue through the building of communities of disciples throughout the world. The commissioning of the disciples was explicit: recognizing the authority given to Jesus, they were to make discples throughout the world, baptize them, and teach them to obey everything that he had commanded (Matt 28.18–20).

RESTORATION

Though Jesus inaugurated the kingdom of God on earth, it is not yet fully established, and will only be fulfilled at the end of time. Still, his life was the vital turning point in the on-going struggle with sin and evil that the Quakers referred to as "the Lamb's War." When he returns as the rightful King—the Lord of heaven and earth—Jesus with the Father and the Spirit will bring about a righteous judgment of all people, vanquish Satan and the forces of evil, overcome death and sorrow, and create a new heaven and earth in which the resurrected people of God from all ages shall dwell in his presence with everlasting peace and joy.

As Batholomew and Goheen point out, it is this great biblical drama, and the place of Jesus within it, with the unifying and detailed emphasis given to it by biblical theology, that provides the foundation of the Christian worldview.[30] It provides the basic ideas, events and moral

---

is during this preparation period, when such destructive ideas are being put forth, that Christian thought and action is most needed.

30. There are many systematic theologies worthy of serious study, among them those by Donald Bloesch, Wayne Gruden, Alister McGrath, Michael Bird, Millard Erickson, and Carl Henry. The Collected Works of Francis A. Schaeffer (5 volumes) are also worth a serious look. C. S. Lewis did not consider himself a Christian theologian, but his influence in the Christian world, Protestant and Catholic, has been immense. Reading through his works, many devoted to some aspect of Christian faith, is an education in itself. The writings of Lesslie Newbigin and G. K. Chesterton, the encyclicals and books of Popes John Paul II and Benedict XVI, though not systematic theologies as such, contain much that is of value to anyone interested in learning more about the historic, orthodox Christian faith. There are as well a multitude of biblical studies and commentaries whose authors, while taking modern biblical scholarship seriously, find the biblical story credible, and a sound basis for living with purpose and meaning. The many biblical writings of N. T. Wright and Richard Bauckham, to cite but two well-known biblical scholars, are exemplars of their tribe.

principles which serve as a grounding for dealing with the issues of life, which vary with time and place. Where the Christian world and life view meets the issues and concerns of a particular time is what Goheen and Bartholomew refer to as "living at the crossroads."[31]

THE BIBLICAL WORLDVIEW

Though Jesus did not use the word "worldview" in his teaching, it is clear that he taught a coherent view of reality rooted in the biblical story. The ideas he shared always did so within the ambit of biblical history. Biblical characters and themes were often on his lips. His stories always reflected the purposes of God, and his actions always furthered God's will for the salvation of the world.

Jesus was not a philosopher in the classical Greek sense, and yet there was wisdom in everything he said and did. His life and teaching revealed a God-centered understanding of the universe that integrated the reality of creation and history with the reality of the spiritual world. As the incarnation of God, Jesus is the perfect integration of matter and spirit, of body and soul, of man and God. This integration is especially important in a time when a multitude of voices are declaring a split between fact and value, between body and person, between sacred and secular. Nancy Pearcey's book, *Love Thy Body*, is an excellent study of scholars and journalists who resist and deny the integration of reality, of fact and value, body and spirit, evident in the life of Jesus of Nazareth. Pearcey very effectively describes the devastating impact of a dualistic (two story) understanding of reality on such issues as abortion, euthanasia, marriage, sexuality and transgenderism. Sadly, one cannot assume that Christians are immune: "Many people who identify as religious or Christian are being co-opted by the secular worldview, often without realizing it."[32]

In their book *Living at the Crossroads*, Goheen and Bartholomew, take a serious look at the nature and importance of worldviews. A worldview includes both the basic beliefs and ideas held by an individual,

---

31. Taken from the title of the book by Bartholomew and Goheen, *Living at the Crossroads*.

32. Pearcey, *Love Thy Body*, 10. (My emphasis.) Pearcey's book should be read by every pastor, every church leader, every parent. This book continues her argument regarding the Christian response to the two storey (dualistic) philosophy of reality given in earlier books: *Saving Leonardo*, and *Total Truth*. (My emphasis)

culture or religion, and the actions and behavior that flows from it. They define the Christian worldview thus:

> Christian worldview sets out the main elements or beliefs that constitute the biblical story and shows how they fit together in a coherent framework. These beliefs can, of course, be analyzed further according to their theological and philosophical categories. The point of a Christian worldview, however, is that the biblical story embodies and implies a framework of basic beliefs that can be set out to equip Christians in their lives. The framework of basic beliefs inherent to the biblical story is not for scholars alone but rather is for all the people of God.[33]

The Bible, when considered not in bits and pieces, but as a coherent whole, provides meaningful and thoughtful answers to the basic questions human beings ask about the nature of reality, of God, of suffering, of good and evil, of meaning. It provides a grand narrative of an infinite and personal God who designed and created the universe in all its complexity, beauty and mystery. As such it provides the basis for a comprehensive and unfolding big picture of reality and history. The biblical worldview is capacious, and being rooted in objective reality calls for and allows a growing depth and breadth of understanding that expands as insight into the nature of things both physical and spiritual increases. Because its parameters are rooted in God, only such insights as reflect his moral and spiritual principles will ultimately prove lastingly fruitful for human flourishing.

That this infinite and personal God truly exists, that he is "there," as Francis Schaeffer put it, that he is the creator of the universe and human beings, is the basis for all clear thinking about nature and human nature.[34] That this God is the source of goodness, truth, love, grace, justice and beauty provides a solid foundation for the understanding of the importance of love and relationships. That this triune God has been revealed (incarnated) on the human level through the Son, the Logos, whose name is Jesus, clarifies as nothing else could the sacred value of human beings to God, their capacity for rationality, and the extraordinary lengths he is willing to go to save them, restore to them their dignity, and to renewed friendship with himself.

---

33. Batholomew and Goheen *Living at the Crossroads*, 27
34. See Schaeffer, *God Who Is There*.

That God has released his Spirit into the world through Jesus for those willing to trust in him and follow him makes clear that he works not by force or coercion, but through the persuasion by which truth operates. It is through practicing the truth in Jesus that human beings become his disciples, and find their true freedom (John 8.31–32). God is working out his plans within human history. He has done so through making covenants, the giving of the moral law, prophetic utterances, the incarnation of Jesus, the giving of his Spirit, the founding of a community of Jesus people, and through his promise of an ultimate glory in a new Heaven and Earth. With the fulfilment of his redemption his people will experience a resurrected body, where suffering, injustice and death will forever be vanquished, and where they will enjoy unending joy and peace in his presence. The unfolding of the different stages of redemption show clearly that God is sovereign, and despite the rebellious inclinations of his human creatures, his plans continue to unfold with a sense of direction and purpose.

Goheen and Bartholomew are right to insist that the basis for worldview thinking is the Bible:

> [T]he primary sources of a Christian worldview should be Scripture and biblical theology . . . We need to be as conscious as possible of the ecology in which we work, including the dimensions of the cultures in which we live. But we must make Scripture and the biblical drama our constant and normative reference points as we map out the contours of a Christian worldview. As we do so, it is important to remember that even at this level a worldview is an abstraction from Scripture and can never replace Scripture.[35]

It is, of course, vitally important to realize that one's grasp of Scripture and the Christian worldview is affected by one's preunderstanding experienced through the culture (family, community, nation) in which one lives. Humility and self-awareness must always be consciously sought. We must remain open to criticism. As we have seen, Scripture has often been *misinterpreted*, and the worldview founded upon it *distorted*. The results have usually been devastating—not only for those who have been the victims of such interpretations, but for the obstacles they present to the acceptance of the Christian faith.[36]

---

35. Bartholomew and Goheen, 27.

36. One need look no further than the history of the churches in America. In the decades prior to the Civil War many orthodox Christian preachers and theologians

Jesus, Discipleship, and Worldviews

The Biblical view of reality has been studied, discussed and debated for two millennia. There have been serious differences. The Reformation and its aftermath afford numerous examples. Differences among Christian traditions must be taken seriously, but it is important to note that there is also widespread agreement on issues of fundamental importance, such as the Trinity, the Incarnation and the Atonement of Christ.[37] Despite the divisions within the Church, C. S. Lewis believed there remained an enormous common ground. In his book, *Mere Christianity*, much of it delivered as a series of talks to men in the Royal Air Force, Lewis sought "to explain and defend the belief that has been common to nearly all Christians at all times."[38, 39]

The Christian faith does not provide a knock-down argument for truth. But it makes sense of things in a way that is compelling, and that draws not only on reason or rationality, but imagination. Jesus said to Nicodemus that a birth brought about by the Holy Spirit was necessary to "see" the kingdom of God. Seeing, which includes both visualizing and understanding, is not just a matter of historical narrative and philosophical propositions, though they are very important, but includes the ability to see or picture connections in a way one could not do before.[40] The Holy Spirit, in my understanding, when indwelling a human being, enables a person through an on-going process of repentance and obedient

---

in the South claimed biblical authority for slavery, and later segregation. In the early decades of the twentieth century many liberal Christians adapted their understanding of the Bible to the latest scientific "advances." Humility, repentance and reform, are always essential. Paul Hiebert reminds us that we cannot equate our understandings of the biblical story with "ultimate realities. Rather, they are partial models or maps that promote comprehension of the underlying unity of divine revelation. Without these tentative models, we have no way to understand the whole of Scripture." Heibert, *Transforming Worldviews*, 267.

37. Evangelicals and Catholics Together is an organization founded in 1994 by Richard Neuhaus and Charles Colson, that has brought conservative Catholics and Evangelicals together on a continuing basis to explore differences and commonalities. Upholding the sacredness of human life is one of the major commonalities they share.

38. *Mere Christianity* has sold millions of copies, 3.5 million in English since 2001, has been translated into 36 languages. In a survey of the greatest Christians books, came in second only to St Augustine's *Confessions*. Marsden, '"Mere Christianity" Still Gets a Global Amen.'

39. Lewis, *Mere Christianity*, 6.

40. For C. S. Lewis the Christian faith provided "a new way of seeing things, and hence a new way of experiencing the world and life . . . Yet this change in the way in which we see things is so great and radical that we need to think of ourselves as a 'new creation.'" McGrath, *Great Mystery*, 49.

learning, to attain a deepening grasp of reality on every level of existence. A grasp that is integrated, such that there are no gaps between reality as understood by science, and reality, and the Christian faith. This is because God is the source of all aspects of reality (save evil), and is present and "revealed" in some measure through every aspect of reality.[41]

It is important to note that the understanding of any aspect of reality involves faith—that is, an openness of mind and heart to the aspect of reality under consideration, marked by the trust that what is gained through sound observation, experimentation, and clear reasoning (as with scientific endeavors), will bring a measure of understanding on the level of physical, material reality.[42] In Prov 2.1–12 there is the understanding that *if* one is receptive to God and his commands, and diligently seeks wisdom, insight and knowledge, he will provide it:

> For the Lord gives wisdom; from his mouth come knowledge and understanding; he stores up sound wisdom for the upright; he is a shield to those who walk in integrity, guarding the paths of justice and preserving the way of his saints. Then you will understand righteous and justice and equity, every good path; for wisdom will come into your heart, and knowledge will be pleasant to your soul . . . delivering you from the way of evil, from men of perverted speech (Prov 2.6–12).

This word is reflected in Jesus's teaching about the Holy Spirit, who he referred to as the Spirit of truth. To the disciples he said, "*If* you love me, you will keep my commandments, and I will pray the Father, and he will give you another counselor, to be with you forever, even the Spirit of truth . . . he will teach you all things, and bring to your remembrance all that I have said to you, . . . and when he comes, he will convince the world

---

41. See Psalms 8, 19, 104 and the book of Job.

42. The twentieth century—and now the twenty-first—has benefited greatly from the findings of science. But it must be remembered that knowledge is a two-edged sword. Scientific knowledge can be used for good or evil, depending on the motives of those seeking such knowledge and the applications that may result from it. The understandings of science (and its daughter, technology) have contributed a great deal to the violence of modern times. Winston Churchill remarked that war had become more terrible through the work of a perverted science. See Alexander, *Medical Science in a Dictatorship*. Tim Keller in his book, *Making Sense of God*, makes the point that the scientific enterprise requires the belief that such endeavors are worth making even when final proof is unavailable. Keller notes that secularists, when they "endorse human dignity, rights, and the responsibility to eliminate human suffering, they are indeed exercising religious faith in some kind of supra-natural, transcendent reality." See Chapter 2.

concerning sin and righteous and judgment, . . . he will guide you into all truth," and "declare to you the things that are to come."[43]

The Christian quest for understanding and wisdom is multifaceted. It is a quest motivated always by a concern for truth, for reality, for that which *is*—-psychologically, morally, physically, and spiritually. It is a quest for learning that requires a growth in character and maturity. It is a moral quest in that learning and wisdom must contribute to a concern for justice, and the love of other people. The love, as Paul wrote, that fulfills the law.[44] It is a relational quest in that wisdom enables one to better know and appreciate those whom one loves—other human beings, and the living God: The Great I Am, and the source of all that is—save evil.[45]

The Christian worldview therefore underlies and complements any human quest for knowledge that contributes to a better understanding of reality, and the betterment of society and creation. But it must also be acknowledged that the quest for wisdom, truth, and maturity, as taught in the Bible, invariably brings conflict with those bent on some form of evil or idolatry, some—as we have seen—willing to promote their view of things through coercion and violence. Those who hold to such views lack wisdom: "For he who finds me [wisdom] finds life and obtains favor from the Lord; but he who misses me injures himself; all who hate me love death" (Prov 8.35–36).

To live out the Christian lifestyle is costly in terms of self-denial and the on-going effort to be disciplined and courageous in obeying his commands. The reward is a life well lived, and the happiness, satisfaction and joy that ensue as one cooperates with the Spirit of God. And one day, hopefully, a personal word from the King, "Well done, good and faithful servant" (Matt 25.21).[46]

What follows are some brief reflections on different aspects of the Christian worldview as it relates to the Biblical narrative, and the light it

43. See John 14.15–17a, and John 16.8, 13.

44. Paul, in his letter to the Christians of Rome, wrote that "he who love his neighbor has fulfilled the law." (Rom 13.8)

45. The Christian faith, the Biblical story and the worldview built upon it, was never meant to be static. In one sense, the history of human life is the long, slow, rocky trek upward toward responsible moral freedom motivated by the inner longing to see, to know, and to delight in the lover of our souls. The King James Version in Isaiah 45.7 states that God creates evil, but which other biblical versions translates to mean the he does not actually create evil, but allows disaster (storms, earthquakes, etc) to occur.

46. It is important to note that life well-lived—a meaningful life—will often involve suffering, as the biblical and historical record make very clear.

sheds on the value of truth, and the sacredness of human life. Philosopher and mystic, Simone Weil, writing in the midst of a dark time wrote:

> If I light an electric torch at night out of doors, I don't judge its power by looking at the bulb, but by seeing how many objects it lights up. The brightness of a source of light is appreciated by the illumination it projects upon non-luminous objects. The value of a religious, or, more generally, a spiritual way of life is appreciated by the amount of illumination thrown upon the things of this world.[47]

ONE: THE CHRISTIAN WORLDVIEW PROVIDES A LENS AND A GUIDE

To bring reality into focus requires clear vision. Human beings without God are spiritually blind, a fact assumed in the many biblical texts which state that the Lord shall open the eyes of the blind.[48] The apostle Paul applied the metaphor of blindness both to unbelievers in general, who were blinded by the god of this world, and in a more limited sense to those Jews over whose minds there was a veil brought on by hardness of heart.[49]

Jesus, speaking in a Nazareth synagogue at the outset of his ministry, conjoined two texts from Isaiah which he applied to himself. "The Spirit of the Lord is upon me," he said, "because he has anointed me to preach good news to the poor. He has sent me to proclaim release to the captives and recovering of sight to the blind, to set at liberty those who are oppressed" (Luke 4.18).[50] To Nicodemus, a Pharisee who appreciated the signs (miracles) Jesus had done, Jesus said, "Truly, truly, I say to you, unless one is born anew he cannot *see* the kingdom of God" (John 3.3). Nicodemus, thinking literally, missed the point, and questioned the physical rebirth of an older man, to which Jesus replied, "Truly, truly, I say to you, unless one is born of water and the Spirit, he cannot enter the

---

47. Weil. *First and Last Notebooks,* 147. Weil, philosopher and political activist, wrote during WWII, She died in 1943, aged 34.

48. See Psalm 146.8; Isa 29.18, 35.5, 42.7, 43.8, 16; Luke 4.18; Rom 2.19.

49. "But their minds [the Israelites] were hardened; for to this day when they read the old covenant, that same veil remains un-lifted, because only through Christ is it taken away." (II Cor 3.14) "In their case [those who are perishing] the god of this world has blinded the minds of the unbelievers, to keep them from seeing the light of the gospel of the glory of Christ . . ." (II Cor 4.4)

50. Jesus here partially quotes Isa 61.1, and Isa 42.7.

kingdom of God. That which is born of the flesh is flesh, and that which is born of the Spirit is spirit . . . The wind blows where it will, and you hear the sound of it, but you do not know whence it comes or whither it goes; so it is with everyone who is born of the Spirit" (John 3.5–8, RSV).[51] Paul, contrasting the wisdom of the world with that given by Christ, wrote: "Now we have received not the spirit of the world, but the Spirit which is from God, that we might understand the gifts bestowed on us by God . . . The unspiritual man does not receive the gifts of the Spirit of God, for they are folly to him, and he is not able to understand them for they are spiritually discerned" (I Cor. 2.12,14).

This spiritual rebirth is often depicted as an emotional experience. But the better explanation is that it is a visionary and cognitive-intellectual experience, in which the Spirit takes away spiritual and mental blindness, and enables a believer to "see"—to perceive, to bring into focus, to discern, to understand—that which was previously impossible.[52] Perhaps not unlike an eye surgeon removing cataracts or inserting a new lens into a patient's eye, and thereby restoring or improving vision. In a way, the Holy Spirit is the lens, and the guide, whereby we are able to discern and understand the purposes of God. Without the proper lens (Calvin referred to it as putting on a pair of biblical glasses), one cannot read or understand—let alone respond appropriately—to Scripture and the Christian worldview and lifestyle.[53] With the illumination and guidance of the Spirit, one is enabled to gain understanding of God's view of things, such as the dignity and worth of an unborn child.

Insight into God's kingdom that the new birth makes possible does not, by itself, bring wisdom or maturity. But without the spiritual sightedness the Holy Spirit provides one cannot be a disciple of Jesus. That many Christians do not become mature disciples with a solid grasp of the

---

51. There is reason to believe that Nicodemus may have experienced the new birth that brings clarity of vision; in John 19.39 it is noted that he accompanies another man, Joseph of Arimathea, in burying Jesus.

52. That the spiritual rebirth may be accompanied by strong emotions (which is often the case) is understandable. But it is unfortunate to promote the new birth as an "emotional" experience. It is obvious that there are many Christians who are able to "see" the things of God's kingdom who say little or nothing about the emotional aspect of that experience. To see clearly—whether physically or spiritually—is of course a wonderful thing, and it is not surprising that for multitudes of new believers it is accompanied with powerful emotions. Nonetheless, the point Jesus was making had to do with enabling believers to understand what God is doing in the world.

53. Calvin, John, *Institutes of the Christian Religion*. Westminster, 7.

biblical story and worldview helps explain why so many find themselves co-opted by other worldviews.

It is important, therefore, for Christians to be mindful of their basic attitude toward God and his Spirit, and also to understand that the guidance the Spirit provides is made known in the company of other clear-sighted Christians. The example of Jesus and that of the apostles, as leaders of the early church, makes clear that the process should, and must, be done within the Christian community, wherein the gifts of the Spirit can be employed in evangelism to foster the new birth of believers, along with encouraging and supporting spiritual formation and maturity as they learn to follow the leading of the Spirit.

To say these things requires recognition of the fact that many people who may be considered Christians—having been baptized, confirmed, and perhaps in some ways involved in church activities—may *not* be Christians in any realistic sense. That is, they may not be able to "see" the things of God's kingdom because, for one reason and another, they have not experienced the spiritual vision and understanding that the new birth of the Spirit brings about. A spiritual birth—the receiving of spiritual vision—cannot be forced. The Spirit blows where it wills. The lack of genuine spiritual vision given by the Spirit helps explain why so many nominal Christians fail to take a stand on the sacredness of human life; they simply do not "see" the issue as important.[54]

TWO: THE CHRISTIAN WORLDVIEW PROVIDES A MAP

Many people who identify as Christians—e.g., evangelical Christians who emphasize the new birth—seem unable to discern spiritual realities, and never venture far in their journey of faith.[55] What pastor has not witnessed new confirmands leaving the church shortly after being confirmed? What pastor or evangelist has not witnessed new believers, caught up in the excitement of conversion, quickly fade away for lack of commitment?

One reason for this is that the spiritual birth of numerous Christians is conditioned largely by emotion. Developing the discipline and courage to actually follow Jesus and obey his commands is to many emotionally daunting. Another reason many believers remain immature is the failure

---

54. It is also true that many who do "see" the value of human life lack the courage to act.

55. See Matt 7.14.

of teachers and pastors to emphasize the importance and cost of becoming a *disciple* of Jesus.[56] The necessary emphasis on God's grace too often lacks emphasis on the importance of Jesus's teaching, and the willingness to be led by his Spirit in actually putting his teaching into practice. To be led by the Spirit of Jesus in the adventure of faith is to follow one who is a trustworthy guide to what we might call the map of reality. It is one thing to express trust in a guide, quite another to follow the guide and learn how to read this map.

The Christian worldview as outlined here, provides a big picture view of life, truth and reality—a living map as it were—to which the Holy Spirit is the guide. The Christian story and worldview carries the claim that this map has universal validity: it is good for all people. It also claims that *all* truth is God's truth. As C. S. Lewis put it so well, "I believe in Christianity as I believe the sun has risen, not only because I see it, but because by it I see everything else."[57]

To say that all truth is God's truth is to say that God—Father, Son and Spirit—is the very ground of truth, and that reality on every level of being and existence—physical, biological, psychological and spiritual—reflects in some way his design and purpose. In the words of Bruce Lockerbie, this means that "nothing is outside the warp and woof of the Almighty's great tapestry. Even the tiniest thread, seemingly unrelated to the central image, has its place in the great pattern of things."[58] This insight is not new. Justin Martyr and Augustine, to name two early Fathers of the Church, shared this viewpoint. In the words of Augustine, "every good and true Christian must recognize that wherever he may find truth, it is his Lord's."[59]

This is not to claim that Christians, as individuals or as a community, always get things right. The history of the Christian Church is replete with events and challenges to which she responded poorly. Ignorance, a misinterpretation of biblical authority, hubris, and corruption, have all played a role. Moreover, the universe is an extraordinarily complex reality, and while the Christian faith offers a framework and a perspective with which to view trends and developments in science, psychology, politics, education, and economics, it is arrogant for Christians to assert

---

56. This was the focus of Bonhoeffer's book, *The Cost of Discipleship*.

57. Lewis, "Is Theology Poetry?" in *Weight of Glory*, 140.

58. Lockerbie, *Christian Paideia*, 50. Lockerbie was Scholar-in-Residence at the highly-respected Stony Brook School on Long Island.

59. From *Christian Doctrine*, quoted by Lockerbie, *Christian Paideia*, 23.

that their understanding of things is always accurate. Humility, the willingness to listen and learn from others, to admit error and wrong-doing, is vitally important. Christians can do this with confidence, trusting that as understanding is gained in any field, it will eventually prove to cohere with other branches of knowledge, and ultimately with God's purposes.

The point here is that the Christian faith and worldview provide an understanding of truth and reality that serves as a reliable map for life when Christians are led by the Spirit. While a good lens enables us to see clearly, a good map provides information, direction and guidance. A map also provides a sense of perspective, a wide-angle view of the countryside to be traversed. The Christian worldview, drawing on centuries of thought, discussion, repentance, prayer, and action, helps provide a big picture of reality, with an understanding of how doctrines, ideas, and historical events that are part of, and impinge upon, the biblical story fit together coherently. When led and taught by the Holy Spirit, who Jesus said would guide us into the truth, Christians can learn the principles of map reading, and make their way through life with a degree of confidence and security.

THREE: THE CHRISTIAN WORLDVIEW PROVIDES THE SCORE TO THE GREAT DANCE

Reality and truth are not exhausted by the metaphor of a map, though maps are of considerable importance. Understanding the realities of God, the universe, and the human drama, through the wise use of reason is of great importance. But the Christian worldview is also to be understood imaginatively and experientially, to be seen and participated in, by opening the door to the great symphony of God's universe. A moral universe, with a beautiful and dynamic weaving together of color, sound, space, structure, ideas, music and personality, in which human beings (as well as other creatures) are meant to live and interact in peace and joy with one another and with God. He who is the very Center—the creative super-genius who is composer and conductor of this great symphonic drama and dance—is the living God who has revealed himself as Father, incarnate Son, and indwelling Spirit. And as his children we are all given a role to play.

At present the great symphony contains a discordant note brought about by those creatures, human and supernatural, who have chosen to play their own tune, to go their own way. From such choices and ideas have come death and travail for the human race and the whole of creation. Yet there remains in the world and universe a rich beauty, with echoes of the unity and harmony that is God's will for his creation, and which will be fulfilled in the coming age when both heaven and earth will be made new.

It is a view of reality that appeals to the imagination because it is embodied in a grand narrative that includes heaven and earth in the dramatic clash between good and evil, love and hate, despair and hope. Creation, Fall, Redemption—a story, a symphony, a dance, that can stir heart, mind and body through giving to each disciple of Jesus Christ a meaningful and satisfying role to play as an instrument of God's grace and truth. Millennia ago one of the psalmists, caught up with a vision of the Lord's love for Israel, expressed the idea well: "Sing to the Lord a new song, . . . Let them praise his name with dancing, making melody to him with timbrel and lyre! For the Lord takes pleasure in his people; he adorns the humble with victory" (Psalm 149.1a, 3).

Ultimately, joyfully and satisfyingly, there will be union with God—Spirit, Son and Father. In the words of Psalm 42:

> As a hart longs for flowing streams,
> So longs my soul for thee, O God,
> My soul thirsts for God,
> For the living God. (Psalm 42.1–2)

FOUR: THE CHRISTIAN WORLDVIEW ENCOURAGES THOUGHTFULNESS

The Christian lifestyle, if it is truly to reflect the teaching of Jesus Christ, requires understanding and thoughtfulness. The map he provides, to continue use of this metaphor, requires skill in making good use of it. The Bible is filled with reminders to seek wisdom. The first Psalm highlights the blessedness of the godly individual who meditates on the law of God, day and night. The first chapter of Proverbs points out that "the fear of the Lord is the beginning of knowledge; fools despise wisdom and instruction." Jesus said that in loving God we should use "all our mind" (Matt 22.37b). The point being that reason is a gift from God encouraging us to use in pondering the revelation he has given in the Bible, and in nature

(Psalm 19). Alister McGrath, with degrees in science and theology, has this to say about the wise use of our rational nature.

> For Christians, God is the best explanation of the world we see around us and what we experience within us. We don't believe in God because we have abandoned rationality but because we see God as both the source and the ultimate goal of human reason. Most of the great writers of the patristic age—including Athanasius of Alexandria and Augustine of Hippo—made this point. God created us with reason in order that our reason might lead us to God, just as following a stream eventually leads us to its source.[60]

The effort to gain a balanced and thoughtful view of the biblical story of creation, fall and redemption, as it relates to the times in which one lives, necessitates much prayer and effort. But it is an effort aided by the strength and illumination of the Spirit, and the support of fellow disciples. It includes, moreover, as one seeks to think things through, the freedom and the encouragement to ask questions.

Questions are found throughout the Bible. The Gospels show Jesus being questioned by his disciples, by strangers, and religious authorities. There were questions about his authority, the miracles he performed, his relationship to God the Father, prayer, and his interpretation of the Law. The Old Testament also records numerous questions: Everyday questions, hard questions. Moses, at the burning bush, is given the task of helping deliver his people in Egypt, but asks God, "Who am I that I should go to Pharaoh, and bring the sons of Israel out of Egypt?" The psalmist, in a time of trouble asks, "Will the Lord spurn forever, and never again be favorable? Has his steadfast love forever ceased? Are his promises at an end for all time?" Habakkuk, noting the violence and injustice of his time, asks why God allows evil to go unpunished. And Job questions his suffering.[61]

Whether considered as a parable or an historical account, the Book of Job is a profound story that raises questions that many find troubling: Is God truly just? Is it right to question God—and with the anger and bitterness that so many feel? The answer this book gives to these questions is that faithfulness to God in the midst of suffering is important, and that truth—even when difficult to grasp—matters to human beings, and to God.

---

60. McGrath, *Enriching our Vision of Reality*, 105.
61. Scriptures in the order used: Exod 3.11, Psalm 77.7–8, Hab 2.13, Job 3.11–26.

Job, the man for whom the book is named, is the story of a prosperous man with a large family whom God allows to suffer at the hands of Satan. Job meets with a series of disasters in which he loses his wealth, his family and his health. His wife suggests he curse God and die, but Job remains steadfast in his faith. In time several friends arrive. For a time they suffer with him in silence. Then in a series of speeches they tell Job that he is suffering because of his sins. Job, angry and bitter, insists that his conscience is clear. Eventually he calls upon God to meet with him face to face, and his request is granted. God appears to Job, and questions him: "Who is this whose ignorant words cloud my design in darkness? Brace yourself and stand up like a man; I will ask questions, and you shall answer. Where were you when I laid the earth's foundations? Tell me, if you know and understand" (Job 38.2–4, NEB). There follows a series of questions to Job that display the extraordinary complexity of the universe and reveal his ignorance (and that of his friends). This brings Job's humble response:

> I know that thou canst do all things and that no purpose is beyond thee. But I have spoken of great things which I have not understood, things too wonderful for me to know. I knew of thee then only by report, but now I see thee with my own eyes. Therefore I melt away. I repent in dust and ashes. (Job 42.2–6, NEB)

The book concludes with the Lord admonishing Job's friends—twice—for not having spoken of God as they should have done. Job, however, despite his angry and bitter words, is *commended* for having spoken of God *truly*. The book ends with Job interceding for his friends, and with his fortunes restored.

It is rather a surprising and curious conclusion, and yet fitting. What individual, having suffered deeply, has not raised anguished questions and complaints to God about the injustices and sufferings they, and/or their loved ones, have experienced? Even for those whose knowledge of great suffering has come through their reading—perhaps with thanksgiving for having been spared—such questions readily come to mind.

The Book of Job provides several insights of importance. One is that the universe is very complex indeed.[62] There is much that we do not know.

---

62. This fact Elihu, speaking for Job's friends, also acknowledged. Their point that we reap what we sow is also true, while their assumption that this was true in Job's case was not; they did not know that his suffering was due to the direct intervention of Satan. Quite often, we reap what others sow.

Humility is always in order. A second is that decent and faithful people such as Job often do suffer. The massive violence of modern times has contributed to suffering on an extraordinary scale, the vast majority innocent victims. A third insight from reading Job is the fact that questions raised by suffering, however bitterly expressed, are not out of place from God's perspective. He does not find questions driven by a desire for the truth, however angrily expressed, offensive. This is a liberating insight.

Biblically speaking, asking questions is always important if they are heartfelt, and express a concern for what is true. That God asks questions of human beings underlines the importance of truth. Following the rebellion of Adam and Eve, God questions them: "Where are you? . . . Who told you that you were naked? . . . What is this that you have done?" (Gen 3.9, 11, 13) When Cain's offering is rejected he becomes angry. God asks him: "Why are you angry, and why has your countenance fallen? If you do well, will you not be accepted?" (Gen 4.1–7) Often through the prophets God questions his people. In Jer 2.4 there is this: 'Thus says the Lord: "What wrong did your fathers find in me that they went far from me?"' Jesus, in his sermon on discipleship asks, "Why do you call me Lord, Lord, and not do what I say?" (Luke 6.36, NIV).

We are saved—set right with God through the atoning death of Christ—but we mature when we begin to cooperate with God. It is a matter of meditating on the Word of God (Psalm 1, Psalm 119), of setting our minds on the things of the Spirit (Rom 8.6), thinking about the things that are true, honorable and just, as well as things that are pure and excellent, lovely, gracious, and worthy of praise (Phil 4.8). Paul rightfully begins this list with pondering the things that are true, that correspond with reality. Paul, it must be noted, also emphasizes that we should not merely ponder these things, for in the next verse, 4.9, he writes that what we learn is to be *put into practice*! As James the brother of Jesus would write, "Faith apart from works is dead" (James 2.26b).

How sad it is that so many Christians fail to seek a mature understanding of the truth of their faith. Nancy Barcus in her book, *Developing a Christian Mind*, has this to say about the failure to seek such understanding.

> Those who embrace the doctrines of Christianity without carefully understanding them sorely limit their own effectiveness as Christians. These believers never assess and understand the Scriptures against the wider context of life. At once they begin to confine themselves within self-imposed limits they do not

fully grasp. Dogma becomes a defense against many things which they do not understand and do not intend to understand. Such people have narrowed the borders of the intellectual life so hazardously that they live thereafter in isolation and ineffectualness. Should an intellectual challenge penetrate their defenses, their whole faith could collapse.[63]

FIVE: THE CHRISTIAN WORLDVIEW PROVIDES A BASIS FOR DEFENSE AND ANALYSIS

Yet another way in which the Christian worldview is of help is in analyzing other worldviews, and the history, ideas, presuppositions, and assumptions which are part of them. This is true whether the focus is on political and cultural viewpoints, religious understandings, or those of the sciences.

One current area of conflict that relates to the issue of abortion concerns sexuality and the Christian view on marriage and family. Gabrielle Kuby, a German scholar, has provided a powerful analysis of these issues in her discerning and well-documented book, *The Global Sexual Revolution*. The very subtitle of the book makes the point: *Destruction of Freedom in the Name of Freedom.*

Historically, as Kuby points out, sexuality was understood biologically in binary terms: a human being was either male or female. Children were produced by the mating of a male and a female who were married. The family, parents and children, were understood to be the foundational basis of human society. This was understood to be the case in all cultures, with regard to every religion, and every form of government. In the last century or so freedom has become untethered from moral principle and common sense, and is understood by those who subscribe to humanist ideals as the ability to make choices without restraint. It is a view, a *construct*, an *ideology* that suits the ambition and desires—the pleasures—of its proponents. One of those desires is to be able to choose one's own gender.[64] Another is the willingness a woman (and man) to have to abort

63. Barcus, *Developing a Christian Mind*, 94.

64. Though sexuality is not the focus of this book, it deserves the serious attention Kuby gives it, especially given the effort of so many in the West to redefine gender as something determined not by biology, but an individual's personal choice. And an issue increasingly to be enforced by law. A recent (June 15, 2020) Supreme Court decision, *Bostock v. Clayton County,* written by Justice Neil Gorsuch (considered a

their unborn child should pregnancy conflict with other desires. This new ideology threatens to become, in Kuby's words, a "new totalitarianism."[65]

A variety of political issues are in need of discussion and analysis. Among them are war and armed conflict, racism, the extreme egalitarians who insist on defacing and destroying public monuments, and the "cancel culture" extremists who express their displeasure with people and organizations by boycotting or withdrawing support from them. These issues are beyond the scope of this book, but cry out for level-headed analysis from a biblical worldview perspective, dealing with the very foundations of law, political governance, public safety, and human rights. Samuel Huntington in his highly acclaimed book, *A Clash of Civilizations and the Remaking of the World Order*, published five years prior to 9/11, describes in considerable detail the escalating conflicts between differing cultures, not least those between "Islamic" nations and Western democracies.[66] Following the terrorist attacks of 9/11 these concerns became more urgent and widespread: ideas, customs, ideologies, values and religions (particularly Islam) became subjects for discussion.

Philosopher David Naugle, in commenting on the events following 9/11, provided a summation that also applies to current events: "At the heart . . . of this current culture war—whether at a local, national, or

---

conservative justice) underlines Kuby's work. Writing for the majority Gorsuch wrote that, regarding employment, a man who *considers* himself to be a woman is "similarly situated" to a woman who actually thinks of herself as a woman, and must be treated as such. To take the man's subjective claim to be a "woman" as fact, as a variety of authorities have done, undermines the truth—the reality—of what gender is. Imagine the confusion that boys and girls will face when they must deny the obvious, and real, biological sexual differences that they will confront every day. See Crawford and Michal Hanby, "The Abolition of Man and Woman," A 17.

65. As Kuby explains in chapter 16, "The Slippery Slope to a New Totalitarianism," this new totalitarianism is soft, borne along not by guns and coercion (at least initially), but by unleashing the human desire for pleasure and self-gratification shared alike by everyday people and cultural elites in art, film, media, and government. Kuby, *Global Sexual Revolution*, 269–78. To disagree with this new ideology, and the tactics taken to re-educate and coerce the world into acceptance of it, is to invite criticism and attack from scholars and politicians, and be labeled intolerant and bigoted. What Kuby describes is a cultural and metaphysical revolution, "a shifting of the fundamental ground upon which we stand and build a culture, even a civilization, instead of desire being subjected to social, moral, and transcendent orders, the identity of man and woman is dissolved, and free rein given to the maximum fulfillment of polymorphous urges, with no ultimate purpose or meaning." (Quote from the back cover of Kuby's book.)

66. Huntington, *Clash of Civilizations and the Remaking of the world Order*, 209–18.

international level—is a clash of worldviews. Sometimes the clash has been more than verbal. More and more, it seems, the conflicts between competitive ways of conceptualizing human existence turn bloody."[67]

Obviously tough, critical questions need to be directed toward all worldviews that claim to explain reality. That includes modern science, and the worldview of scientific materialism held by many scientists. It is widely acknowledged that modern science, and the technological applications derived from it, have contributed in numerous ways to human betterment. However, some scientists (and a good many non-scientists) go further, and claim that the most important questions humans ask about life and its meaning can be—and will be in time—answered satisfactorily through the further developments of science. This view, which is called 'scientism,' claims that science is the only source of truth about reality. Religious claims about the nature of reality are viewed as irrational and superstitious.[68]

Numerous scientists and theologians disagree. Nobel laureate Peter Medawar, who is not a Christian, believes there are questions that science cannot and will not be able to answer.[69] Alister McGrath, Stanley Jaki, Stephen Meyer, and John Polkinghorne, to name several, are Christians with a background in science whose many writings take the findings of science seriously, while rejecting the reductionist claims of the advocates of scientism, and upholding the truth claims of the Christian faith.[70]

---

67. Naugle, *Worldview*, p xvii.

68. Biologists Richard Dawkins and E. O. Wilson, among others, have strongly criticized Christianity (and other religions) as superstitions unworthy of commitment. Such views are particularly prominent among biologists, the majority of whom are committed to a neo-Darwinian interpretation of nature.

69. See Medawar, *Limits of Science*; also Le Fanu, *Why Us?*; Behe, *Darwin's Black Box*; Meyer, *Signature in the Cell*; Nagel, *Mind & Cosmos*. The origin of biological information, the complexity of the human brain, and the place of moral values are a few of those issues that he and others think that science cannot answer.

70. McGrath calls for a new natural theology, in which the insights of natural science can be seen in conjunction with the big picture of reality provided by the Christian worldview. McGrath cites theologian Jonathan Edwards, who centuries ago offered this insight: "When we are delighted with flowery meadows and gentle breezes of wind, we may consider that we see only the emanations of the sweet benevolence of Jesus Christ; when we behold the fragrant rose and lily, we see his love and purity. So the green trees and fields, and singing of birds, are emanations of his infinite joy and benignity; the easiness and naturalness of trees and vines [are] shadows of his infinite beauty and loveliness; the crystal rivers and murmuring streams have the footsteps of his sweet grace and bounty." Cited by McGrath, *Enriching our Vision of Reality*, 178.

A Christian response to the worldview of secular or scientific humanism, given its extraordinary influence in the world, is especially important. This worldview gave birth to the eugenics movement, and continues to have great influence not only in science, but in medicine, education, government, psychology and law. It is probable that secular humanism is today the most influential philosophy or worldview in the world. To a considerable degree it permeates cultures East and West Communist and Capitalist, Asian, European, African and American. That this is so is due in large part because nations around the world are embracing modern science and technology. Unfortunately, those who embrace modern science and seek the benefits of the industrial-technological advances derived from it, often embrace the atheistic and morally relativistic worldview that drive it.[71]

Poorly discipled Christians, however, are unable to respond effectively to the public challenges presented by other worldviews. J Gresham Machen, in words relevant to this day, describes the effect on public affairs when Christians fail to speak the truth in a timely manner:

> False ideas are the greatest obstacle to the reception of the Gospel. We may preach with all the fervor of a reformer and yet succeed only in winning a straggler here and there, if we permit the whole collective thought of the nation to be controlled by ideas which prevent Christianity from being regarded as anything more than a harmless delusion. What is to-day a matter of academic speculation begins tomorrow to move armies and pull down empires. In that second stage, it has gone too far to be combated; the time to stop it was when it was still a matter of impassioned debate. So as Christians we should try to mold the thought of the world in such a way as to make the acceptance of Christianity something more than a logical absurdity.[72]

The Christian worldview, and the theological and philosophical positions based upon it, when strengthened and illumined by the power of the Holy Spirit, provide reference points by which Christians can engage

---

71. See Professor John West's book, *Darwin Day in America*, on the public policy consequences in the United States (and much of Europe) that have followed from Charles Darwin and his philosophy of evolution, which today belongs to the secular humanist worldview. As he notes in the introduction, "This book is intended to offer a sober warning about what can happen when policymakers—and the general public—uncritically accept a materialistic understanding of human nature advanced in the name of science." *Darwin Day in America*, xvii.

72. Cited in Craig, *Reasonable Faith*, 17.

life and the world in such a way that they are able to remain faithful to Christ. St Paul's words to the Christians in Corinth (I Cor. 10.3-5a) are right to the point: "For though we live in the world we are not carrying on a worldly war. For the weapons of our warfare are not worldly, but the divine power to destroy strongholds. We destroy arguments and every proud obstacle to the knowledge of God, and take every thought captive to obey Christ . . ."

SIX: THE CHRISTIAN WORLDVIEW PROVIDES A FOUNDATION FOR HUMAN RIGHTS

The American Founders claimed that fundamental human rights are based on natural law, the moral law that God has infused into the human heart, and understandable through reason. Because of the pervasive, corrupting influence of human sin, God clarified and strengthened this understanding through the teachings of the Ten Commandments, and the ethical teachings of the New Testament. The Founders took this to mean that such rights are objective, universal and *inalienable*. They are incapable of being reduced or surrendered because they are given by God and not by the state.[73] Novelist Ayn Rand, somewhat surprisingly, wrote, "The most profoundly revolutionary achievement of the United States of America was *the subordination of society to moral law*."[74]

In Western politics today, however, the idea of objective, inalienable rights has yielded to the emphasis on progress and innovation. Though human rights are a concern often discussed in government circles, intellectual journals, schools, and media outlets, agreement on what these rights are, and who is protected by them, has been elusive. China, for example, has expressed grave concerns about the violation of the rights of immigrants and refugees in the European Union, Britain, Australia, Canada and the United States.[75] These same western nations are on re-

---

73. There are many people who believe in natural law who are not Christians or Jews, but for them natural law is but God's law implanted in the human heart and mind. It may be ignored or denied, but it remains. Rom 2.14-16 is the New Testament text that grounds it. See Robert Reilly, *America on Trial,* for a well-documented defense of the importance of natural law to the Christian Church, and America's founding.

74. Cited by Rhodes, *The Debasement of Human Rights,* 160. (Rhode's emphasis).

75. "China gravely concerned over human rights violations against migrants by some western nations/diplomat, Xinhaunet, August 26, 2022. See www.xinhaunet.com/english/2021_06/25/c_1310026375.htm#.

cord protesting the human rights violations of the Uyghurs (Muslims), the practitioners of the Falun Gong religious movement, and the people of Tibet, by China.[76]

In December 1990 a United Nations World Conference in Vienna expanded the field of human rights by insisting on the inclusion of economic and political concerns. This had the effect of *downgrading* the traditional understanding of human rights, which emphasized the intrinsic value of human beings, protection from unjust government infringement, and most important, the right to life.[77] A nation that held to a traditional understanding of human rights would not remove the *human* rights of their people—the right to life, the right to free speech, and just laws that ensure freedom—even though certain economic or social benefits might be reduced during an economic downturn.[78] It is worth remembering that Germany's euthanasia program, and the murder of the Jews, was justified in part by financial concerns. More recently, one of the arguments made to justify an abortion in this country is that a mother might not to be able to afford a child.

The value of knowing the biblical story and the Christian view of reality is that it provides a solid foundation for human rights. Biblical history, with the events and teachings it describes, along with the history of the church from earliest days until the present, is the history of a long conversation with regard to the nature of humanity. Legal historian John Noonan, begins his essay, "An Almost Absolute Value in History." with these words: "The most fundamental question in the long history of thought on abortion is: How do you determine the humanity of a being?"[79] What follows is a brief synopsis of Noonan's essay (7–59).

---

76. "Severe Violations of Human Rights in China," May 5, 2018. See https://editorial.voa.gov/a/severe-violations-human-rights-china/4378252,html. Accessed August 25, 2022.

77. Rhodes, *The Debasement of Human Rights,* 81–84. Ironically, most of the nations represented at this conference had authorized abortion, thereby denying the unborn the right to life.

78. See Rhodes, *Debasement of Human Rights.* The rise of economic and political rights is a fairly recent development, and subject to contradictions. Consider the transgenderism movement. If, as advocates of transgenderism assert, gender is malleable and unrelated to biology, then on what basis can feminists claim human rights for women? See Pearcey, *Love Thy Body,* 227–64.

79. Noonan, *Morality of Abortion,* 1.

Jewish and Christian scholars, in the earliest reflections on biblical teaching regarding the nature and value of human beings, agreed on these fundamental points:

1. The value/worth of all human beings is that, alone among created beings, God has created them, male and female, in his image.
2. Each human being is brought into being—knit together in the mother's womb—through the reproductive process God has designed.
3. The unborn child throughout pregnancy, from conception to birth and beyond is a unique being made in God's image, and created for the purpose of gaining the wisdom necessary to love God and neighbors.
4. The unborn child, though hidden till birth, is a neighbor to be loved in keeping with Jesus's second great command to love our neighbors as we love ourselves.

The early Christian church, in contrast to Roman culture which allowed for aborting and exposing unwanted children, prohibited abortion. It did so based on the first Christians' understandings of biblical teaching, and the writings of the early church fathers. This view prevailed until the fifth century. From 450 to about 1150 the prohibition basically continued, though the question of ensoulment (the idea that God implanted a soul in the unborn child 40 to 80 days after conception) allowed for a somewhat more permissive stance. The development of Canon law by the Catholic Church (roughly 1140–240), was used by countries influenced by Christianity as a basis for public law, and continued to about 1750. Despite the tumult and violence associated with the Reformation (1517—1750), its leaders largely upheld the Catholic stance on abortion. This period was marked by a vigorous casuistic discussion of abortion's prohibition based on the level of medical knowledge, and the level of accommodation church leaders (popes, bishops, church councils) thought to be appropriate.[80] The period from 1750 to 1965 witnessed a tightening of the prohibition in Catholic thought. As noted earlier understanding of the process of conception as the union of egg and sperm, coupled with increased knowledge of genetics, particularly in the later decades of the nineteenth century, led Catholic leaders to view abortion (and infanticide) as "horrible crimes."

---

80. Casuistry is a method for balancing concerns of conscience with the need to resolve issues involving right and wrong conduct.

Noonan in his closing remarks on the near absolute value of prohibiting abortion emphasized two points. (1) At conception a new human being is formed with his or her own genetic code, and with it all the potentialities for development which come with it.[81] (2) For the Christian community this new being, with its unique potentialities, is from conception a neighbor, to which the Lord's command to love your neighbor as yourself immediately applies.[82]

In any discussion of human rights, whether it takes place in the public sphere or in the churches, it is always to be remembered that it is God who has conferred worth and value on all things, and declared that human life is sacred. As David Gushee writes:

> I have argued that in biblical thought the character of God, together with the free decision of God to decide and declare the unique incalculable value of human life, entirely grounds any ascription of sacredness of human life. Therefore, it is wrong to say that human beings and their lives are somehow intrinsically sacred . . . if we are not at the same time saying that what makes human lives sacred is God's action and declaration toward them.[83]

Jesus Christ, through his incarnation, bestowed upon the human race an extraordinary blessing. In the words of philosopher Nicolas Wolterstorff, "To each of us the Second Person of the Trinity pays the honor of assuming our nature, thereby sharing our nature with us. We each have no greater dignity than that.[84]

SEVEN: WORLDVIEW DISCIPLESHIP REQUIRES UNITY AND RECONCILIATION

The twentieth century, as with earlier centuries, has been rife with division and strife between nations, ethnic groups, and families. It also exists

---

81. Noonan, "An Almost Absolute Value," 57.

82. Noonan, "An Almost Absolute Value," 59.

83. Gushee, *Sacredness of Human Life*, 400. (my emphasis) This understanding of the worth and dignity of every human being is one that conservative Evangelical and Reformed Protestants, Roman Catholics and Orthodox Christians, all strongly uphold. It is a source of hope for greater cooperation among them in the future. That there are genuine differences among these branches of the Christian faith is indisputable. That there is a fundamental agreement on the sacredness of human beings is, however, cause for thanksgiving.

84. Wolterstorff, *Journey Toward Justice*, 139.

within, and among, the different branches of the Christian churches. Tragically, division among Christians grieves the Spirit and undermines the credibility of the Gospel. Jesus, during the Last Supper, prayed that the apostles would remain united with him and the Father, and united with one another, "so that the world may believe that thou hast sent me" (John 17.21). It is a prayer often unrealized.

For much of the nineteenth century millions of men, women and children of color suffered the violence and dehumanization of slavery. Many of their owners were Christians. Integrating newly freed slaves who were Christians into white churches following the Civil War was strongly resisted for more than a century. In World War 1 the "Christian" nations of Europe, as they were then considered, fought one another in a brutal and devastating war that consumed the lives of millions. In Rwanda Christian Hutus (nearly 200,000 of them) murdered their Christian Tutsi neighbors. In the closing decades of the twentieth century and the early decades of the twenty-first multitudes of Christian husbands and wives found it easier to divorce one another than to work out the problems that divided them. And millions of mothers (and fathers) who have identified themselves as Christians have broken the unity of the church by having their child destroyed by abortion.

There is no excuse for these things. In the pages of the New Testament there are numerous references to the importance of unity among Christians, and the spiritual means and help to attain it, The vital importance of unity that Jesus stressed in his prayer often was echoed by the New Testament writers. James the Lord's brother, in his letter to the early church (James 2.1–9) strongly denounced the partiality that would divide rich from poor. The apostle John in a letter to fellow Christians emphasized the importance of love, self- honesty, and confession to the experience of continuing fellowship. Paul in his letter to the Ephesian fellowship described how the blood of Christ provided the basis for peace and unity between Jew and Gentile. He begged his readers to eagerly pursue "the unity of the Spirit in the bond of peace" with patience, forbearance in love, and the use of God's spiritual gifts, "until we all attain to the unity of the faith and of the knowledge of the Son of God, to mature manhood, to the measure of the stature of the fulness of Christ . . ." (Eph 4.13).

This passage, and others throughout the New Testament, lay out the basis for reconciliation on every level—of sinners with God, of brother with brother, husband with wife, parent with child, neighbor with neighbor, Jew with Gentile, and Christian with enemy. The foundation on which a practical unity among Christian people is to be sought. In Colossians 1, Paul lays out a brief summary on the radical nature of the reconciliation that Jesus Christ has wrought.

> He is before all things, and in him all things hold together . . . For in him all the fullness of God was pleased to dwell, and through him to reconcile to himself *all* things, whether on earth or in heaven, making peace by the blood of his cross" (Colossians 1.15–20).

Despite grave differences that exist in our modern world, this passage asserts that all human beings have much in common: we are all creatures of God. We are inhabitants of the same planet, we share a single gene pool, and we share the same rational nature. Every human being is loved by God. He demonstrated this not just with words, but through the historical actions of his only begotten Son, Jesus, who gave his life for the salvation of the world. And he did this because he "desires all people to be saved and come to a knowledge of the truth" (1 Tim 2.4). It is obvious that some people will turn away from the Good News, and the meaning and hope that it brings. Even so, the relationships that Christians have within the Christian community, as well as those outside the community, are in a substantial way to mirror the reconciliation that God has wrought in Christ.

Abortion is a special case. For a mother and father who consider themselves Christians to seek the death of their unborn child is to break the commandment not to kill. It is also to break perhaps the deepest human bond, that between mother and child. For a mother and father to seek the death of their own child is to disobey Jesus's command to love their neighbor—an unborn child being the most intimate neighbor one could have. (This is not to deny or overlook the great difficulty that an unexpected pregnancy brings. It is to say that personal discomfort and difficulty do not warrant taking the life of an innocent human being) Further, to disobey the command to love is to mock/disparage Jesus's deep concern for oneness among his followers. Oneness among the followers of Jesus, in which men, women, and children of varying backgrounds could get along, and care for one another practically, was evidence that Jesus had been sent to proclaim God's love for the world (John 17.23). Without this, words mean little. Jesus in praying in this way acknowledged a simple truth: It is hard to believe people who do not practice what they preach. I am convinced that the failure of many Christians to practice what they say they believe may be the primary reason for the decline of western churches.

For unity to be restored there must be reconciliation and renewal. There must be repentance for those who have sought abortions. There must be repentance for those who have been judgmental of them. And there must be repentance on the part of all Christians who, in times of division and violence, have chosen the path of least resistance and remained bystanders. God's grace and mercy is abundant, and available to us all. It is important for Christians to take their civil responsibilities seriously, and to participate in the democratic process—to use voice, vote and action to build a culture of life. But we must get our own house in order.

Roland Warren, the president of Care Net, one of the leading prolife organizations in the United States, takes note of the fact that the end of slavery did not bring an end to racism. As Warren notes, "when the slaves were freed, they entered into a culture that had no interest in integrating them into any part of civil society in neither the North nor the South. They faced brutality, discrimination, a lack of equal access to education and economic opportunity, and many other severe challenges."[85] For many former slaves the Jim Crow era which followed was exceedingly difficult. The failure of so many churches, south and north, to pursue a course of biblical reconciliation of white with black, was a major contributor to the difficulties faced by former slaves. Thankfully, decades of prayer and work by pastors, churches, community leaders and politicians have done much to help people of color to integrate fully into American society.

The struggle over abortion continues. The goal, as Warren puts it, is not just to end abortion—though this is of great importance—but to help create an environment where post-abortive women (and men) know they can find grace and forgiveness. Where single women and couples facing an unexpected pregnancy receive, with their unborn child, the opportunity and the help they need to experience the abundant life that Christ offers to the world.

> This means that we not only embrace life by reaching pregnant mothers. But we must also reach, engage, and train fathers of unborn children, and help couples facing unplanned pregnancies build low-conflict, healthy marriages and strong families as much as possible. In addition, and importantly, we must deploy the Christian Church's central and transformative mission of

85. Warren, "Pro Abundant Life."

offering compassion, hope, help, and discipleship to those at risk for abortion outside and inside the church.⁸⁶

It is the hope and prayer of every Christian who understands the Gospel's emphasis on life, and grace, that there will come a time when American and world culture will come to the realization that every human being is worthy of life, and the full protection of the law. Abortion is not the only threat to human life and dignity, though it is the deadliest. Euthanasia, cloning, genetic engineering, along with terrorism and war, also threaten life. Christians who understand the Gospel and the Christian worldview with its emphasis on the sacredness of human life, must become what it is God's will for us to be: ambassadors of reconciliation. We must do what we can, where we are—as individuals, parents, and citizens—to build a culture of life that honors the human dignity and right to life for all people. As Bartholomew and Goheen put it, Christians are to live in such a way that the truth of the Gospel can be seen as beneficial for individuals, families, and the wider community.

EIGHT: THE CHRISTIAN WORLDVIEW IS TO BE LIVED

At the close of the Sermon on the Mount Jesus makes a statement which, if not denied, is often ignored or watered down: "'Not everyone who says to me, 'Lord, Lord,' shall enter the kingdom of heaven, but he who does the will of my Father who is in heaven. On that day many will say to me, "Lord, Lord, did we not prophesy in your name, and cast our demons in your name, and do many mighty works in your name?' And then I will declare to them, 'I never knew you; depart from me, you evil doers'" (Matt 7.21–23). Jesus went on to say that for a person to hear these words and *not do* them would be foolish; in a crisis their life would crumble. To *hear* and *do* them, however, is as wise as building one's house on rock. Those who do so will have the character to withstand the storms of life.⁸⁷ To emphasize faith in Jesus without a corresponding emphasis on

---

86. Warren, "Pro Abundant Life."

87. In saying this Jesus was addressing individuals with his blueprint for living a faithful and meaningful life within a community of disciples. It is this way of life, lived out by men and women committed to Jesus that does much to provide strength, help and perspective in the face of adversity. The Amish, though not perfect, provide an observable example of the support a community can offer to its members.

Jesus, Discipleship, and Worldviews

obeying what he taught is to contribute to what Dallas Willard called the "great omission."

The apostle John, based on the fellowship he shared with Jesus and the other apostles described the relationship between the *knowing* and *doing* of the discipled life economically and profoundly:

> Beloved, let us love one another; for love is of God, and he who loves is born of God and knows God. He who does not love does not know God; for God is love. In this the love of God was made manifest among us, that God sent his only Son into the world, so that we might live through him. In this is love, not that we loved God but that he loved us and sent his Son to be the expiation for our sins. Beloved, if God so loved us, we also ought to love one another. No man has ever seen God; if we love one another God abides in us and his love is perfected in us . . . We love, because he first loved us. If anyone says, "I love God," and hates his brother, he is a liar; for he who does not love his brother whom he has seen, cannot love God whom he has not seen." (I John 4.7–12, 19–20)

I understand this to mean that obedience to the command to love God and neighbor—which includes the stranger and the enemy—is vitally important in learning to *know* God in a deeply personal way. The very nature of God is that of love. The Greek word agape in this context denotes a love that is gracious, strong, and disposed always to meet the actual needs of those who need help. This is the love God has shown the world through giving his Son as an expiation for sin. It is the love he wants his people to put into practice, a love that is more than words (though words can be appropriate and helpful). It is a love that includes actions—providing food, shelter, financial help, or a listening ear. John clarifies this with a question: "If anyone has material possessions and sees his brother in need but has no pity on him, how can the love of God be in him?" (I John 4.17 NIV) To obey God's command to love others—an obedience empowered by the indwelling Holy Spirit—produces a *double* benefit in those who do so. Love that is practical truly helps others, and we come to know God better in doing so. What John describes here is a dynamic, and elegant, connection between faith and works, such that God's love is perfected (matured) within the believer as he or she seeks to care for others. It is this balance that is the mark of the discipleship Jesus commands of those who would follow him (Matt 28.19–20).

The absence of concern for others, however, suggests that the Holy Spirit is not present, or only minimally so. It also means, if obedience is half-hearted or lacking, that we do not love God—whatever we might say. The apostle's words are clear: "For he who does not love his brother whom he has seen, cannot love God whom he has not seen" (I John 4.20b). An individual might well believe in God in some sense, but failure to practice the command to love suggests that they do not truly *know* him. The commands to love and forgive others are meant for *this life*. When we pray the Lord's prayer, we are praying that God's will be done on earth—*now*—as it is in heaven.

Love of this nature, that responds to problems and responsibilities such as an unexpected pregnancy seriously, provides the sense that God is with us, that he is alive, that he loves us. Moreover, love, when it is practical and visible among Christians helps build and sustain the unity that gives non-believers reason to take the Gospel message seriously. Further, loving actions are evidence of new life within a Christian—"[He] who loves is born of God and knows God" (I John 4.7). This is a point which requires discernment.

Some new believers are living lives of decency at the time of their conversion, while for others faith is a pretense. Only time will tell if their lives are truly aligned with that of the Lord. If the new life is truly of the Spirit, and mentoring is available, then in time the fruit of the Spirit will be seen. The Lord said that a good tree would (eventually) bear good fruit (Matt 7.17), though there must be allowance for immaturity. Conversion does not bring instantaneous maturity. Becoming a *disciple* is a *process* in which apprehension of the truth of Jesus brings a renewal of the mind, and results in a change of behavior.[88] The law of the harvest applies to believers as well as a field of corn. This process, however, is often short-circuited in church fellowships where the teaching and mentoring necessary to foster spiritual formation is for some reason lacking. The key is the willingness to follow Jesus. John put it clearly: 'He who says "I know him" but disobeys his commandments is a liar, and the truth is not in him; but whoever keeps his word, in him truly love for God is perfected.

---

88. Paul's letter to the Ephesians, chapters 2 through 6, set forth one of the best descriptions of the discipling process in the New Testament. Chapters 2 and 3 describe being made alive in Christ, available now to Gentile as well as Jew. In chapter 4 Paul describes the teaching of the truth in Jesus (which presupposes Spirit-led teachers and mentors), and the renewal of the mind and habits which truth makes possible. Then in the remainder of his letter, he describes the changes in behavior that follow—all of which require a continual replenishment of the Spirit (5.18).

By this we may be sure that we are in him: he who says he abides in him ought to walk in the same way in which he walked' (1 John 2.4-6).[89] There is no substitute for learning to think and act as Jesus did.

It may be that no amount of effort by Christians will prevent or end abortion, war, crime, the abuse of people, or the environment. Although true, I am convinced that the prayers, words, and actions of Christian disciples can, and do, make a significant difference. In any event, we are to obey God's commands, not that it will necessarily end human violence, but because it is *right*. And doing what is right, with whatever degree of faith and maturity we possess, is what pleases and honors the Lord in a way that deepens our fellowship with him. One of the reasons Dietrich Bonhoeffer is so widely respected is due to the fact that, though an able theologian and writer, he took an active part in opposing the Nazi movement and its treatment of the Jews. He took the Word of God seriously, and sought to live what he believed and taught. One text he took seriously was Proverbs 24.11–12, a word relevant then, a word equally relevant today:

> Rescue those who are being taken away to death; hold back those who are stumbling to slaughter. If you say, "Behold, we did not know this," does not he who weighs the heart perceive it? Does not he who keeps watch over your soul know it, and will he not requite man according to his work?

To rescue those being taken away to death, to seek justice, to care for others—family, friends, strangers, even enemies—is an emphasis running throughout the Bible. It applies to all human beings—born, preborn, young, old, male, female, black, white, yellow, red, handicapped or able-bodied—because each one bears the image of God. Each one is loved by God, who demonstrated his love for all people through Jesus, the Word of God, who "became flesh, and made his dwelling among us" (John 1.14a NIV). God did so, as Jesus said, because of his love for the world (John 3.16 NIV). Paul, in a letter to his young associate, Timothy, wrote that Christians should pray for those in authority, and added an important point: "This [prayer] is good, and pleases God our Savior, who wants all men to be saved and to come to a knowledge of the truth. For there is

---

89. That countless number of Christians have been—one might say, in the neighborhood—when the dehumanization and violent treatment of fellow human beings took place is to me a sign that the process of discipleship described above was, if not completely absent, largely ineffective. A deeper study of seminary curricula, sermons, church school teaching, and confirmation practices, in situations where mass violence took place would be instructive.

one God and one mediator between God and men, the man Christ Jesus, who gave himself as a ransom for all men . . ." (I Tim 2.3–6 NIV). Though many people will resist God to the end, it remains true that God wants people to be treated fairly, and to discover the blessings of salvation.

It is God's will for human beings, not merely to exist, but to know the truth in Jesus, to live wholeheartedly. Irenaeus, one of the early church fathers, wrote. "The glory of God is man fully alive." To put it another way writes Nicolas Wolterstorff, is to see that God wants his people to *flourish*. His will for us is shalom, for peace. In the words of Wolterstorff, "Shalom is not just peace but flourishing, flourishing in all dimensions of our existence—in our relation to God, in our relation to our fellow human beings, in our relation to ourselves, in our relation to creation in general." And in this life here and now, not merely in the life to come. Wolterstorff goes on to say that flourishing is genuinely present "only when we no longer wrong one another, and oppress one another. Shalom has justice as its ground floor. Shalom goes beyond justice, but shalom is never less than justice."[90] There will be shalom, wrote Isaiah, when

> [T]he Spirit is poured upon us from on high . . .
> Then Justice will dwell in the wilderness,
> and righteousness abide in the fruitful field,
> And the effect of righteousness will be peace [shalom],
> and the result of righteousness,
> quietness and trust forever. (Isa 32.16–17)

CONCLUSION

It is the way of life that Jesus lived and taught, rooted in the biblical story, that provides the framework for Christian discipleship. It is this view of reality that enables us to see that life is sacred. It is this view of human life and dignity that should be central to the work of discipleship. It is the view of life that, once understood, gives direction and purpose to life. It is the view of life that brings reconciliation and peace with God, and encourages the new believer to become an agent of reconciliation. The Gospel of Jesus Christ is the Gospel of life.

The Gospel is also a story, and not just a body of facts or ideas or concepts to be learned. Rather, it is *the story* of the world and the universe.

---

90. Wolterstorff, *Journey Toward Justice*, 114–15. My emphasis.

Understood in this way life becomes an adventure story in which each disciple has a meaningful role to play regarding how the story turns out.

A primary concern of this book has been abortion, the largest assault on human life in world history, and which continues daily. We dare not ignore any threat to human life, whether crime, terrorism, human trafficking, war, or abortion.[91] Christians must do what they can wherever people are dehumanized or treated violently.[92] Our violent and chaotic world needs disciples, Christians able and willing to do what they can to protest violence, to rescue those in danger of slaughter, to support those who need comfort and support, to share the Gospel of life in all its fulness and beauty.

David Gushee in his book, *The Righteous Gentiles of the Holocaust*, in a section entitled, "A Century of Mass Murder," clarifies the challenge that lies before the Christian churches.

> The threat of mass death is still very much with us . . . Throughout human history we have proven ourselves morally capable of murdering as many people as our technology enables us to kill. Technology now enables us to obliterate human existence and destroy the ecosystem upon which all life depends. The future can no longer responsibly be assumed; instead it must be chosen, day after day. Our ability to "choose life, so that [we] and [our] children might live" (Deuteronomy 30.19) remains in doubt. Learning how to choose life—despite having the capacity to choose not only death but mass death—is the profound moral challenge facing humanity at the end of our century of mass murder.[93]

---

91. Wars and civil conflicts, terrorism, drug violence, and crime, consume many lives every day. And there are a multitude of other political and cultural activities that deride and demean people with regard to race, ethnic groups, nationality, or political views. Any such idea or activity is contrary to the biblical view of human beings made in the image of God.

92. Sin of any kind is an affront to our love for God, as well as our neighbors, whether impatience, refusal to forgive, prejudice, greed, or materialism. Violence, however, particularly when the death or serious injury of the intended victim(s) is sought—and which includes all those who contributed to the violence, such as the industrialists who supplied the weapons (or took advantage of slave labor, as did the Communist and Nazi regimes), and "desk murderers" who wrote out the plans and orders of the politicians and officers responsible for them—is more serious.

93. Gushee, *Righteous Gentiles*, 3. Gushee, in his later book, *The Sacredness of Human Life*, expands on this earlier book by focusing on the moral and spiritual foundation of efforts to choose life. As he makes clear this is not an easy or simple task, given the numerous assaults on human life and dignity during the twentieth century.

It is a profound moral challenge to which the Gospel of Jesus, when practiced by his followers, can provide hope and direction. We must choose life, and we must trust in God, confident that his will shall prevail, that "the haughty looks of man shall be brought low, and the pride of men shall be humbled, and the Lord alone will be exalted in that day" (Isa 2.11). Embracing and embodying the Christian biblical worldview and lifestyle is the only way that Christians—in the face of the moral fluctuations of modern cultures—can uphold the sacredness of human life, and honor God as the giver of life, from generation to generation. As Christians we are to be salt and light in the world (Matt 5.13–14). The world does not expect Christians to be perfect, but it is not unreasonable for the world to think that the lives of Christians will reflect in a substantial manner what they say they believe.

Nonetheless, it must be noted that in many countries serious efforts have been, and are being, made, to promote a concern for human rights for all people, including preborn children. For that we can be thankful.

5

Making Disciples
Shaping Hearts, Minds, and Behavior

Go therefore and make disciples of all nations, . . . teaching them to observe all that I have commanded you.

—Jesus, Matthew 28.19b, 20a

Above all else, guard your heart, for it is the wellspring of life.

—Proverbs 4.23 (NIV)

Him we proclaim, warning every man and teaching every man in all wisdom, that we may present every man mature in Christ. For this I toil, striving with all the energy which he mightily inspires within me.

—Paul, Colossians 1.28–29

My little children, I am writing to you so that you may not sin, but if any one does sin, we have an advocate with the Father, Jesus Christ the righteous; and he is the expiation for our sins, and not for ours only but also for the sins of the whole world. And by this we may be sure that we know him, if we keep his commandments. He who says, "I know him" but disobeys his commandments is a liar, and the truth is not in him; but whoever keeps his word, in him truly love for God is perfected. By this we may be sure that we are in him: he who says he abides in him ought to walk in the same way in which he walked.

—I John 2.1–6

INTRODUCTION

Discipleship is the responsibility of the Church as a whole. This includes theologians, seminary professors, and pastors, who must embody and teach the biblical story, explain the Christian worldview built upon it, defend it against its enemies, and encourage those they teach and work with to embrace this story and worldview and make it their own as followers of Jesus. Concern for discipleship also includes parents, whose responsibility it is to bring up their children "in the discipline and instruction of the Lord" (Eph 6.4), teaching them the Word of God through the daily circumstances of daily life. Lastly, it includes believers themselves, who—once they have become a Christian—have the responsibility of appropriating the truth of the Gospel and integrating it into every aspect of their lives. If discipleship is to be given the attention that Jesus Christ commanded, an understanding of what it is and how it can be done is vitally important.

There is no manual on discipleship in the New Testament. Instead, we have the teaching of Jesus scattered through the Gospels, and the approach he took in making disciples of the twelve men he called to be with him. This includes numerous episodes from the life of Peter, as well as many references to the work of the Holy Spirit. There is, moreover, Paul's teaching on the renewal of the mind, his reflections on the fruit of the Spirit, and love (agape). These ideas, with the thoughts of John in his gospel and letters, provide an in-depth look at the nature of love, which are further amplified in Peter's list of virtues. The marks of discipleship elicited in these different perspectives share several commonalities: One, they are all God-centered, God glorifying, and God-enabled. Two, they all involve a renewal of the mind with the truth in Christ, and three, each approach emphasized a change in moral behavior. What we learn, we are to do. We are saved by God's love in Christ, and we are sanctified—matured—as our worldview is transformed, motivating us to embrace a moral lifestyle characterized by a wise and courageous love. It is the manifestation of this love in our lives that is needed if the churches are to be makers of peace and protectors of the unborn.

It is one thing to talk of the importance of Christian discipleship, another to actually achieve it in a substantial way as the early church was able to do. Discipleship was obviously a matter of great importance for first-century Christians, which for decades had the example of the apostles. Preaching the Good News, resisting persecution, founding home churches that would integrate Jewish and Gentile believers, and the practical sharing of possessions as described in the early chapters of Acts, show that the changes in people's lives brought about through the apostles' teaching and example was remarkably effective.[1] But there were problems. There were tensions between Greek and Hebrew disciples over help given to widows. Peter struggled with prejudice toward Gentiles. The Corinthian church was admonished by Paul about their divisions, sexual immorality, and the proper preparation for the Lord's Supper. James, the brother of Jesus, was concerned about the connection between faith and works. The seven churches of Asia Minor mentioned in the Book of Revelation were each confronted with a particular sin.

A TIME FOR TEACHING

Rev. Paul Stallsworth is a friend and colleague on the National Pro-Religious Council, and executive director of the United Methodist Task Force on Abortion and Sexuality, who shares a deep concern for the sanctity of life and the importance of discipleship. In a recent edition of the Task Force's newsletter, he asserted the need for bishops and pastors of the United Methodist Church to uphold the truth of the Gospel, and the church doctrine and discipline which follow from it with regard to abortion and human sexuality.

> For years we have shirked that responsibility. *Now is the time to teach. The Council of Bishops needs to step forward and be the first to teach church doctrine. Then all the rest of us need to follow—resident bishops, district superintendents, professors, pastors, and lay leaders.*[2]

---

1. See Acts 2.43–47.

2. *Lifewatch*, 9/1/17, 2. It is encouraging to note that the recent (2019) General Conference of the United Methodist Church upheld the traditional Christian view of marriage and sexuality. (Author's emphasis). Stallsworth is editor of the newsletter.

Stallsworth's call for teaching is pertinent and important, and applies to every branch of the universal Church. It will not be easy. Teaching the truth of the Gospel in a balanced and in-depth way is challenging in every age. To do so in modern times with regard to any doctrine that is currently under attack by the culture—whether the objectivity of truth and moral values, marriage, sexuality, climate change, or the life issues—takes understanding and courage. Sadly, when it comes to the issue of abortion many pastors lack both understanding and courage.

In numerous conversations about abortion with fellow pastors I have found few that have preached on the issue, or undertaken a serious study on the issue for their congregations. For decades the National Prolife Religious Council has led workshops at annual conferences for the National Right to Life Committee (NRLC), the nation's largest pro-life organization. These workshops have typically focused on providing biblical and theological guidance to the pro-life attendees, who represent different denominations from around the country. Discussions have always prompted thoughtful responses, one of the most common concerns being the unwillingness of their pastor (or priest) to preach about abortion. Pastors are the gatekeepers for congregational concerns, and their reluctance to address abortion usually forestalls support for women hurt by abortion, and other pro-life ventures that might be undertaken. The reason for this reluctance, most often, is fear.

An article for Care Net Pregnancy Centers highlighted five fears that hold pastors back from speaking on abortion. (1) "My congregation will think I'm being political." (2) "I do not want to be pegged as a crazy right-wing conservative." (3) "I feel inadequate to address the issue of abortion." (4) "I'm already overwhelmed, and if I preach on the issue of abortion it will open the floodgates of hurt and bondage, and I won't be able to handle the fallout of the sermon." (5) "I am afraid I will alienate and drive away women hurt by abortion."[3] Such fears help explain why many churches fail to stand strongly for life.[4] They also suggest the need

---

3. Campbell, "Five Fears That Keep Pastors From Preaching About Abortion," June 15, 2018, *Focus on the Family*. Article reprinted from Care-Net.org.

4. A Pew Research Poll in May 2022 stated that support for abortion since 1995 has remained strong. Sixty-one percent of those polled supported keeping abortion legal in all or most cases. Sixty-six percent of Black Protestants agreed, as did 60% of white (non-evangelical) Protestants, 56% of Roman Catholics, and 24% of Evangelicals. See htpps://www.pewresarch.org/religion/fact-sheet-public-opinion-on-abortion. Accessed September 3, 2022.

Making Disciples

for more effective discipleship. Dallas Willard, in remarks given at Fuller Seminary that remain relevant, had this to say:

> I know of no current denomination or local congregation that has a concrete plan and practice for teaching people to do "all things whatsoever I have commanded you." Very few regard this as something we should actually try to do, and many think it to be simply impossible. Little wonder, then, that it is hard to identity a specifically Christian version of spiritual formation among Christians and their institutions. As we depart from the mark set by the Great Commission, we increasingly find it harder to differentiate ourselves *in life* from those who are non-or even anti-Christians.[5]

The process of discipleship must be such that it helps pastors, other church teachers, and parents, grasp the biblical story and worldview along with the understanding of how Christians are to think about issues such as abortion. Further, it must include an understanding of spiritual formation that would enable them to overcome their selfish tendences (fears, prejudices, etc.) and actually put the truth of their faith into *practice*. As James the apostle wrote, we are to be "doers of the word," lest we deceive ourselves (James 1.22). Becoming a doer of the Word, a disciple of Jesus, will for many be a struggle, as I can attest from my own experience.

A PERSONAL STORY

There is an interesting passage in the book of Ecclesiasticus (or The Wisdom of Jesus Son of Sirach) which reads: "Do not aspire to be a judge, unless you have the strength to put an end to injustice; for you may be intimidated by a man of rank and so compromise your integrity" (Sir 7.6, NEB).[6] I thought, upon reflection, that it applied to me. A pastor is not a judge, though I possess a concern for justice, a concern shared by many pastors. Unfortunately, in the early days of my ministry I felt intimidated by people of rank, namely, the nine Supreme Court justices

---

5. His talk was given in 1993. Willard, *Great Omission*, 72–73. (Author's emphasis) Abortion and pre-marital sex are two areas where this is currently true. See Ayers, "Sex and the Single Evangelical," August 14, 2019; Sessions, "Evangelicals Struggle to Address Premarital Sex and Abortion," July 13, 2017.

6. Sirach is from the *Apocrypha*, a number of books and letters from the intertestamental period, and not included in most Jewish and Protestant versions of the Old Testament. They are, nonetheless, insightful, and worth reading.

who had authorized abortion, as well as the leaders of the denominations I served which supported it. Moreover, there were the people of the two congregations I served who I feared might be pro-abortion. Then one summer while on vacation I read the book, *Handbook on Abortion*, and concern grew into conviction.[7] The witness of the Bible, Christian history, and medicine was quite clear: Abortion destroys an innocent life, and it is a grave sin. I became convinced that I should address it, but this sense of conviction made me miserable because I lacked the courage to act. The fears highlighted in the Care Net article were also mine, and they compromised me. This inward discord continued for a considerable length of time. It gradually dawned on me that a pastor afraid to face things that must be faced, afraid to bring the insight of the Bible to bear on issues of importance, might as well resign. Much prayer (mine, and that of my wife and friends), the baptism of the Holy Spirit, and the counsel of friends who taught me some of the principles of cognitive therapy, liberated me from the fearful thinking that held me back. There finally came the day when I was able to preach (very nervously) about abortion. The response was less dire than I feared. With time, study, and prayer, my understanding deepened, along with the courage necessary to preach and teach about it.

I suspect there are other pastors who struggle as I did. To them I would say pray for wisdom, and for the direction and strength of the Holy Spirit. I also think an understanding of cognitive therapy, which has deep roots in biblical teaching, is imperative. The New Testament has much to teach us in this regard.

PETER'S STORY

In the life of Peter, one of the great leaders of the early church, we can see something of the process that Jesus (and the Spirit) used to disciple him. It began with Jesus's call to Peter and his brother Andrew, to follow him, to live with him, to be his companions, in order that they might learn to become "fishers of men" (Matt 4.18–20).

For several years these men followed Jesus throughout Israel. They observed him in conversation with others, answering questions, healing the sick, and bringing deliverance to the possessed. They listened and thought about his teaching and parables, observed him at prayer,

---

7. The authors were Dr. and Ms. Jack Willke.

in the synagogue and in the temple. They ate their meals together and asked questions of their own. They took note of the crowds that gathered around him, as well as the controversy his words and actions provoked with Jewish leaders. On several occasions Peter and the other disciples were sent out by Jesus with the authority to teach and heal. They did well, and on one occasion he responded with joy and thanksgiving at their success (Luke 10.1-22). In every instance Jesus modeled for them a life of wholehearted trust in God his Father. As Peter said of Jesus in his meeting with Cornelius and his friends, "He went about doing good and healing all that were oppressed by the devil, for God was with him" (Acts 10.29). To be a disciple of Jesus was—and is—to belong to a community of committed servants.

On one occasion Peter was commended personally by Jesus for having understood that he was the Christ, the Messiah (Matt 16.13-20). Yet, on the night Jesus celebrated Passover with the disciples—knowing Peter better than he knew himself—Jesus said to him that he would fall away. Peter denied it vehemently, declaring that neither prison nor death would hold him back. When Jesus was arrested the disciples scattered, except for Peter, who followed Jesus and the crowd who had arrested him to the home of the high priest. There, he was noticed and identified as a follower of Jesus, and there—three times—Peter denied knowing him (Luke 22.31-34, 47-62).

With Jesus's crucifixion, the disciples despaired, realizing that Jesus was not going to redeem Israel as they had hoped (Luke 24.13-21). When, on the third day several women informed them that Jesus had risen from the dead, they were astonished and unbelieving. Shortly thereafter, when Jesus appeared to them, they were startled and frightened. But he ate with them, invited their touch, assured them that having flesh and bones he was not a spirit, and opened their minds to all the scriptures had to say about him as the Messiah (Luke 24.36-49). Later, as the disciples gathered at Lake Tiberius, Jesus spoke with Peter, and gave him the opportunity to reaffirm his love for him, once for each denial (John 21.15-23).[8] Through this conversation Peter experienced, in a

8. It is interesting in reading this account to take note of the fact that Jesus, in asking if Peter loved him, used the word, *agapas,* the Greek word for the love that is rooted in God. Peter answered affirmatively, but he used the work *philo,* the Greek word for brotherly love. Jesus asked him twice again, but the third time he used *philies,* understanding that Peter was responding on the level that his faith enabled him to do. Years later, however, in his second letter written toward the end of his life, Peter in encouraging his fellow Christians to seek maturity, writes that the pinnacle is love—and

personal way, the power of God's grace. Grace not as a doctrine, but as a transforming reality.

Though Christians and Jews shared a substantial common ground in their belief in God and his commands, there were significant differences. Peter's life is the story of a clash over those differences, the ones he grew up with as a believing Jew, and the ones introduced by Jesus and his message of the Kingdom of God. Peter, like other Jews of his time, held to a worldview in which the incarnation of God in Jesus, and his crucifixion, constituted a great stumbling block (I Cor 1.23). The Jewish Law and the traditions based upon it were binding. Gentiles were considered unclean (Acts 10.28), and women were viewed as second class citizens. Jesus, however, though a Jew, was different. Peter had observed Jesus speaking well of a Roman centurion, a soldier belonging to the army of occupation (Luke 7.9). On another occasion Peter and the other disciples found Jesus talking with a woman—a Samaritan woman—and "marveled" that he was actually speaking with her (John 4.27). When Jesus asked the disciples, "Who do you say that the Son of Man is?," they provided a variety of answers, but it was Peter was said, "You are the Christ, the Son of the living God." An insight, said Jesus, given not by other men, "but by my Father who is in heaven" (Matt 16.13–17). That Jesus, the Christ, would later be crucified, and then resurrected bodily from the dead, were undoubtedly the most astonishing events Peter was ever to witness.

After living and working with Jesus for three years, and witnessing his crucifixion and resurrection, Peter's worldview had begun to change radically. The learning process deepened with the events on the Feast of Pentecost. Following the ascension of Jesus to the Father, the disciples gathered with other believers in Jerusalem to pray. There, on the day of Pentecost, the Holy Spirit, as Jesus had promised, descended upon them with tongues of fire. They were baptized with the Holy Spirit. A great crowd, in Jerusalem for Pentecost, and hearing the commotion, gathered about. Peter addressed them, saying that this was the fulfilment of a word by the prophet Joel (Acts 2.14–42), and urged them to repent and be baptized. Thousands, deeply moved, responded in faith and were baptized. The Christian Church was born, and Peter became its primary leader.

His sermons and bold response to the opposition of the priests and Sadducees, provided strong evidence of courageous leadership. But he had not yet reached his maturity. There were stumbles.

---

employs the Greek word *agapain,* the love that flows from the heart of God. Perhaps a small sign of the maturity that he had attained through the work of the Spirit in his life.

Paul, a fellow apostle, in his letter to the Christian community in Galatia, described an occasion in which Peter ate with some Gentile Christians, but separated from them when some Jewish Christians arrived. Paul confronted him, and said, "'If you, though a Jew, live like a Gentile and not like a Jew, how can you compel Gentiles to live like a Jew?'" (Galatians 2.11–14) It was a question which made clear that Peter had yet to fully integrate the worldview and lifestyle of Jesus into his life.

Another story which helps show this maturing process in Peter's life is to be found in Acts 10.1–43. It began with a Roman centurion named Cornelius, stationed in the coastal town of Caesarea. Cornelius was a man with a deep faith in God (a "God-fearer"), and generous in helping others.[9] One afternoon Cornelius had a vision in which an angel appeared to him. The heavenly messenger commended Cornelius for his prayers and alms, and then told him to send for a man named Simon Peter, who would be found in a house in Joppa, another city near the Mediterranean Sea. Cornelius complied, and sent three men to find Peter. The next day, about noon, as these men were nearing Joppa, Peter went to the housetop of the home where he was staying to pray. He became hungry, and while waiting for food to be prepared, fell into a trance, during which he too experienced a vision. In this vision a sheet was let down before him, containing a wide variety of animals, reptiles and birds. There was a voice saying, "Get up, Peter. Kill and eat." But Peter, mindful of Jewish custom, said, "Surely not, Lord; I have never eaten anything impure or unclean."[10] The voice spoke to him a second time, "Do not call anything impure that God has made clean."

The vision was repeated a third time, and as before, Peter refused. Peter said this even though he had been present with Jesus when he spoke with a group of Jewish leaders and teachers about the fact that it is not the food we eat, but what comes out of our minds that defiles us (Mark 7.14–19). As Peter pondered the meaning of this perplexing vision, the men from Cornelius arrived. The Spirit told Peter to accompany them, saying that he had sent them. Having explained Cornelius's vision, they

---

9. According to the NIV Archaeological Study Bible, "God-fearers were non-Jews who believed in one God, attended the synagogue and respected the moral and ethical teachings of the Jews but who did not fully embrace all of the Jewish customs, such as the rite of circumcision . . ." Note to Acts 10.2, 1785.

10. Peter's comment was very much in keeping with Jewish teaching as found in the Old Testament book of Leviticus, chapter 11, in which the Lord tells Moses and Aaron which animals may be eaten, and which may not.

invited Peter to accompany them to his house in Caesarea. Peter complied, and when the next day he, with several Christian brothers and the visitors, arrived at the house of Cornelius they found relatives and friends of Cornelius gathered to hear him. Peter began by saying, "You are well aware that it is against our law for a Jew to associate with a Gentile or visit him. But God has shown me that I should not call any man impure or unclean. So when I was sent for, I came without raising any objection. May I ask why you sent for me?" Cornelius answered with the story of his vision, and invited Peter to share all that the Lord had commanded him. Responding to this invitation Peter said,

> I now realize how true it is that God does not show favoritism, but accepts men from every nation who fear him and do what is right. You know the message God sent to the people of Israel, telling the good news of peace through Jesus Christ, who is Lord of all. You know what has happened throughout Judea, beginning in Galilee after the baptism that John preached—how God anointed Jesus of Nazareth with the Holy Spirit and power, and how he went about doing good and healing all that were under the power of the devil, because God was with him. We are witnesses of everything he did in the country of the Jews and in Jerusalem. They killed him by hanging him on a tree; but God raised him from the dead on the third day and caused him to be seen. He was not seen by all the people, but by witnesses whom God had already chosen—by us who ate and drank with him after he rose from the dead. He commanded us to preach to the people, and to testify that he is the one whom God appointed as judge of the living and the dead. All the prophets testify about him that everyone who believes in him receives forgiveness of sins through his name (Acts 10.34–43 NIV).

Because Peter overcame his initial reluctance, and obeyed the Lord's command, Cornelius, with his relatives and friends, were given the opportunity to hear and respond to the Gospel. They did so, and received the Holy Spirit, and were baptized (Acts 10.44–48).

This brief overview of Peter's life sheds light on several aspects of discipleship. First, as the accounts in Gal 2 and Acts 10 make clear, it is difficult for a person to put off the sinful inclinations everyone shares, to overcome ignorance, to put aside the view of the world that he/she had been brought up with, and embrace the understanding that Jesus revealed. The world *as it really is,* as N. T. Wright is wont to say.[11] The clash of one's worldview with that of Jesus, and the process of thinking things through, and developing the courage, wisdom and discipline to live it out, requires the power of the Holy Spirit, and time. Conversion can happen suddenly, and a powerful insight or experience can change the direction of a person's life, as Jesus's call to Peter to be a disciple did, but there was no overnight maturity. Other experiences and reflections concerning their meaning, all illuminated by the Spirit, were necessary in Peter's life, as they are in every Christian's life. Discipleship is the process of sanctification—putting off the old nature and old responses to circumstances, and putting on the new—wherein old habits are repented of, and increasingly replaced by the development of new understandings and habits rooted in Jesus' life and teaching—a new worldview and lifestyle. It is a process—a life-long process—in which one increasingly dies to self, and embraces the new life of Christ.

Second, the vision given to Peter that led to meeting with Cornelius and company, all of them Gentiles, illustrates that God was serious about renewing Peter's worldview. For Peter to be the leader God wanted him to be—and for the Christian Church to be the universal community he intended it to be—meant that Peter's prejudice toward Gentiles had to be replaced with the idea that God "accepts people from every nation who fear him and do what is right" (Acts 10.35 NIV). The apostle Paul put it succinctly in Ephesians 2.11–22, describing how God had broken down the wall of hostility between Jew and Gentile through the death of Christ, that Jew and Gentile might become "one new man in place of the two" (Eph 2.15). Prejudices of various kinds were prevalent in biblical times, much as they are in today's world. Prejudices, now as then, often prove deadly when they consider certain classes or groups of people—whether Jews, Slavs, people of color, women, the handicapped or the preborn—as a threat, as subhuman, disposable, a surplus people.

A third point is that the change in Peter's understanding was meant to change his *behavior*. Obedience was necessary. When the three men from Cornelius arrived, the Spirit said to him, "Rise and go down, and accompany them without hesitation; for I have sent them" (Acts 10.20 NIV). Peter did so. So it must be with disciples of every age.

---

11. Wright, quoted in Bartholomew and Goheen, *Living at the Crossroads,* 27.

A fourth point is made by Peter himself in a letter sent to dispersed members of the early church,[12] in which he makes clear that our faith, in response to God's grace and power, calls for serious *effort* in seeking spiritual maturity (2 Pet 1.5).

A fifth point is this: Lives were at stake. The Almighty's plans are for the salvation of the human race, and in good time the restoration of all things. The Gospel of God's kingdom is to be shared with the world, and it must be shared by people whose lives of love and service lend credibility to the message. That Peter acknowledged his prejudice, and yet obeyed the vision God gave him in speaking to those with Cornelius, most certainly contributed to the credibility of his words and the wonderful receptivity of those present to the Holy Spirit (Acts 10.44). Being a disciple of Jesus Christ is a very serious matter.

In pondering this a comment by a professor at Union Seminary, Hans Hoekendijk, came to mind. A number of us were in a restaurant with him to talk following a class. During our conversation he shared his experience as a member of the Dutch resistance during World War II. It was fascinating to learn that he had met with members of the German resistance to Hitler, including Dietrich Bonhoeffer. Hoekendijk also talked about his sister. She had been a missionary serving in the Dutch East Indies (if memory serves), and had been murdered by the Japanese. I'm paraphrasing, but in words that remain with me he said, "Her death, as nothing else, taught me that being a Christian is not a game." Peter would have agreed.

Peter's life illustrates that becoming a disciple is an on-going, and frequently challenging process. A process that is rooted in enabling believers to grasp and integrate the truth into their thinking and their behavior. Peter's life has encouraged me with my own struggles to understand the Christian worldview and what it means to be a disciple of Christ. A struggle shared, no doubt, by a countless number of Christians.

---

12. It is likely that Peter's second letter is addressed to the same Christians he mentions at the outset of his first letter, "the exiles of the Dispersion in Pontus, Galatia, Cappadocia, Asia and Bithynia" (1 Pet.1.1–2).

THOUGHTS ON THE DISCIPLING PROCESS

In Dallas Willard's insightful book, *The Great Omission*, there is the chapter, "Spiritual Formation in Christ,"[13] in which he offers several suggestions with regard to spiritual formation which deserve our thoughtful and prayerful consideration. As he points out, the goal of the Great Commission is to help the disciples of Christ actually *obey* what Jesus commanded, in the sense of changing behavior. This is something they must *learn*, and something they must *do* if they truly love him. As Jesus himself put it, "They who have my commandments and keep them are those who love me; and those who love me will be loved by my Father, and I will love them and reveal myself to them" (John 14.21). This I believe is what the story of Peter's life shows us.

The Holy Spirit initiates the process that leads us to Christ and the way of discipleship. There may be a sense of conviction about our lives and our sins, or a growing hunger for meaning. Our observation of a committed Christian may arouse in us a desire to experience life as purposefully as they do. The beauty of a sunrise, the loveliness of some melody, the carefree play of a child may awaken within us a sense of gratitude, and the desire to express it. A conversation, a movie, or reading a good book may somehow draw our attention to God. The Spirit has a way of awakening us to our need for God, our true Father, and bringing us to the revelation of himself and his purposes in Jesus, and the call he makes on our lives.

The actual training begins, writes Willard, with redirecting the will, the heart, and mind from the outlook and habits of the pre-Christian life to the new life in Christ.[14] The new birth restores spiritual sight, so that we are able to begin to see Jesus as he is, the Son of God, the wellspring of truth, life, and love. He is the Liberator, the Friend of sinners, the Lord. Like Aslan, the Great Lion of C. S. Lewis's Narnian Chronicles, he is not safe—nor is he reluctant to call his followers to noble, difficult, and (when circumstances demand it) dangerous tasks. But he is good. In Jesus the Christ we see the beauty, righteousness and grace of God the Father. To follow him, to be in his company and that of the Father and the Spirit, is to experience life as God meant for it to be lived, to become our true selves (John 8.32), to work with him and his people in being ambassadors

---

13. His book is composed of a series of addresses brought together with a focus on discipleship, or perhaps more accurately, the failure of so many Christians to make disciples.

14. Willard, *Great Omission*, 73.

of God's kingdom. A kingdom that when fulfilled will bring about the vanquishing of evil, and the reconciliation of all things in a new heaven and earth (Revelation 21.1–5). I believe we must regain the idea that following Christ is a great and wonderful *adventure*. A great drama about the conflict between good and evil, in which he invites each of his followers to join his band of disciples; for each of them there is an important role to play.

Accompanying, overseeing and directing the various "steps" in the spiritual formation of a disciple is the presence of the Holy Spirit, the Spirit of Christ.[15] At the Last Supper Jesus promised the apostles the Holy Spirit, the Spirit of truth, who would teach them, and make possible a continuing communion with him and the Father even after he left them (John 14.15–26). Paul makes the same point in Ephesians 5.18 with this word: "And do not get drunk with wine . . . but be filled with the Spirit." The tense in Greek indicates a continual, on-going infilling of the Holy Spirit.

The Spirit, added Jesus, would "convince the world concerning sin and righteousness and judgment" (John 16.8a). And by guiding the apostles into the truth, as well as the things to come later, the Spirit would glorify Jesus (John 16.12–15). The promises of the Holy Spirit began to be fulfilled some weeks later, when the Holy Spirit came upon the apostles and those gathered with them on the feast of Pentecost. (Acts 2.1–42).

This reorientation of the will, mind and heart enables the new Christian to make use of the spiritual practices that help reshape the whole personality. Such practices help shape the mind, heart, will and body—the whole person—to love Jesus and his commandments.[16] This necessarily requires a transformation of life—a *metamorphosis*—through *the renewal of the mind* (Rom 12.2a). This means putting off old ways of thinking, and embracing the worldview of Jesus. New Christians must develop the habit of setting the mind on the truth and wisdom taught and assumed by Jesus.[17] Proverbs 3.5 puts it well, "Trust in the Lord with all your heart, and do not rely on your own insight. In all your ways acknowledge him, and he will make straight your paths." This is a command that is also a promise. As we look to God for help and insight, he will guide our steps

---

15. Willard, *Great Omission*, 74–76.

16. Willard, *Great Omission*, 74

17. This really includes the whole Bible, but there are numerous references throughout that particularly emphasize the importance of seeking wisdom and truth in Proverbs, Psalms, and passages such as Rom 8.5–6, 12.1–3, 15.4, 1 Cor 1.30, Eph 4.17–24, Phil 4.8–9, Col 3.1–2.

through life.[18] As we follow his guidance, and focus on God and his will, we begin to develop a taste for the living God (Psalm 63.1–4), a willingness to acknowledge our sin (Psalm 32.1–5), and a hunger and delight in understanding his Word and commands (Psalm 119.24).

This is perhaps the first of the steps that must be taken, for it is with the mind that we are able not only to grasp the truth, but to recognize falsehood and its roots within the self. But it is also with the mind that we learn to develop the self-control and strength of will to control both one's emotions and actions, and to persevere with the process of becoming a disciple.[19]

Paul, through his own struggles, clearly understood the importance of the renewing of the mind. In his letter to the Christians in Ephesus he provides an overview of this process:

> Now this I affirm and testify in the Lord that you must no longer live as the Gentiles do, in the futility of their minds; they are darkened in their understanding, alienated from the life of God because of the ignorance that is in them, due to their hardness of heart; they have become callous and have given themselves up to licentiousness, greedy to practice every kind of uncleanness. You did not so learn Christ!—assuming that you have heard about him and were taught in him, as the truth is in Jesus. Put off your old nature which belongs to your former manner of life and is corrupt through deceitful lusts, and be renewed in the spirit of your minds, and put on the new nature, created after the likeness of God in true righteousness and holiness (Ephesians 4.17–24).[20]

---

18. This is one of many Old Testament passages that characterized Jesus's relationship with his Father. The Gospel of John contains numerous passages which speak of Jesus's trusting and obedient relation with God his Father: John 5.19–23, 10.37–38; 14.10–11. The passages in Luke 23.46 and John 19.30 show that his commitment and trust in his Father endured to the end.

19. The principles of cognitive-behavioral therapy understood in biblical terms are complementary, in that the put-off/put-on process of which Paul writes asserts that our thinking determines our emotions, which in turn motivate much of our behavior. The Bible, of course, presupposes that this can only be done with the help of the Holy Spirit who provides direction and strength.

20. A darkened understanding and a hardened heart with regard to the sacredness of life is widespread in the twenty-first century. Terrorism, and the fear of terrorism, is common to the Middle East and much of the West. Threats of nuclear war are being heard in Ukraine, North Korea, China, and Iran. In nations all round the world there is a hardness of heart and a darkness of mind when it comes to the rights of preborn children to live, a darkness of mind and heart that, sadly, is not limited to non-Christians.

To speak of "putting off " the old nature, "putting on" the new nature, and being renewed according to the truth in Jesus, is the central task of discipleship. It is a spiritual-intellectual-emotional-relational process that necessitates the effort of the Christian, while also drawing on the wisdom and revelation given by God the Father, and strengthened by the same power that he used in raising Christ from the dead (Eph 1.15–20). It is a loving and merciful power (Eph 2.4), and a fruitful power that enables one to be rooted and grounded in love—the love of Christ (Eph 3.17–20.) It is an enlightening and truth-giving power (Eph 1.18, 4.21) that demonstrates the universality of the Gospel (Eph 2.11–22), and the unity that is to be the hallmark of the Church (Eph 4.1–6). And it is also a very practical sort of power which enables Christians to move toward maturity—Christlikeness—and the ability to work with others in building up the Church, the Body of Christ (Eph 4.11–16). The renewal of the mind is personal, but not private. The aim is to enable all Christians to work cooperatively, each individual utilizing their spiritual gifts, for the richness of God's revelation in Christ can only be fully displayed through the Christian community.

In Eph 4.25, and throughout the remainder of his Ephesian letter, Paul spells out some of the specifics involved in putting on the "new nature," to clarify further that the renewal of the mind must involve the *renewal of behavior*:

> Therefore, "putting away falsehood, let everyone speak the truth with his neighbor, for we are members of one another. Be angry but do not sin; do not let the sun go down on your anger, and give no opportunity to the devil. Let the thief no longer steal, but rather let him labor, doing honest work with his hands, so that he may be able to give to those in need. Let no evil talk come out of your mouths, but only such as is good for edifying, as fits the occasion, that it may impart grace to those who hear. Do not grieve the Holy Spirit of God, in whom you were sealed for the day of redemption, but be imitators of God, to walk in love as Christ loved us and gave himself up for us, a fragrant and offering and sacrifice to God" (Eph 4.25—29).

Paul goes on to mention behavior in marriage and family, between slave and master, and in carrying on spiritual warfare. This is just one of many passages in the Bible that tie the renewal of the mind to the renewal of behavior, and both to the truth that is in Jesus.[21]

---

21. Though the groundwork for the universality of the Gospel, with its emphasis

The aim of discipleship is always to help believers become disciples of Jesus, willing and increasingly able to *obey* his leading with regard to the responsibilities and relationships that are theirs. While salvation is a gift, once possessed it is to become a way of life calling for the active participation of each disciple. As Willard emphasizes, receiving the grace of God is not opposed to the effort of followers of Jesus to understand his truth, and to integrate it into their worldview and lifestyle. As the apostle James put it so clearly, failing to become a doer of the word leads to self-deception (James 1.22).

It is important to note that the renewal of the mind in applying the truth of Jesus to one's life means developing control and discipline of one's body. Not infrequently those whose faith brings an eagerness to follow Jesus, stumble because their body is weaker than their will to follow. Paul admitted (as any Christian serious about their faith will admit) that while he wanted to do what was right, there were times that he failed to do so (Rom 7.7–23). Jesus, the night of his betrayal, asked Peter, James and John to be with him as he prayed, but they repeatedly fell asleep. He said to them, "Could you not watch one hour? Watch and pray that you may not enter into temptation; the spirit indeed is willing, but the flesh was weak" (Mark 14.37–38). The author of Hebrews, well aware of the challenges the early Church faced, emphasized the importance of keeping their eyes on Jesus. "Consider him who endured from sinners such hostility against himself, so that you may not grow weary or fainthearted. In your struggle against sin you have not yet resisted to the point of shedding your blood" (Heb 12.1–4).[22]

Peter, in his second pastoral letter to the early Christian community—those of equal standing in faith in Jesus Christ—provides another perspective on what might be called the discipling *process* in his opening address. It includes a graduated list of virtues, or character traits, that enable one to develop a fruitful relationship with Christ.[23]

---

on the worth of all people, is laid down in the New Testament, it would be centuries before the Christian Church in its various branches worked out more fully its response to slavery. See Jaffa, *New Birth of Freedom*, 151–52; also Stark, *For the Glory of God*, chapter 4, "The Sin of Slavery."

22. It's worth noting that in the first century, and often in the centuries that have followed, Christians have often shed their blood. According to modern scholars, never more so than in the twentieth century. Millions of Christians have been among the victims of twentieth century violence.

23. Though scholars have debated Peter's authorship for centuries, I lean toward the conservative view that these letters are the work of the apostle. In any case, the

May grace and peace be multiplied to you in the knowledge of God and of Jesus our Lord. His divine power has granted to us all things that pertain to life and godliness, through the knowledge of him who called us to his own glory and excellence, by which he has granted to us his precious and very great promises, that through these you may escape from the corruption that is in the world because of passion, and become partakers of the divine nature. For this very reason make every effort to supplement your faith with virtue, and virtue with knowledge, and knowledge with self-control, and self-control with steadfastness, and steadfastness with godliness, and godliness with brotherly affection, and brotherly affection with love. For if these things are yours and abound, they keep you from being ineffective or unfruitful in the knowledge of our Lord Jesus Christ (2 Peter 1.1–8).

THE FOUNDATION IS GOD

The steps toward maturity of which Peter writes rest entirely on God. God calls people to himself, and shares with them his power, making possible a growing maturity that brings a growing knowledge of himself, and his son, Jesus Christ the Lord. The resources he provides include the promises he has given, which undoubtedly include the gift of the Holy Spirit, and the many promises and insights contained in his Word. These things provide the foundation on which a godly life can flourish. But it is important to notice the emphasis on individual effort. It is this emphasis on growing spiritually, on developing the qualities that Peter highlights in vss 5–7 that produce a mature knowledge of the Lord. God provides all the resources needful for being a disciple of Jesus, but it is necessary for each believer to use these resources, to draw on God's power, and to persevere in the effort. There are no shortcuts to being a disciple.

MAKE EVERY EFFORT TO SUPPLEMENT FAITH WITH VIRTUE (GOODNESS)

The first virtue Peter mentions (2 Peter 1.5) is the importance of making a serious effort to supplement one's faith with virtue.[24] Being set right with God through faith in Jesus Christ is a gift, but attaining Christ-like

---

identity of the author makes no difference to the value of the argument made here.

24. The word "virtue" as used here refers to moral excellence.

character is a fruit. Though this process is God-ordained and supported at every point through his Spirit, it is not coerced. One must choose to join hands with God in order to pursue goodness, and that requires a serious and sustained effort. One cannot mature without God's help, and God will not provide maturity without personal commitment. Striving for maturity is a joint endeavor.

To choose to obey, to grow and mature as the Spirit leads, is—to use a word made popular by author Stephen Covey—to be proactive.[25] It means taking seriously one's "response-ability." It includes the willingness to set one's heart on the things of the Spirit, learning to make wise choices, and refusing to blame others or circumstances for the consequences of one's decisions. It is, all in all, the effort to become a good person.

There is much that pastors, teachers, and parents, can do to nourish this attitude. Perhaps the most important thing they can do to show the value of effort in spiritual growth is by modeling it. Paul worked hard in his effort to bring believers to maturity in Christ (Col 1.28–29), and he modeled what he taught: "What you have learned and received and heard and seen in me, *do;* and the God of peace will be with you" (Phil 4.9). Words are powerful, especially when they are lived out.

VIRTUE WITH KNOWLEDGE

The second virtue or habit is closely related to the first, in that it clarifies the end or goal of the efforts to be made. Knowledge is essential. Peter writes that the knowledge and promises God has provided were granted in order that disciples "may escape from the corruption that is in the world because of passion, and become partakers of the divine nature" (2 Pet 1.4).

What is meant here is the importance of gaining knowledge and wisdom that is practical, and applicable to daily life. It is the knowledge that informs a world and life view. This means giving thought to God's plans for his kingdom, and the kind of person God wants us to be, and—if we are parents, pastors, or teachers—the kind of person we want our children or those we work with to become. This means setting goals that will move us (children, students, etc) in the right direction in terms of

---

25. Covey has written a series of influential books that highlight seven principle-based habits that build character and enable people to live effectively. See *7 Habits of Highly Effective People*, *7 Habits of Highly Effective* Families, and *The Leader in Me*. They resemble in some ways the virtues or habits of which Peter writes.

things to be learned, skills to be developed, and work to be achieved. This includes not only decisions to be made, and actions to be taken, but developing the capacity to appreciate and enjoy life, other people, and the Lord, who is the source of every good.

An invaluable aid to knowledge is developing the habit of thoughtful reading of the Bible, and other literature, that contributes to a love of what is noble, beautiful, just, and good. A habit that fosters the development of the Christian worldview, with an attitude that seeks a coherent understanding of every level of reality. Developing the habit of prayer, of thanksgiving, petition and confession is the proper complement to that of reading and seeking knowledge, especially one's personal knowledge of Christ.

Obviously, goals will need to be adjusted as life goes on, given life's varying circumstances, but each goal should in some way reflect the end in mind: becoming a person of sound Christian character, able to employ one's gifts and talents in helping others, in being in some way a servant (John 13.1–16).

A powerful tool that can aid in this process is developing a personal mission statement.[26] Stephen Covey suggests that a mission statement take into account one's roles in life—e.g., family member, student, employee—as well as the goals appropriate to each role. A thoughtful mission statement provides balance (e.g., work, family, learning, health), specific and achievable goals, with on-going attention to the ultimate goal of "becoming a partaker of the divine nature," a mature disciple of Christ.

KNOWLEDGE WITH SELF-CONTROL

To keep God's will for our life in mind, and the things we need to learn and work on, requires self-control. This means self-restraint in sexual matters: identifying those things—the things of passion—that lead to corruption and must be avoided, or rooted out of one's life. No easy task in the eroticized world of today.[27] But, as Paul noted, self-control also meant avoiding the misuse of the freedom given to us in Christ: "For you were called to freedom, brethren; only do not use your freedom as an opportunity for the flesh, but through love be servants of one another" (Gal

---

26. Covey, *7 Habits of Effective People*, 136–39.

27. Thanks to the internet (and popular music) many children are exposed to pornography while of elementary school age.

5.13). To mature on this level means developing the discipline to keep in mind the kind of person one chooses to be, to keep first things first, and to set priorities accordingly.

The temptations that lead to corruption, sexual and otherwise, and the misuse of spiritual freedom have been present in every century, but they do not compare to those of the twenty-first due to the omnipresence of TVs, computers, smart phones, and the ever-increasing number of websites that appeal to personal and sexual appetites of every kind. They are accompanied by a cornucopia of other activities that clamor for attention, including sports, political events, travel, entertainment, and social media. Nearly all are heralded by a veritable blizzard of advertisements. Without self-discipline one's priorities can easily be overwhelmed. Consider the variety of actions that call for our attention, and which require discipline concerning their order of priority:

- Many activities, such as a crisis, special times with spouse, family, and friends, as well as work or school responsibilities, that are both important and urgent.
- Other activities, such as texting, phone calls, and social events, are urgent though not important.
- Still other activities, which often absorb our attention and time, are neither urgent nor important—watching TV, busy work, social get-togethers, and all manner of fun activities.
- There are, however, another category of activities which, though not urgent, are important. Things such as recreation, study, building relationships, making plans for important occasions or commitments, and relating our activities to our priorities.

The challenge for every Christian, pastor, parent, or child, is to take time periodically to think things through and determine which activities are truly important, and should come first, in light of their goals, and the person God wants them to be. Without discipline little progress can be made in maturity, or in gaining competence in any field.

SELF-CONTROL WITH STEADFASTNESS

Developing self-discipline or self-mastery requires steadfastness—fortitude and perseverance. If a virtue is to become habitual, a permanent aspect of one's character, there must be a continuation of faith and effort. It takes no effort to be lazy. It requires a persistent willingness to keep on in the face of tiredness, boredom, as well as times of difficulty or danger. Steadfastness also includes courage. Courage does not mean feeling brave, but doing the brave thing no matter how one feels.

The author of Hebrews presents Jesus as the example we are to follow, he who is "the pioneer and perfecter of our faith, who for the joy that was set before him endured the cross, despising the shame, and is seated at the right hand of God" (Heb 12.2). Keeping the end in mind, as Jesus did, is an important incentive to endurance. So too is contemplating his example in facing opposition and hostility. This is no small matter in a day when hostility to religion, and Christianity in particular, is so widespread. The temptation for many of us will be, if not to give up, to ease up on our convictions, to hold back on speaking out or taking action on issues of importance. To say this is also to acknowledge that discipline and steadfastness require control of one's thoughts.

To support the right to life of all people, and especially the unborn, in the face of modern culture's disregard of their right to life, is a most important matter. To do so, and not to give in, to think for oneself, to speak up when a defense of life and justice is necessary, to take whatever other actions may be warranted requires fortitude and courage. It was a quality Peter learned well.

STEADFASTNESS WITH GODLINESS

The term "godliness" that Peter uses here (a term rather rare in the New Testament), coupled with steadfastness, is a reminder that the whole process of pursuing a Christ-like character must be thoroughly God-centered. It is an important aspect of keeping first things first. We seek to grow in maturity not as a pursuit of self-glorification, but as a means to honoring and serving God, a concern that is to permeate all our doings.

It was a concern that God's people have at times neglected. Our Jewish forebears were often drawn to idolatry (Hos 8.4), were known to sacrifice their children to Molech (Jer 7.30–31), to pursue greed and exploit the poor (Amos 5.10–12), to prophesy but falsely (Jer 23.16), and to forget to thank God for his help (Ps 106.19–21). There were times, as Isaiah pointed out, they worshipped God with fasting and praying, while at the same time oppressing others and seeking their own pleasure (Isa 58.1–5).

Jesus, confronted by a number of Pharisees for allowing his disciples to eat with unwashed hands (for them an important tradition), responded by saying, "This people honors me with their lips, but their heart is far from me, in vain do they worship me, teaching as doctrines the precepts of men. You leave the commandment of God, and hold fast to the traditions of men" (Mark 7.6b–8). To the church in Ephesus, one of seven churches in Asia mentioned in the Revelation to John which had gone astray, this message was given: "I know your works, your toil and your patient endurance, . . . But I have this against you, that you have abandoned the love you had at first. Remember then from what you have fallen, repent and do the works you did at first" (Rev 1.2, 5).

Similar occurrences are to be found in the history of the Church down to the present day, where Christians have ignored or forgotten God. They may have wrapped themselves in religious clothing, but in reality excluded God. We must be thankful for all those who possessed the steadfastness necessary to seek the truth and reformation.

In every age, in the life of every Christian, steadfastness and courage are essential to keeping first things first. Above all it means keeping the command to love God with heart, soul and mind, which Jesus called "the great and first commandment." This command, and the second, to love the neighbor as oneself, form the very foundation of the moral order (Matt 22.38–40).

The most effective aids in keeping to one's priorities are setting the mind on the things of the Spirit, on the Word of the Lord, and making and keeping smaller commitments, which when honored and achieved, lead to those that are greater. To this I would add the practice of making times of confession. We often fail to do the right thing, even in small matters. The only way forward is to admit our failings, ask forgiveness, and commit with the help of the Spirit and our brothers and sisters in Christ, to do better.[28]

---

28. Another aid in making steadfastness a part of our character, is that of finding an accountability partner, someone we trust, someone willing to be honest with us about the commitments we make. I believe this is the point of Eph 4.1–16 with its emphasis on unity, and the importance of speaking the truth in love. Likewise, I John 5.7 which asserts that walking in the light, in truth, brings fellowship, and the forgiveness Christ brings when we're honest with ourselves. Pondering the lives of faithful believers set out in the eleventh chapter of Hebrews, as well as the lives of other faithful Christians down through the ages is another worthwhile exercise.

SUPPLEMENT GODLINESS WITH BROTHERLY AFFECTION (PHILEO)

The discipline of keeping God in mind as one grows spiritually is essential, because it is meant to lead increasingly to a love of the brethren, to one's Christian brothers and sisters. The words "brotherly affection" are one word in Greek—*philadelphia*. As the Interpreter's Bible commentary has it,

> Brotherly affection means literally the love brothers by common descent have for one another. Early Christians thought of themselves as having become sons of one Father through their spiritual union in Christ. Brotherly affection for them signified the love Christians should have for one another as members of the church . . .[29]

In the book of Acts, following Pentecost, there was an immediate and lasting concern for this kind of brotherly affection, something good in and of itself, but also a necessity if there was to be the lasting unity that Jesus had emphasized. An early practical manifestation of this love is seen in the sharing of goods and possessions among the first Christians following the coming of the Spirit (Acts 2.42–47). It was to be a continuing emphasis, as noted by a number of New Testament authors. Paul was later to write to the Christians of Rome, "Love one another with brotherly affection; outdo one another in showing honor" (Rom 12.10). The author of Hebrews wrote, "Keep on loving each other as brothers" (Heb 13.1, NIV).[30]

The Good News of Jesus Christ is not just information, but a powerful Spirit-inspired message that makes of believers a "new creation" (2 Cor 5.17)), and a new community where moral goodness is to be the norm. While most people are inclined to care for their siblings, it is another step to consider fellow disciples as "brother" and "sister." In any family there are differences to be accommodated, but even more in a congregation where members will include individuals from different backgrounds, and with a variety of personal issues they need help with. The willingness to accommodate those differences, to the point of providing help with such practical needs as counseling, rent, food or clothing, certainly requires the help of the Holy Spirit, but it also requires the efforts of each Christian to

---

29. Albert E. Barnett. "The Second Epistle of Peter. Exegesis." In *The Interpreter's Bible* ed. Geoge A. Buttrick (Nashville: Abingdon Press, 1957), 12:177.

30. Though the authorship of Hebrews has been widely disputed, the point is the same no matter who the author may have been.

actually do what is needed. In the apostle John's first letter there is this: "If anyone has the world's goods and sees his brother in need, yet closes his heart against him, how does God's love abide in him" (I John 3.17–18)?

The fourth of Stephen Covey's seven effective habits is what he calls "Think Win/Win."[31] This habit offers an insight that complements the emphasis Peter gives to brotherly love. The Win/Win attitude "is a frame of mind and heart that constantly seeks mutual benefit in all human interactions. Win/Win means agreements or solutions which are mutually beneficial, mutually satisfying."[32] When one person is the beneficiary of another's help, it is not a matter of creating dependency, or of one looking down on another, but the realization that both are members of the same family, and share an equal footing and an equal value before God the Father.

Another point that Covey makes is that the Win/Win habit, where differences exist, encourages an negotiation such that all parties benefit. As Covey puts it, "It's not your way or my way' it's a *better* way, a higher way.[33] Better, because it reflects the Jesus way of life. This may seem a natural occurrence in biological families, but often it is not. The same is true of some Christian fellowships, where brotherly love has been too weak to sustain the unity that is God's will. The willingness to seek understanding through empathy, sensitive and careful listening, the willingness to forgive, and the humility to ask for forgiveness are all emphases necessary for sustaining brotherly affection.[34] Romans 12.9–21 should be memorized and taken to heart by every disciple.

Put another way, the brotherly love of which Peter writes requires learning the skills of peacemaking. In the Sermon on the Mount Jesus said, "Blessed are the peacemakers, for they shall be called sons of God" (Matt 5.9). Ken Sande, the president of Peacemaker Ministries, is a lawyer who has taken Jesus's word seriously. His book, *The Peacemaker,* and the ministry he founded, sets out four basic principles that, applied thoughtfully, have helped hundreds of families, churches and businesses, resolve disputes in a biblical manner.[35]

31. Covey, *7 Habits,* 204–34.
32. Covey, *7 Habits,* 207.
33. Covey, *7 Habits,* 207.
34. The book of Proverbs is a treasure trove of practical knowledge on such things as understanding, careful listening, wise speech, and humility. A sampling: Prov 10.12; 12.18; 15.1; 16.18; 17.17; 19.11; 25.11; 28.13.
35. Sande has also published a shorter, but equally helpful, version of this book:

- "Glorify God." The basic motive in life, and in dealing with conflict, is to please and honor God (I Cor 10.31). Problems, looked at from this perspective, and handled wisely and with love, are opportunities to bring glory to the Lord.

- "Get the log out of your eye." Self-awareness and self-honesty with regard to our faults should come before pointing out the faults of others (Matt 7.5).

- "Go and show your brother his fault." Confronting another person with a concern does not come easily for most, but there will be times when it is important to do so (Matt 18.15). To do so, graciously, calmly and fairly, may well resolve the issue. If not, further action involving a trusted friend or church leader may be necessary.[36]

- "Go and be reconciled." With every dispute the purpose of these biblical principles is to deal with the conflict fairly and satisfactorily, such that the issue at hand is resolved in a way that restores the relationship (Matt 5.24).

BROTHERLY AFFECTION WITH LOVE (AGAPE)

Brotherly affection (*phileo*) clearly overlaps with love (in the Greek, *agape*), and yet they are not quite the same. When agape is used, it is always linked to God, "for God is love" (*agape*, I John 4.8). It is his very nature, the fountainhead of his grace and mercy, and yet firm and principled. Another difference is that whereas brotherly love is primarily directed toward members of the Christian community, agape is more universalistic and inclusive. As one biblical scholar put it, "It transcends the confines of the Christian community. It describes the right Christian attitude and behavior toward all men as persons."[37]

This universality—the love of God for *all* people, the just and the unjust—is of crucial importance to the Gospel. In a book about the Hitler youth movement I was struck by the comment of a young woman who was imprisoned after the war for "miseducating Germany's young

---

Resolving Everyday Conflict. Both books are very practical. Every Christian and family should have a copy for easy reference.

36. Sande, *Peacemaker*, 10–11.

37. Albert E. Barnett, "The Second Epistle of Peter. Exegsis." In *The Interpreter's Bible*, ed. George A. Buttrick (Nashville: Abingdon Press, 1957), 12.177.

people," a task for which she had been trained, and for which she sacrificed much. Years later, reflecting on her work, she said, "When we strove to be unselfish, humble, industrious, friendly, and ready to help others, all this was only with regard to our own people. What good are kindness, self-sacrifice, energy, and a sense of responsibility if they are so jealously guarded that only one's brothers and sisters may benefit from them?"[38] Concern for one's family and community is good, but not sufficient. Jesus's parable of the Good Samaritan makes the point very clear.

When Jesus speaks of love, whether God's love for the world, the love of people for God, or the love to be shown to the neighbor (including strangers and enemies), he always uses some form of agape-love. It is a noble and powerful love, and though in one sense a gift, in another it is something that Christians are to seek, to pray and strive for. As with the other virtues it involves a continuation of the mind's transformation, the effort to look with respect and compassion at other people—in principle, all other people regardless of color, age, sex, political stance, or birth status—and the willingness to act on behalf of those one personally interacts with.

On this interpersonal level, agape-love requires effort to see others as persons of equal value before God, along with the willingness to understand them. Perhaps the most effective approach is through careful listening and observation. Observation is important because most of us communicate with body language (tone of voice, facial expressions, etc.), as well as words. Quite often these forms of communication do not coincide. To gain understanding would require exploring the difference. As the proverb reminds us, "The hearing ear and the seeing eye, the Lord has made them both" (Prov 20.12), and we must make use of both in our relationships with others.

The point or goal of this approach is to gain an accurate perception or understanding of others in order that whatever response is made is appropriate. One can have a loving attitude toward another person, and yet not understand them in a way that would produce an appropriate response. Many parents, talking with a child who is upset, attempt to solve the problem, when what the child desires is for their mother or father to listen carefully and support them in thinking through the problem for themselves. As Covey points out in a chapter on his 5th habit, "Seek first to understand, then to be understood," it is important to diagnose situations

---

38. Bartoletti, *Hitler Youth*, 150–51.

before we offer advice.[39] Like most things, this is easier said and done. To listen and observe effectively requires control over our thinking, much prayer, and lots of practice.

This form of love is especially important where human rights are concerned, as it often involves those who are strangers: those who are different, and in some way distant from us. To take the stranger seriously requires the love that flows from the heart of God, love that is empathic, disciplined, and imaginative, that understands that we are to treat others—even those we don't know (or don't know well)—as we ourselves would like to be treated. People from a different ethnic group, with a different skin color, who worship differently, or do not speak our language, can and do present barriers which make connection and love difficult. With abortion, for example, this is especially important, in that the preborn child is not easily observed by most people.[40] Many human beings, Christians among them, themselves a preborn child at one point, cannot—or will not—make the effort to understand, and to love, their preborn neighbors. Where agape-love is absent, injustice often prevails.

Love for others also includes love for enemies. Jesus, in the Sermon on the Mount, using agape-love, said

> You have heard that it was said, 'You shall love your neighbor and hate your enemy.' But I say to you, love your enemies and pray for those who persecute you, so that you may be sons of your Father who is in heaven; for he makes his sun to rise on the evil and on the good, and sends rain on the just and on the unjust (Matt 5.43–45).

---

39. Covey, *7 Habits*, 239–55. There are many good sources for anyone desiring to better understand listening skills, e.g., Wright, *Communication: Key to Your Marriage*, Tannen, *That's Not What I Meant!*

40. However, the increasing use of ultrasound by the medical community has given many parents the opportunity to view their child before birth. A growing number of crisis pregnancy centers that utilize ultrasound have given mothers the ability to observe their preborn child in vivo. A prolife colleague, Tom Glessner, head of the National Institute of Family and Life Advocates (NIFLA), told me that crisis pregnancy centers that use ultrasound with pregnant women find that a higher number of these women, once they view the child within their womb, decide to forego abortion and keep their child. Others too have been impacted by observing ultrasound technology. Abby Johnson's dramatic shift in perspective began with observing (via ultrasound) an abortion. Dr Bernard Nathanson said of himself, "When ultrasound in the early 1970s confronted me with the sight of the embryo in a womb, I simply lost my faith in abortion on demand." (See *Hand of God*, 140; Johnson's story is in her book, *Unplanned*, 1–8.

Not a few Christians have viewed these words, along with much of the Sermon on the Mount, as an unattainable moral ideal. Love for the enemy is difficult to grasp. Why put yourself out, or forgive, someone who seeks to harm you, or someone who is an enemy of life? For most people avenging wrongs seems more sensible than love and forgiveness. Though this command is idealistic, Jesus clearly meant his disciples to take it seriously, as he was to do himself. Despite the unfairness and brutality of his trial and crucifixion, he was heard to say before his death, "Father, forgive them; for they know not what they do" (Luke 23.34).

Shining through all Jesus said and did as the incarnation of the Father, was God's costly love for the sinful people of the world (John 3.16), that they might be reconciled to him (Col 1.20). We are part of that world. We are among those with whom he wants to be reconciled, for we have all fallen short of what the Lord has intended for us. We have been, one way and another, his enemies. We need and desire his love and forgiveness. What we need and desire, he has given us. And what we have received through God's grace and love, he wants us to extend to others. It is treating others as God has treated us.

To be specific, love for the enemy must encompass those responsible for the killing of the unborn. While we may strongly oppose their words and actions, we must also pray for them, and seek their conversion. Difficult? Unquestionably. But not, with God's help, impossible. The ministries of Abby Johnson, Silent No More, and Project Rachael, among others, while doing all they can to comfort those wounded by abortion, are open to those involved in the abortion industry. Their prayers and personal witness, motivated by the love of God for those who, in a real sense, are his enemies and the enemies of life, have often proved successful. Hundreds of doctors, nurses, and aides have been won over by love. Dr. Barnard Nathanson, a physician who worked hard to legalize abortion, and practiced it for years, left the movement when he became convinced of the humanity and worth of the child in the womb. He later became a Christian, won over in part by the deep love, joy and prayer of Christians he witnessed protesting at an abortion facility. Their love and prayer astonished him: "They prayed for the unborn babies, for the confused and frightened women, and for the doctors and nurses in the clinic. They even prayed for the police and the media who covering the event.

They prayed for each other but never for themselves." In the final years of his life, he spoke often in support of the preborn child's right to life.[41]

Jesus was, and is, the friend of sinners: outcasts and wrongdoers, strangers, thieves, and the murderers. Difficult and costly though it may be, it is the way of agape-love that Jesus commands his followers to embrace if they would be his disciples. Dealing with evil, hating the sin and loving the sinner, embracing the stranger, and seeking what is appropriate and right for all concerned is a complex and difficult task. It requires great maturity, great forbearance, perseverance, and courage. Difficult and challenging though it may be, we must—if we would be disciples of Jesus—think and pray it through. "If," as Peter writes in his letter to first century Christians, as well as those of the present day, "these things are yours and abound, they will keep you from being ineffective or unfruitful in the knowledge of our Lord Jesus Christ" (2 Pet 1.8).

It is our willingness to take the truth of Jesus seriously in the making of everyday decisions—regarding our responsibilities and circumstances, and resisting the selfish urges of our former selves—that reshapes our worldview, our character, and our very lives. The person who is able to treat others as he/she would like to be treated, to resist the allure of a materialistic society, or the pressures of a violent and racist culture, is very likely an individual who has gained the discipline, strength, and courage, to do so through numerous smaller decisions to be obedient, to do the right thing. Such people are disciples, those who—habitually, even if not perfectly—practice what Jesus lived and taught. We cannot practice what we do not understand, and we cannot practice what we lack the discipline and courage to actually *do*. Abstract faith and obedience are not enough. If they were, "we could be virtuous while asleep."[42]

The Bible has much to say to Christians, young and old, who are willing to follow Jesus as his disciples. Though training in discipleship is not presented systematically in the Good Book, as it might be in a seminary setting, it is rich in spiritual wisdom and guidance. As we've seen in this chapter it involves teaching the truth of Christ, putting off the old nature and its corruptions, the renewal and transformation of the mind through setting it on the things of the Spirit of truth, and making a serious effort to appropriate the moral virtues taught by Jesus, and in a graduated, step-by-step approach in Peter's letter.

41. Nathanson, *Hand of God*, 192. See chapter 19, "The Hand of God," 187–96 for the full story.

42. A comment Guinness attributed to the Greeks. Guinness, *Time For Truth*, 87.

To ponder these virtues is to realize their interconnection, and how they contribute to the fulfillment of the great commands of Jesus. They are truly the mark of the Christian disciple. In the words of a biblical scholar from an earlier generation,

> This series of seven graces is a unity. They are beads upon a chain; each is distinct and separate, and yet each is bound to others by a golden thread of unity. In these the Christian is to excel. He seeks to appropriate them with all diligence. The discipline involved will make his life rich and effective not only in terms of influence upon others but in his knowledge of Jesus Christ. The blindness, lack of insight, and shortsightedness of many Christians can be largely traced to the fact that they never add to their faith any of the disciplines of Christian living.[43]

This is spiritual common sense. In fact many Christians are more deeply influenced by the influences and distractions of the culture in which they live than by the truth of the Gospel.[44] Millions of Christians spend more time watching TV or searching the internet in one day than they give to prayer, worship, bible study, and charitable activity in a week. This is especially true of the young Christians of the western world, many of whom eat, drink, and socialize with cell phone or iPad in hand. The challenge, as in every age, is to disciple them. To set before them, time and again, the lifestyle and world view of the biblical story. To encourage the renewal of their mind and heart, to encourage them to embrace these disciplines and reach toward maturity in Christ. To stand against the rogue worldviews of our time that would denigrate and destroy the most vulnerable among us.

For those of us who love Christ, who seek to protect the life of the preborn and help their mothers and fathers, and to support those wounded

---

43. Elmer G. Homrighausen. "The Second Epistle of Peter. Exposition." In *The Interpreter's Bible*, ed. George A. Buttrick (Nashville: Abingdon Press), 12:177-78.

44. The Barna research organization undertook a research project for Summit Ministries in Colorado on the impact of a non-Christian worldview on the lives of practicing Christians. The results were troubling, and provide further evidence that discipleship is not what it should be in many churches: 61 percent agree with ideas of the new spirituality. 54 percent agreed with postmodern views. 36 percent found Marxist ideas agreeable, and 29 percent believe ideas based on secularism. "Competing Worldviews Influence Today's Christians," Available at https://www,barna,com/research/competing-worldviews-influence-todays-christians/. Accessed September 20, 2022.

by abortion, this must be our aim. We must do what we can to change our culture, but change must begin and flourish in the house of God.

6

Home Discipleship

Hear, O Israel: The Lord our God is one Lord, and you shall love the Lord your God with all your heart, and with all your soul, and with all you might. And these words which I command you this day shall be upon your heart; and you shall teach diligently to your children, and shall talk of them when you sit in your house, and when you walk by the way, and when you lie down, and when you rise.

—DEUTERONOMY 6.4–8

Jesus's teaching is not intended only to enrich us intellectually. It does that, but head knowledge alone is insufficient. Learning from Jesus should make us more like him. Jesus rarely taught his followers things to do or not to do. Rather, he taught them new ways of seeing, thinking, and understanding. He knew that if many people understood how things really worked, they might alter their behavior accordingly. Jesus is interested in our transformation, in our gradually becoming more like him in our thoughts and vision. This will lead to better behavior, but behavior is the effect, not the cause.

—KENNETH BOA AND JOHN ALAN TURNER[1]

---

1. Boa and Turner, *Hearts and Minds*, 32–33.

INTRODUCTION

The *Dobbs* decision by the Supreme Court has greatly encouraged the pro-life community, and validates the many prayers and extraordinary labors undertaken in the last fifty years by millions of men, women and children, to protect the unborn and to provide support and help for mothers. But the struggle to protect preborn human lives by law, and to make abortion unthinkable is far from over. With the return of the abortion issue to the states a new chapter has just begun.[2] For abortion to become unlawful will require a great deal of work on many levels: law and government, media coverage, medicine and health care, and providing effective support for mothers and children. It will also require stronger support from churches, in teaching the prolife message, providing counseling support for post-abortive mothers (and fathers), and greater financial support. It will not be easy. Gallup released a new poll conducted in May 2022, not long after the leak of Supreme Court Justice Alito's draft on the *Dobb's* decision that suggested the Court would overthrow Roe. The poll revealed that for the first time 52 percent of respondents thought abortion to be "morally acceptable." Only 38 percent thought abortion to be "morally wrong," a new record low.[3] It is clear, moreover, that the Court's overthrow of Roe and Casey has already, in these early days, given new energy to pro-abortion supporters committed to keep abortion legal, and if possible, codify it in federal law.

To make abortion unthinkable will require not only the passage of laws, but helping parents—and grandparents—and the citizens of this country realize that abortion is a violent and inhumane procedure that not only destroys preborn children in great numbers, but tears everyone apart. With the easy availability of abortifacients, and interstate travel to states that will allow it, it is quite possible that abortion will continue to be popular. It is not unlikely that the efforts to build a culture of life will be a generations-long struggle. This is a task that will require the churches of this nation to take discipleship far more seriously that is now the case, as well as the solid, biblical worldview teaching that must be its

---

2. Concern for abortion must also include concern and support in the effort to prevent the widespread legalization of euthanasia. The efforts of genetic engineers to design babies according to the desires of parents presents another, and more radical, challenge,

3. Foley, "Most Americans think abortion is 'morally acceptable' for the first time, Gallup poll finds." See https://www.christianpost.co,/news/most-americans-think-abortion-is-medically-acceptable-poll.html/Accessed 7/24/22.

foundation. What is needed is a moral renewal of the churches, and a renewal that encourages parents to take seriously their responsibility to disciple their children. The best place for faith in God and moral values to take root in the minds and hearts of children is in the home. For that to happen a growing number of parents must prepare themselves for what I call home discipleship, the focus of this final chapter.

For parents to teach their children the way of faith and discipleship is a theme that runs through both Old and New Testaments. As Jesus called a small group of men to be with him for a time, to learn the ways of kingdom discipleship, so children for a time are with their parents, whose responsibility it is to love them and disciple them. The truth that all children, and all human beings, are made in the image of God is a truth that children should learn as early in life as they are capable of understanding. A truth that should be part of their understanding of reality. The earlier children learn this truth, the more likely it is that they will be inoculated against any form of prejudice.

Discipleship is for everyone who has responsibility for teaching and mentoring. As Paul Stallsworth noted above, this is a time for teaching. The work of scholarship with regard to the biblical story and the Christian worldview is the particular responsibility of the philosophers, theologians, ethicists, teachers, and pastors of the Church. But this responsibility also belongs to Christian parents (and grandparents). Biblically speaking, the *primary* responsibility for the moral and spiritual development of our children belongs not to the church, and not to the school—public or private—but to parents themselves.[4]

Unfortunately, the teaching of the biblical story and worldview to their children is a responsibility that many Christian parents leave to their church, a task that many churches fail to do effectively, in part because time is limited. The hours a child will spend in worship, Sunday School, youth groups, or Vacation Bible School, were every such opportunity taken advantage of, might amount to only several hundred hours in a year. For most children today—given the shrinking attendance figures at

---

4. Private Christian schools for those who can afford them can be an excellent choice. The Classical Christian School movement has much to offer. Such schools emphasize the Christian worldview. Christopher Perrin provides an excellent summary: "Classical (and Christian) education is a traditional approach to education that blends Christian theology with the historic curriculum and pedagogy of the seven liberal arts in order to produce societal leaders characterized by wisdom, virtue and eloquence." Perrin, "What is Classical Education? Part III. See also Monica Whatley and Shawn Whatley, *Shaping Hearts and Minds*.

worship and Sunday School in recent years—the hours will be considerably less. In contrast, the hours a child will spend in a public (or private) school during an academic year (typically 180 days) amounts to well over one thousand hours.

Most children with Christian parents attend public schools, and it is not unreasonable to think that the many hours they spend in these schools will have a major impact on shaping their worldview in ways that will run counter to that of the Christian faith. Millions of Christian (and non-Christian) parents are troubled by the state of affairs in their local schools. Common concerns among Christians include bullying, the removal of prayer and Bible reading, the presence of drugs, the predominance of the secular mindset with regard to history, social subjects, science, technology, and the acceptance of changing moral values with regard to sexuality and gender.

Homeschooling, legal in all 50 states since 1993, has been driven in part by such concerns, but has increased considerably in the last several years due to the Covid pandemic. To protect them from disease millions of school children were forced to undertake virtual learning at home. Many parents, concerned about the effectiveness of virtual learning and the content of some of the classes their children were taking, turned to home schooling. For Christian parents with the willingness and time to invest it is a wise and worthwhile undertaking. The greatest benefit of home schooling for Christian parents is being able to integrate each and every subject—from the Bible to history to literature to math to science to art—with the Christian perspective, and to do so within the family culture. A number of studies have shown that children who are homeschooled do better academically than those who are not.[5] There are a variety of organizations available to help parents get underway with curricula, teaching methods, and educational resources for teachers and students.[6] In spite of these concerns most children will remain in a public school due to financial and time constraints of the parents.

---

5. According to the National Home Education Research Institute (NHERI) home educated students typically outscore those educated in public schools by 15–30 percentile points. See https://www.nheri.org/research-facts-on-homeschooling/.

6. A number of Christian groups have developed state-wide associations that can be of help with the various issues that homeschoolers will face. A web search will provide information. These organizations can also provide help in locating area teachers with special expertise in such subjects as math, science, art and music, should parents lack expertise in these areas.

HOME DISCIPLESHIP

It is, however, important for Christian parents to realize—whether their children go to public or private schools (including Christian private schools)—that it is their responsibility to do *spiritual* home schooling, what I refer to as *home discipleship*. This is not a new concern. William Wilberforce, the great anti-slavery statesman, in his book *Real Christianity*, published in America in 1829, shared his concern about this issue, and the importance of teaching the Bible and applying its principles to life. His concern continues to be relevant.

> In an age in which infidelity abounds, do we observe [parents] carefully instructing their children in the principles of faith which they profess? Or do they furnish their children with arguments for the defense of that faith? . . . When religion is handed down among us by hereditary succession, it is not surprising to find youth of sense and spirit beginning to question the truth of the system in which they were brought up. And it is not surprising to see them abandon a position which they are unable to defend. Knowing Christianity chiefly by its difficulties and the impossibilities falsely imputed to it, they fall perhaps into the company of unbelievers . . .[7]
>
> Understanding Christianity is not something that comes without effort. Almost every example in the natural world teaches us this principle . . . No one expects to reach the heights of success in education, the arts, finances or athletics without a great deal of hard work and perseverance. . . . Carefully studying the Bible will reveal to us our own ignorance of these things. It will challenge us to reject a superficial understanding of Christianity and impress on us that it is imperative not to simply be religious or moral, but also to master the Bible intellectually, integrate its principles into our lives morally, and put into action what we have learned practically.[8]

Every parent would do well to take these words seriously. Christian churches can, and do, help parents teach the principles of faith in the biblical story and the worldview grounded in it.[9] Even so, I believe that no

---

7. Wilberforce, Cited in Moreland, *Scientism and Secularism*, 40.

8. Wilberforce, *Real Christianity*, 22–23.

9. Church education programs, such as Sunday Schools, Vacation Bible Schools,, and after school programs, while of value, are limited in several ways: attendance is voluntary; time with children is very limited compared to public or private schools; the level of expertise among teachers (also usually volunteers) is less than that of

one can better evangelize and disciple their children than concerned and committed parents. But they must be clear about its importance, willing to seek the knowledge and wisdom necessary to do it well, and be committed for the long haul.

The word of Moses to his people at Mt. Sinai following the giving of the Ten Commandments, emphasizes the great command to love God, the importance of obedience, and the responsibility of parents. Deuteronomy 6.1–9 is their charter,

> Hear, O Israel: The Lord our God is one Lord, and you shall love the Lord your God with all your heart, and with all your soul, and all your might. And these words which I command you this day shall be upon your heart, and you shall teach them diligently to your children, and shall talk of them when you sit in your house, and when you walk by the way, and when you lie down, and when you rise. And you shall bind them as a sign upon your hand, and they shall be as frontlets between your eyes. And you shall write them on the doorposts of your house and on your gates.[10]

As Kenneth Boa and John Alan Turner point out in their book, *Hearts and Minds,* this passage has much to teach us, and should be of special value to parents who want to bring their children up with a Christian understanding of the world. "*These words* which I command you this day" are part of the worldview given by God to the human race. The biblical worldview articulated by Moses, understandably primitive and limited at that point in salvation history, was centered upon God as Creator and Redeemer. It was an understanding which honored his Word as the source of moral and spiritual truth, righteousness, and grace. It was a worldview that included an account of God's creation of the world, the

---

professional teachers, and less than what committed parents can provide, given the motivation most parents have for the well-being of their children, and the greater amount of time they have with their children.

10. Paul in his letter to the Ephesian Christians had a word for fathers: "Fathers, do not provoke your children to anger, but bring them up in the discipline and instruction of the Lord" (Eph 6.4). In another letter, this one addressed to Timothy, a young leader in the church, Paul reminds him to hold fast to his faith in Jesus Christ, made known to him by the faith of his mother and grandmother. It seems reasonable to assume that both fathers and mothers were involved in discipling their children. In Timothy's case it appears that the discipling efforts of his mother, Eunice, and his grandmother Lois, had been quite effective (2 Tim 1.5–6). One suspects that they took Deuteronomy 6 seriously.

unique value of human beings and the responsibility he had given them, along with the fact of their rebellion against him, and his plan to save them. It also included the moral commands that were to govern their relationships and responsibilities. Central to everything was the command to love God whole heartedly and unreservedly. To choose life, and do so faithfully, wisely and courageously in the face of whatever problems, crises and struggles may come along.

This passage makes clear that teaching children the content of their faith is the basic responsibility of the parents. "*You* shall teach them to your children" (Duet 6.7). Who loves children more than parents and grandparents? Who spends more time with children than parents? Who cares more for preparing children to live meaningfully, purposefully and faithfully than parents?

We show our love for our children in many ways. We clean them up, play with them, put them to bed, prepare breakfast and other meals. We talk with them, and listen to them. We teach our children to speak our language (a complex task that most parents do quite well), to bathe and toilet themselves, to carry out a variety of personal and household chores, to learn safe ways of doing things, to love and respect others.

Parents give names and labels to a thousand things, and answer a host of questions about nature, life, and family. Sooner or later questions such as these turn up: What are things for? Where did we come from? Who made the moon? What is God like? What is truth? Why do bad things happen? How do we know what's right and what's wrong? Did the things in the Bible really happen? What happens to us when we die?

As children grow older there will also be questions about sex, education, college, jobs, work, politics, and marriage. All these questions and more are daily fare for parents as their children seek to make sense of reality and their lives from the stance of the Christian faith and worldview. The questions that children and youth ask are often fundamental questions, and honest questions deserve honest answers—answers that committed and thoughtful parents are capable of answering.[11] Answer-

---

11. Children are capable of asking serious questions, and I believe it is important for parents to take them seriously. Francis Schaeffer often emphasized the point that honest questions deserve honest answers. And if, as parents, we can't answer them, as will sometimes be the case, we can direct them to authorities who can. A local pastor or teacher, a good library, and a wise selection of websites are all possibilities we can utilize. Brushing aside honest questions is a failure to take the one who asks them seriously. And may lead to a lack of confidence in the truth and adequacy of the Biblical story and worldview.

ing them biblically, wisely, and coherently is essential if children are to develop a worldview that truly reflects God's will for them. A worldview that teaches the sacredness of human life, and the responsibility we have to uphold it in our daily lives. The teaching that God commands parents to do includes all of these things. But to do it wisely and effectively they must first work out their own understanding of the biblical worldview: "These words which I command you shall be upon *your heart*."

This passage, and numerous others in Scripture, address the question of God's purpose for human life. What is the goal of Christian education, and the spiritual home schooling that parents are responsible for? Is it to help children gain the knowledge and skill necessary to make a living for themselves—and their spouse and family when married? Is it to become a good citizen and contribute to making a better society? Craig Bartholomew and Michael Goheen in their book on the Christian worldview cite a study that points out that Christian education should not consist of putting "religious icing on an otherwise secular educational cake. Those who confess the Name of Christ are called to develop learning and teaching which is based on the Word of God."[12] And that teaching, though it will include such things as making a living, or being a good citizen, must be directed toward—and seen in the light of—helping our children know and love God. Education, as Bartholomew and Goheen view it—whether done in a Christian school or in a home setting—should prepare children to bear witness to the Gospel: "As God's people, we are called to witness throughout our lives to the coming rule of God. Education is for the purpose of equipping students to witness faithfully to the gospel *in the whole of their lives*.[13] This means, among other things, preparing our children to stand against the culture where it clashes with the Gospel. Thankfully, many thousands of parents are doing so, a fact made plain at the annual March for Life held in Washington, DC, each year to mark the anniversary of the Supreme Court's *Roe* v. *Wade* decision. Among those present are a great number of families, with parents and children marching together in support of life. Children are quite capable of understanding and grasping the importance of the life issues if their parents are willing to make the effort.

A powerful example of this is to be seen in a series of videos on abortion recently created by the daughter of a friend and colleague,

---

12. Mechielsen. "Preface," vi., cited in Bartholomew and Goheen *Living at the Crossroads*, 169.

13. Batholomew and Goheen, *Living at the Crossroads*, 170. (My emphasis)

Navin Mathews. Navin's daughter, Sanaya, fourteen years old, worked out the script for an 8 session video series, each session of which responds to an argument for abortion. These videos are thoughtful and persuasive.[14]

In today's multicultural, morally relativistic world, the children of Christian parents will meet with numerous criticisms and challenges to the Christian faith. They will come while watching TV, through events and discussions in public school, at college or at work, in talking with friends, through listening to popular music or viewing a movie, and increasingly on social media accessed through their cell phones and computers.

There is no way for our children to avoid the blizzard of information that floods the internet, radio, TV, social media, and daily conversations with friends. Parents would do well to monitor their children's use of the internet, and make use of internet filters where possible. There will be questions and confrontations. What parents must do, what the Church must do, is *inoculate* their children with a sound understanding of the truth—the drama of the biblical story and the worldview built upon it (see chapter 4). This means helping children and youth learn to think Christianly, i.e., morally, thoughtfully, wisely, biblically. Of equal importance, is helping them develop the corresponding traits of character—the moral virtues highlighted above—that will enable them to respond compassionately and courageously to the questions and challenges they will inevitably face.

The 7 Habits of Highly Effective Families, by author Stephen Covey, is filled with suggestions that can aid parents in helping their children become principle-centered individuals. The habits of which he writes overlap in significant ways with the moral virtues of the New Testament. To me, one of the more helpful suggestions in the book is encouraging families to develop a mission statement, in which family priorities and goals can be discussed and established by parents, and children when they are old enough to take part. A mission statement which everyone contributes to can do much to foster cooperation and unity within the family. The chapter on this habit offers a wealth of practical information on how to develop and apply a family mission statement.[15]

---

14. Sanaya's videos can be accessed at https://youtube.com/channel/UCUINVBXWSRNsuX2jOiOz9IA.

15. Covey, *7 Habits of Effective Families*, 70–112. Each chapter in this book concludes with suggestions for sharing the ideas of the chapter with adults, teens, and younger children.

Accompanying, and underlying all of these activities, should be the development of a time of conversational prayer, spiritual reading, and discussion. The daily reading of the Bible, or a wise devotional guide, is invaluable. So too is encouraging children to ask questions. This is a practice easily begun early in the lives of children with a time of reading and prayer before bed, or before a meal.

Children are born hard-wired for love and learning. Treating them with respect, with love and affection, can do much to help children embrace the Christian faith and worldview. Children are a gift from God, and are to be enjoyed for their own sake. Learning should not be forced. Children want to learn to walk, to talk, and to experience the life around them, and everyday life offers a multitude of experiences for learning. It includes such things as getting along with other members of the family, with pets, and neighbors. It involves learning to express and receive affection.

An essential part of growing up for every child is learning to respect and obey their parents, and other proper authorities (e.g., teachers, church leaders, police). The ultimate authority of course is God the Father, Jesus the Son, the indwelling Spirit. This aspect of learning necessarily involves the opening of mind and heart to an understanding of God's kingdom through the birth of spiritual vision—the ability to see life spiritually brought about by the Holy Spirit, and which involves committing one's life and will to Christ. Though parents, pastors and others can do much to encourage this process, it must be done with a light touch. The Spirit, like the wind, moves where he will. The Spirit in drawing a child toward becoming a disciple of Jesus may use a conversation, the reading of a book, a worship service, a lovely sunrise, the blossoming of a tree, the pang of conscience, a dream, or observing the lives of their parents and other admired individuals.[16] Parents who are attentive to their children can be of great help to them in making sense of such experiences.

---

16. Brother Lawrence attributed his conversion to viewing a tree blossoming in spring. C. S. Lewis attributed his to books that deeply affected him, and to a moving conversation with friends Hugo Dyson and J. R. R. Tolkien. Thousands of others to reading the books of C. S. Lewis. Countless numbers to the preaching crusades of Billy Graham. In recent decades many Muslims have become Christians in response to dreams in which Jesus appeared to them. Other people from around the world have given their lives to Christ as the result of a near death experience in which they report having met with a Being of Light they understood to be Jesus. See for example, the book, *Seven Lessons From Heaven.* by orthopedic surgeon Mary Neal, who drowned while kayaking,

Self-honesty, the willingness to admit mistakes, to be humble, is another vital aspect of growing up. The ultimate goal of discipleship is helping believers, of whatever age, to love God, and others. Learning to do this necessarily includes forgiveness—both in forgiving others their mistakes and sins, and the humility to ask forgiveness for one's own sins and shortcomings. Our sins and those of others may be slight, but some will cut deeply, and without forgiving and being forgiven there will be no going forward. This can be a difficult lesson for any child to learn, but the health of their faith and that of their relationships depend upon it.[17]

A crucial aspect of the growing up process, and to which the internal work of the Holy Spirit contributes greatly, is that of helping individuals develop self-discipline. There is no substitute for discipline, a virtue often encouraged in the Bible.[18] Without it there are many things that can never be learned, and many problems that can never be solved. It means not only doing things habitually, but doing things that are often difficult, and doing them whether one feels like doing them or not. Developing this habit is crucial to every aspect of life, and the sooner children attain it the better. There will be numerous situations in life which are unpleasant and difficult, and none more than developing the ability to think and act Christianly. The author of Hebrews well understood this: "For the moment all discipline seems painful rather than pleasant; later it yields the peaceful fruit of righteousness to those who have been trained by it" (Heb 12.11). To lack the faith and discipline to face and overcome problems is the road to perpetual immaturity.

The first section of psychiatrist Scott Peck's book, *The Road Less Traveled*, entitled "Discipline," is worth serious reflection. As he points out:

> Life is a series of problems. Do we want to moan about them or solve them? Do we want to teach our children to solve them? Without discipline we can solve nothing. With some discipline

---

17. Several books worth reading come to mind which offer insight into the importance, and the practical difficulties involved in forgiveness. One is *The Hiding Place* by Corrie ten Boom, in which she describes her struggle to forgive the treatment of a brutal prison guard experienced by her and her sister in Ravensbruck, a Nazi concentration camp for women. Another is *From Red Earth,* by Denise Uwimana, a survivor of the Rwandan genocide in which she describes her efforts to work with other genocide widows to "tell their stories, find healing, and rebuild their lives." It is the story of encouraging repentance on the part of the murderers (many just teenagers), and forgiveness for those who suffered great losses. See article by Uwimana, "Cancilde and Emmanuel. How far does forgiveness reach?" 76–78.

18. See Prov 3.11–12; Prov 12.1; Gal 5.23; 2 Pet 1.6; Heb 12.3–11.

we can solve only some problems. With total discipline we can solve all problems. What makes life difficult is that the process of confronting and solving problems is a painful one. Problems, depending upon their nature, evoke in us frustration or grief or sadness or loneliness or regret or anger or fear or anxiety or anguish or despair . . . Indeed, it is *because* of the pain that events or conflicts engender in us that we call them problems. And since life poses an endless series of problems, life is always difficult and full of pain as well as joy. Yet it is in this whole process of meeting and solving problems that life has its meaning . . . Problems call forth our courage and our wisdom; indeed, they create our courage and wisdom. It is only because of problems that we grow mentally and spiritually.[19]

Courage is a discipline as well as a virtue. It is the trait of character that enables a person to do the right thing even when they are afraid. Life for most people will include situations where a choice will be necessary between going along with something that is wrong, illegal or evil, or standing firmly for what is true and right. Clarity about the right thing to do is very important, but *doing* the right thing is essential if courage is to become part of one's character. One of the challenges for parents is helping their children see the importance of courage, and supporting them in making courageous choices. For most parents it is tempting to shelter or coddle their children rather than helping them stand on their own two feet. As an old folk saying has it, "Prepare the child for the road, not the road for the child."[20] The best way to prepare for the road ahead, whatever might come, is to meditate on the life of Jesus, the "pioneer and perfecter of our faith, who for the joy that that was set before him endured the cross . . ." (Heb12.2).

---

19. One can quibble with the idea that discipline can solve all problems, or become truly wise without the help of the Holy Spirit. But there is much wisdom in Peck's writing that echoes that of the book of Proverbs, e.g., "My son (daughter), do not despise the Lord's discipline or be weary of his reproof, for the Lord reproves him whom he loves, as a father the son (daughter) in whom he delights (Prov 3.11. (Author's emphasis)

20. This quotation is cited as an epigram for the book, *The Coddling of the American Mind*. Authors Kukianoff and Haidt point out that in recent years three ideas they consider bad have increasingly taken hold among hundreds of thousands of college students. They argue that these ideas are both unwise, and serve to weaken those who hold them. The three ideas: (l) "What doesn't kill you makes you weaker." (2) "Always trust your feelings." (3) "Life is a battle between good people and bad people." *Coddling*, 4.

Home Discipleship

Jesus did not call his people to be isolationists and live inside a protective bubble. He told his followers that they were to be *in* the world, but not *of* it, protected by God from the evil one, and consecrated by his truth. This was his prayer for them.

> My prayer is not that you take them out of the world, but that you protect them from the evil one. They are not of the world, even as I am not of it. Sanctify them by the truth; your word is truth. As you sent me into the world, so I have sent them into the world. For them I consecrate myself, that they too may be consecrated in truth (John 17.15–16, NIV).[21]

For children to be in the world but not of it means that as parents (and grandparents) we must seek to understand and live out the biblical worldview ourselves. We cannot share what we do not possess. We cannot teach or model what we do not believe or understand or take seriously ourselves. We cannot expect our children to love God, and others, if we as parents fail to do so. We cannot expect our children to become thoughtful citizens if we do not make the effort. We cannot expect our children to respect the sanctity of human life if we do not.[22]

No parent (or church or Christian school), can teach or model everything necessary for a child or young person to think and act Christianly, whether as a student, factory worker, carpenter or entrepreneur, whether as a farmer, a politician, professional athlete, or as a citizen.[23] What I believe they can, and should do, is work toward helping their child become a disciple of Jesus, to pray that they will be indwelt by the Holy Spirit, and grounded in the biblical and Christian worldview with the understanding that Jesus Christ is Lord over all walks of life. This must include the understanding that respecting and serving others, at all times and in all places, as would be appropriate to the relationships involved, is paramount. And as such to prepare, or begin to prepare them, for the inevitable tensions that will arise in whatever walk of life they may

---

21. The words "consecrate" and "consecrated" in v. 17 are from the RSV.

22. Morton Kelsey, an Episcopalian pastor for many years, made the same point about Christian educators, which of course includes pastors: "A teacher can only communicate as much Christianity as he or she has assimilated and is *living*." Kelsey, *Can Christians Be Educated? A Proposal for Effective Communication of our Christian Religion*. 10. (Kelsey's emphasis.)

23. As I see it, local congregations, and Christian schools, share a complementary responsibility for discipleship with parents, though a church or school will also have special responsibilities with respect to their charter and history.

choose. This must be done not only by teaching, reading or discussion, but through example.

My wife, Carol, for years an elementary school teacher in our local community, faced just such a situation when she learned that the National Education Association, which all teachers were encouraged to join, supported abortion. To join meant that her association dues would help pay for the NEA's support for abortion on demand.[24] Not to join would mean having to cross a picket line should the local teachers association (in conjunction with the NEA) ever go on strike. She gave the matter considerable thought and prayer, then discussed the matter with the local NEA representative and her school principal, and told them that she would not join the NEA. Though a strike never came during her years of teaching, she was respected for the stand she had taken. In standing her ground as a Christian public school teacher, our children came to understood something of the importance of courage.

Obviously, parents aren't perfect, and they don't know everything. But they do need, and are capable of gaining a solid grasp of the Biblical story, and the big picture that the Christian worldview provides, with some understanding of the strands of evidence which support it. And there must be a good faith effort to practice its teachings that is worthy of our children's respect. As Ken Boa and John Turner put it, *"the kind of parent you are will have a longer-lasting effect on your children than your parenting techniques."*[25]

Parents for much of their children's lives will have the opportunity to spend a great deal of time with their children. Far more in fact than other persons such as school teachers, pastors, or church school teachers, and far more than their children will spend with TV or the Web—*if* they choose to make wise use of the opportunities these hours afford them. Unfortunately, many parents allow TV, smart phones, and computers to use up time that they could be spending with their children.

Prior to school age, as mentioned above, parents literally have thousands of hours to spend with their children, enjoying them, teaching them, and with the opportunity to model for them the life they hope their children will adopt. In the passage in Deuteronomy the emphasis is on everyday activities and everyday relationships which take place with the family. As the Good News Bible puts it, "Teach them to your children.

---

24. Lewis, "Here's Why Teachers' Unions Support Abortion, Planned Parenthood."
25. Boa and Turner, *Hearts and Minds*, xx. (Authors' emphasis)

Repeat them when you are at home and when you are away, when you are resting and when you are working" (Duet 6.6–7). To every parent this means that wherever you are, and whatever you are doing, there are opportunities for teaching.

"Faith is better caught than taught" is a saying with a great deal of truth in it, and one of the best ways for that faith to be caught occurs when children observe their parents living and practicing their faith in God day by day through the splendors of the ordinary. As numerous educators have pointed out, by and large, children learn what they live.

Family meals, sharing chores, games and sports, vacations and travel, bed time rituals, worship and fellowship activities with their church, viewing movies and TV together, as well as special meals, events and holidays, reading, and casual times of play and talk, all provide opportunities for parents to model and share their faith in a relaxed, informal manner. Families also provide an abundance of opportunities for children to experience differing relationships, face a variety of challenges, and to develop their talents and gifts in an atmosphere of love, acceptance and appreciation for who they are as unique individuals.

Of course, to work together as parents assumes that husbands and wives are also seeking to build a solid marriage—not an easy task in the world of today.[26] A mother and father who love one another and treat one another with respect provide an atmosphere and an example in which love can flourish in a child's heart. A mother and father who are honest in their dealings with one another, and those outside the family, provide an example that children can easily observe and take seriously.

---

26. Of special importance in living out the Christian world and lifestyle is modeling a Christian marriage. Nancy Pearcey in her book, *Love Thy Body* includes a section she entitles "Western De-Civilization." (LTB 248) In recent decades the homosexual community has made considerable headway in distorting the whole concept of marriage. Journalists, judges and academics have foisted a new definition of marriage on the public. The Obergefell decision of the Supreme Court in 2017, in particular, "demoted marriage to nothing but an emotional attachment and pronounced it to be identical for opposite-sex and same-sex couples." (LTB 247) Many now ask, if emotional attachment is the only criterion for marriage, why limit it to two individuals. Why not threesomes, or small group marriages, or even human-animal relationships? Perhaps few go as far as journalist Masha Gessen, who asserts that the real goal of homosexuals is not same-sex marriage, but the *elimination* of marriage. Sadly this is a goal that many evangelical Christians have aided, having lost sight of the biblical view of marriage. Pearcey cites Abigail Rine, who teaches at an evangelical college, as saying that her students tend to hold a same-sex position "with only a thin religious veneer . . . The students fail to recognize that what is at stake is not a few scattered [Bible] verses but an entire worldview." Pearcey, *Love thy Body*, 249.

When a mother and father experience conflict and say things better left unsaid, but then apologize, they give their children a lesson in humility and making amends. Parents who give generously to their church, as well as to personal concerns of other family members or neighbors, provide a powerful example of generosity.

Involvement in a small group and regular worship show children the importance of worship and fellowship. A mother and father who laugh often—who can laugh at themselves—express the importance of humor and humility. A mother and father who honor their parents demonstrate the bonds that tie one generation to another. So too, parents who make visits to a nursing home demonstrate concern for those who may be unable to fully care for themselves. And a mother and father who provide a thoughtful Christian perspective to issues such as consumerism, the environment, education and abortion, give their children the opportunity to see that moral truth is important, and that courage is necessary to defend it. All these things, and many others besides, provide living examples that any child can observe and ponder and imitate. Further, these activities demonstrate love and respect for others, in ways that are genuinely pro-life. Blessed is the child whose mother and father practice what they believe day in and day out.[27]

Hospitality can be a big part of everyday life, and a practice that most families are very capable of. It is an activity with which children and youth can easily share, in preparing for the gathering, helping with a meal or snack, fellowshipping with visitors when they arrive, and cleaning up afterwards. Rosaria Butterfield argues convincingly that hospitality—opening one's home to friends, neighbors and even strangers—is key to living the gospel and sharing the Christian faith and way of life. She and her husband, Kent, a Reformed Presbyterian pastor, seek to practice this in their home, and do so with the help and involvement of their children. Hospitality, as Butterfield points out, is thoroughly biblical. It is also practical, and when done with warmth and affection is appealing to

---

27. Jean Garton, a devoted prolife leader in the Lutheran Church, tells the story of her son coming into a room where she was viewing photographs of children who had been aborted, and seeing them, asked: "Who broke the baby?" That question became the title of her celebrated book, which makes the point that children are sensitive to the issues of life, as they will continue to be if they live with parents who indwell the biblical worldview of Jesus. See Garton, *Who Broke the Baby,* Preface.

Home Discipleship

those seeking meaning and fellowship. It is evangelism in a down to earth approach that demonstrates discipleship.[28]

Viewing the heavens, enjoying the stars or a moonlit night, is something people have done from earliest times. Sigmund Brower, a Christian writer, viewing the moon in the company of his daughter one evening, was brought up short by her question: "Who made the moon?" In answer to his daughter's questions—wanting her to understand that the moon, and everything else, was made by God, and that there were good reasons for thinking so—he wrote the book, *Who Made the Moon?* He was concerned, as any Christian parent should be, that his daughter's faith be well grounded in the Christian worldview—strong and reasonable enough to withstand the influence of today's secular culture, particularly the influence of scientism. His book sets forth a view of science from a Christian and biblical perspective that any parent would do well to read, and can serve as an introduction to the Intelligent Design movement. Though few parents will write a book, this one serves as an illustration of how to take Deuteronomy 6 seriously, in relating everyday experiences of our children to the things of God.[29]

The arguments of the Intelligent Design movement are not proofs for the truth of the Christian faith, but taken together provide a powerful inference to the existence and power of a super-genius, i.e., God. There

---

28. See Butterfield, *Gospel Comes with a House Key.*

29. See Brower, *Who Made the Moon? A Father Explores How Faith and Science Agree.* There are also a great variety of resources available when serious discussions regarding science, intelligent design, history, economics, politics, philosophy, religion, human and civil rights occur. Daily events locally, nationally and internationally, will often provide a pretext for such discussion. Within driving distance of many communities are a variety of museums that deal with local, regional or national history, art and sculpture, technology, archaeology, politics, sports and more. Movies, videos, lectures, concerts, and documentaries on nearly every conceivable subject are available through YouTube, as well as other cable outlets. C-SPAN provides coverage of many political events. Many local libraries stock not only books, but videos, movies and music, that would appeal to a wide audience. The wise usage of such resources by parents and children, intertwined with the thoughtful daily conversations of a household can provide a relaxed, low-key, upbeat, and cheerful atmosphere in which the basic assumptions/principles of the Christian world and life view can be discussed, pondered and observed. Pastor Rick Warren has mentioned talking of worldviews with his children, and giving them a coin if they can identify the worldview of the advertisements they watch. Integral to this can be a sharing of prayer concerns, readings of biblical passages, saying grace at meals.

are a variety of resources on Intelligent Design that any thoughtful parents could use.³⁰

One of the best times for families to enjoy and learn from one another is meal time. Asking each member of the family what it is that they are thankful for that day, and including these things in saying grace is a way to encourage in everyone the habit of gratitude. Jokes, questions, and ideas flow naturally if parents are intentional about this. Asking children their opinion about what they learned during the day is a great question to spur discussion.

This was a common practice in our home, as was reading. Over the years our family read many books together. There were Bible story books, and books about people who lived lives of faith, compassion, courage and meaning.³¹ Quite often following the meal, while some members of the family cleaned up after dinner, one of us would read a chapter of a book, or an article from a magazine, and occasionally a good discussion would follow. On weekends we often would have a special tea time, where with tea and a good snack we would take turns reading from a good book.

Encouraging the love and enjoyment of good books is one of the most helpful things parents can do for their children. Fortunately, there are hundreds of books that portray a worldview and its consequences in ways that are both entertaining and insightful. A biography or novel, skillfully written, can provide an inside look at the thinking, emotions, values, actions and worldview of the characters involved. Moreover, a good book can show the consequences of the actions taken by the various personalities portrayed from a moral and spiritual point of view.

Educators William Kilpatrick, Gregory and Suzanne Wolfe, make this argument cogently with their book, *Books That Build Character*. Its

---

30. See, for example: Meyer, *The Return of the God Hypothesis*, Behe, *Darwin's Black Box*, Denton, *Miracle of the Cell*, Flew, *There Is a God*, Demski, *Mere Creation*, Wells, *Icons of Evolution*, Le Fanu, *Why Us?*, McGrath, *A Fine-Tuned Universe*, Meyer, *Signature in the Cell*, and the Discovery Institute's videos that illustrate these ideas. Thomas Nagel's book, *Mind & Cosmos: Why the Materialist Neo-Darwinian Concept of Nature is Almost Certainly False*, is of special interest given the fact that he is an atheist. The Ben Stein documentary, *Expelled*, provides a look at these issues through a series of interviews with scientists and historians.

31. We read Christmas stories, stories about Easter and the resurrection, and stories of Christians from different eras. We read a number of Newberry Award classics. We read books about history, books and articles on slavery and race, along with many human-interest stories. A book on Christian resistance to the Nazi regime in the Netherlands prompted the question as to when Christians might support their country, and when they should not.

subtitle, *A Guide to Teaching Your Child Moral Values Through Stories*, makes the point that reading good books can help our children love and embrace what is noble and true. It is a volume that deserves a place on the bookshelf of every family. Amitai Etzioni, commenting on the book, wrote, "Values do not fly on their wings. They are communicated, effectively, around stories, historical narratives, legends and such. Here is *the* source book of moral tales for educators and parents and grandparents."[32] Reading and pondering noble ideas, and observing or reading about men and women who have lived noble, courageous and selfless lives is a powerful form of inspiration.

This book by Kilpatrick and the Wolfes is a family guide to reading, not only in setting forth the many good reasons for reading with children, but also in including an annotated list of over 300 books listed by category, with the appropriate age for them to be read. The stories such books tell provide clarity about right and wrong, and an appreciation of virtue and its importance. These stories also show that turning from selfishness, however expressed—as prejudice, meanness, dishonesty, violence, cowardice—toward what is right and good (in many books God is seen as their source) is a struggle, and often a difficult struggle. Furthermore, such stories make clear that ideas produce consequences in keeping with the ideas. Good stories make virtue attractive, and also make clear that selfishness does not bring happiness. Moreover, they do these things in a way that help shape a reader's worldview—their way of seeing the world—while encouraging and inspiring the reader to emulate what they are learning.

C. S. Lewis, the renowned literary scholar, and perhaps the greatest Christian apologist of the twentieth century, was convinced that one of the best ways to avoid being caught up in the shifting currents of one's time in history was to read *old* as well as new books. As Lewis said in his essay, "On the Reading of Old Books," writers of old books certainly made mistakes and held views incompatible with the Christian life, but it was highly unlikely that their mistakes would be those made by writers and journalists of modern times. In reading older books one can gain perspective on one's own moment in history, and thereby avoid some of the mistakes made by those caught up in what Lewis called "chronological snobbery," the idea that what is newest is best. Some things are

---

32. Etzioni is the author of *The Spirit of Community: Rights, Responsibilities, and the Communitarian Agenda*. His comment is on the flyleaf of the Kilpatrick-Wolfe book. (His emphasis)

of permanent value—the eternal things, the values and ideas rooted in eternity. As Lewis said, "The only palliative is to keep the clean sea breeze of the centuries blowing through our minds, and this can be done only by reading old books."[33] One old book worth reading is, of course, the Bible.

Among the works recommended by Kilpatrick and the Wolfes are Lewis's seven volume series, *The Chronicles of Narnia*. These seven books tell the stories of some English children called from time to time into the land of Narnia by its rightful sovereign, Aslan, who to their surprise turns out to be a great Lion. Aslan is not at all a tame Lion, but he is good. Once in Narnia the children are caught up in a series of adventures given by Aslan that challenges them, when faced with difficulties and dangers, to act faithfully and courageously. Each of these fairy stories is delightfully readable. They are also morally and spiritually enlightening, and will reward many re-readings. As Lewis commented, "sometimes fairy stories say best what's to be said."[34]

Good stories can be enhanced by acting them out. On one occasion, while reading *The Lion, Witch and Wardrobe* with our children (and due to read the chapter where readers learn something of the history of Narnia and its future) my wife came up with a wonderful suggestion.[35] Her idea was that we act out the scene where the history of Narnia is given, which happens to be in the home of two talking beavers, husband and wife (many animals in Narnia can talk). There, in the snug little home of the Beavers, following a lovely dinner complete with tea and sticky buns, the four English children—Peter, Susan, Edmund and Lucy—-learn of Narnia's domination by the White Witch, and the identity of Aslan, the great Lion and rightful king of Narnia, who would return to set Narnia free. To do this Carol and I set out signs for the kids when they arrived home from school directing them to the "Beaver's house," set in an upstairs bedroom. One important sign was the warning to beware of the White

---

33. Lewis, "On the Reading of Old Books," in *God in the Dock*, 202. Edited by Hooper.

34. This phrase is the title of an essay by the same name, In Lewis, *Of Other Worlds*, 35.

35. In 2015 the BBC listed the eleven best children's books of all time. *The Lion, Witch and the Wardrobe* (the first book of the Narnia books written by Lewis, but chronologically the second according to Narnian history) was listed No. 2, following E. B. White's *Charlotte's Web*. See "BBC chooses best children's books of all time -do you agree?" Author and Episcopal priest, Morton Kelsey, has said that the richest account of Christ's atonement in twentieth century literature is portrayed in this book, where Aslan, the Great Lion, gives his life for that of a traitor.

Witch (and Fenris Ulf, a vicious wolf, the head of her secret police). There in our upstairs bedroom they discovered the "Beaver's House" (a shelter built out of bedroom furniture). Inside this little "house" Carol served tea and sticky buns while we read the relevant chapter from the book. It was a lovely and memorable time that our children enjoyed immensely.

There are numerous other scenes in the *Chronicles of Narnia* which stand out in my mind as vivid reminders of what is good and true, and the joy that accompanies the faith and courage of doing the right thing. One such scene is from *The Silver Chair* (sixth book in the series). In this book two children, Jill Pole and Eustace Clarence Scrubb, with the aid of a Marshwiggle named Puddleglum, are given a mission by Aslan (the rightful king of Narnia) to rescue a lost prince. After many adventures and missteps—caused in part because they fail to follow the signs given to them by Aslan—they discover the prince in a dark underground world, bound by an evil enchantment given by the Queen of the Underland. No sooner do they set him free and make plans to return to Narnia and the Overworld, than the Queen (who is really an evil witch), appears and seeks to cast a spell over them by throwing an enchanting powder in a fire. Growing drowsy and thick-headed by the enchantment the children and the prince find themselves slowly accepting the Queen's view of things—one could say, her worldview. All their talk of Narnia, the sun, and Aslan, she considers a dream, an illusion, a "pretty make-believe." Until Puddleglum courageously stamps out the fire with its sleep-inducing effect, and says:

> One word, Ma'am. All you've been saying is quite right I shouldn't wonder. I'm a chap who always liked to know the worst and then put the best face I can on it . . . But there's one more thing to be said, even so. Suppose we *have* only dreamed, or made up those things—trees and grass and sun and moon and stars and Aslan himself. Suppose we have. Then all I can say is that, in that case, the made-up things seem a good deal more important than the real ones. Suppose this black pit of a kingdom of yours is the only world. Well, it strikes me as a pretty poor one. And that's a funny thing, when you come to think of it. We're just babies making up a game, if you're right. But four babies playing a game can make a play world which licks your real world hollow. That's why I'm going to stand by the play-world. I'm on Aslan's side even if there isn't any Aslan to lead it. I'm going to live as like a Narnian as I can even if there isn't any Narnia.[36]

---

36. Lewis, *The Silver Chair*, included in the one volume *The Chronicles of Narnia*, 633.

At this point the Queen, alarmed at Puddleglum's courage, assumes her real appearance as a witch—now in the form of a green serpent—and attacks the prince. In the struggle that follows the witch is killed, and Jill, Eustace, Puddleglum and the Prince make their way to freedom, the over land of Narnia, the real world of beauty, truth and goodness—Aslan's kingdom.

This scene often brings to mind the enchantments of today's secular materialistic worldview with its constant inducement to self-interest, pleasure seeking and moral relativism—and its disparagement of truth, goodness, and their source in the living God.[37] To resist takes faithfulness to the truth, which also requires—as Puddleglum the Marshwiggle demonstrates—courage. *The Silver Chair,* by today's standards an old book, is a wonderful story and a marvelous morality tale.

Reading together is a great way to create memories, strengthen the bonds of family, and discuss ideas and issues of importance. Of particular importance are the issues related to building a culture of life, and the biblical truth that all people are made in God's image, including preborn children. One of the attractions of developing the habit or reading together is that the cost is small.[38]

Good books and good stories can be a powerful aid in discipling our children (and ourselves). To encourage them in becoming life-long learners, and readers of books that build character, is one of the wisest things parents, teachers and pastors can do.

Discipling children (for certainly Jesus meant for them to be discipled)—helping them understand the biblical story and worldview, and their place within it—means that parents must make a concerted effort to utilize every resource available to them. Michael Goheen and Craig Bartholomew's books, *The Drama of Scripture,* and *Living at the Crossroads,* provide an excellent introduction to the biblical story, and its connection to the Christian worldview. They provide a solid grounding for helping children become faithful disciples of Christ, and understanding that

---

37. To disciple children also requires awareness of other worldviews that our children will inevitably be exposed to through school, their friends, reading, advertisements, TV, movies and the internet. We live in a global society that celebrates consumerism, sports, entertainment, and the pursuit of pleasure. Access to the internet means access to the world: to customs, practices, lifestyles and ideas from every quarter of the globe. It is up to parents to monitor activity.

38. The pro-life ministry of our congregation established the tradition of giving parents, at the baptism or dedication of their child, a one volume copy of *The Chronicles of Narnia,* with the encouragement to read it to their children.

to be a Christian means helping the family, the church—and the wider community—work together to build a culture of life. Pope John Paul II's book, *The Gospel of Life*, though a bit old for children, is worthwhile reading for parents, clarifying as it does that standing strong for the value of all human life is integral to the good news of Jesus Christ.

Another book that should be on every parent's reading list, particularly those with children in college, is *The Fabric of Faithfulness*, by Steven Garber. This book is one of the best books on spiritual formation and worldviews of which I am aware. The focus of Garber's book is helping young people connect what they believe with how they live in the world. The stories and personal experiences Garber shares provide powerful, and inspiring, examples of individuals struggling to find meaning and direction in situations which challenge their faith. One particularly moving story is that of Hans and Sophie Scholl, siblings of college age in Germany during World War Two. Upon becoming Christians they became convinced that they must act to counter the growing corruption and violence of their country, and with the help of a few friends founded a resistance movement they called The White Rose. The purpose of their small movement was to publish newsletters to be sent to college campuses criticizing the actions of the government. The response was lively for a time, but ended when they were caught distributing The White Rose at the University of Munich and arrested. Following a swift trial they were beheaded. Was it worth it? Sophie's response at their trial, "Somebody, after all, had to make a start."[39]

When rooted in the biblical story the books I have recommended, the activities that I have listed, and others like them, reveal the sacredness of human life—as well as the respect and care proper to animals, indeed, all of creation. And especially when done with humility and humor. I do not think most children expect their parents to be perfect, but they do expect them to be real and authentic, people who are making a solid and persistent effort to act in accordance with what they say they believe. There is hardly a better place for children to be discipled—loved, mentored, and disciplined—in the ways of faith, love, beauty and truth than a home where parents have learned the importance of using everyday life, and the splendor of the ordinary, as the school of Christ.[40]

39. Garber, *Fabric of Faithfulness*, 184,

40. Though single parents do not have the advantage of demonstrating a relationship in the way a married couple can, there remain a multitude of experiences that they can take as seriously as any couple, including their relationships with others,

Nicolas Wolterstorff in a series of talks about Christian education has much to say about the importance of a community of love for educating children and youth Christianly. Of particular value is a Christian community in which men, women and children of different ages and occupations live lives of compassion and respect for all those around them, in which there is taught an understanding of the Christian story and worldview. Modeling that is authentically Christian, writes Wolterstorff, when accompanied with reasons for such behavior, are together much more effective in helping children live the life of faith than a community where nominal faith and hypocrisy are rife. There is no substitute for seeing disciples of Christ in action.[41]

Rod Dreher in his recent book, *The Benedict Option*, is of the opinion that the church today has lost sight of the gospel, and argues for the development of small, intentional communities of deeply committed Christians who will support and care for one another in a way that truly reflects what Jesus meant by discipleship.[42] Would that every Christian congregation was such a community. Would that every family was itself a small intentional Christian community. Committed parents can help lead the way.

It would be good for every mother and father (and every pastor and youth leader) to be aware of the national study on youth and religion led by sociologist Christian Smith that is described above. Through surveys of thousands of religious young people it was discovered that a large percentage of them, though they claimed to believe in Jesus Christ as

---

and the way they deal with moral issues. The way in which a single mother or father practices their faith at home, at work, in their attitude toward money and personal responsibility, can have a powerful impact on any child. Hospitality is something that almost any parent can do. And the relationship a single parent has with their children is itself of great importance in the faith development of a child. It is important to note further, that parents who are divorced—a difficult situation that sadly is increasingly common—-have the opportunity, the challenge, to act maturely with regard to the divorced spouse. Too many children of divorce observe bickering, resentment, anger and abuse between their separated parents. Sadly, many divorced parents use their children as pawns in the divorce process. To treat a divorced spouse with respect, even if the disagreements and hurts are serious, can be a powerful witness to a child who still loves both parents. In any Christian community there will undoubtedly be other committed Christians who can complement and assist parents, whether married or single, in the ongoing adventure of inculcating the Christian world and life view in their children.

41. Wolterstorff, *Educating for Life*, 180.
42. Dreher, *Benedict Option*.

Savior, gave little evidence of being his disciples. An uncritical tolerance of other worldviews and lifestyles was common; an understanding of the Christian faith as the worldview that best depicts moral and spiritual reality—very uncommon. One wonders what their congregations were teaching, and what their parents understood their responsibility to be in terms of discipling their own children.

However, as Smith also noted, the children and youth who became serious about their faith in God usually belonged to families and church communities where parents took their faith seriously. To an extraordinary degree children are drawn to their parent's lifestyle (and that of their friends) *if* that lifestyle is rich in goodness, patience, kindness, honesty, laughter, and faith in God. When children grow up in the home of parents, or even one faithful parent, who look at life from the standpoint of the Christian worldview and the lifestyle built on it, a lifestyle that shows evidence of the fruit of the Holy Spirit, they often learn to "see" the world in much the same way.

CONCLUSION

The issue of worldview discipleship is of the utmost importance. Perhaps the most important reason is that a worldview, particularly the Christian worldview, helps provide perspective about reality on all levels—physically, historically, psychologically, and spiritually. Indeed, an accurate spiritual perspective encompasses all the other perspectives within it, just as an elevator which can reach to the top floor of a building has access to all the floors beneath it. There was a time when theology was considered the queen of the sciences, for the very reason that it was thought to encompass the insights of all the other disciplines. To quote C. S. Lewis once again, "I believe in Christianity as I believe that the sun has risen, not only because I see it, but because by it I see everything else."[43] The explanatory value of the Christian faith, and the teaching of the triune God and the incarnation, is capacious, comprehensive—and lasting. Simone Weil put it well, "To be always relevant, you have to say things that are eternal."[44]

---

43. Lewis, "Is Theology Poetry?" in *Weight of Glory*, 140. The analogy of the elevator also comes from Lewis's book, *Miracles*, 179.

44. Cited by Guinness, in *Prophetic UnTimeliness*, 105.

The meaning that Christianity and its worldview provides is of particular importance because it provides a balanced view of the salvation needed by every human being, an understanding of what is involved in personal transformation, as well as a solid foundation for human rights. It provides the insight necessary to understand that respect for all human beings of whatever age (including the preborn) is both objective and universal, and that living in accordance with its truths means not only believing it to be true, but practicing its moral principles in daily life. This, in utter contrast to the rogue worldviews surveyed in Chapter Two. Practicing the truth of Jesus, with his command to love God, and others, makes life rich and good. Practicing the truth of Jesus encourages every Christian, young and old, to share their faith with others, to serve them, to bring healing and help where they can, to work at being faithful in marriage and friendship, and to strive for justice and fair dealing. Further, it offers hope—hope that life can be meaningful here and now despite the pain and suffering and evil and injustice that abound. Hope that in the life to come these things, along with the suffering involved, will be overcome. God promises to make all things new (Revelation 21.1–5).

My wife, Carol, reminded me recently of the subtleties of the worldviews we face. She also has emphasized the importance of keeping an awareness of the work of the Evil One, and the need to engage in spiritual warfare. Spiritual warfare is no small matter, though in our modern, secular age the idea is usually downplayed or dismissed entirely. Nonetheless, it is an important thread in biblical teaching, especially in the New Testament. Jesus' ministry included many instances of deliverance from evil spirits. St Paul in his letter to the Christians of Ephesus and Colossae specifically highlighted the importance of engaging in spiritual warfare, building on the work of Jesus in disarming the principalities and powers that threaten the will of God, and the flourishing of human beings.

We must emphasize that this understanding of the Christian worldview will only be possible if it remains rooted in the biblical story, and our children are indwelt by God's Holy Spirit. It is the Spirit which brings life, it is the Spirit which brings conviction about sin and evil, it is the Spirit which enlightens about truth, and it is the Spirit which pours the love of God into their hearts and motivates and strengthens them in the on-going process of the renewal of mind, heart and *behavior*. That our children be filled with the Holy Spirit should be our constant prayer, as it should be our constant desire for ourselves. We cannot give what we do not have, and we cannot give witness to that which we have not in some measure experienced for ourselves.

The overall purpose of knowing the biblical story and the Christian worldview is that the understanding and strength it gives should contribute, through the power of the Holy Spirit, to lives of genuine compassion and service—faith working through love as Paul put it in Galatians 5.6. A love and respect that extends to all people, including the most vulnerable—the preborn child. The wonder and joy of this way of life is that in loving others for Jesus' sake we come to know God more deeply (see 1 John 4.7–11).

Richard Weikert, in his book, *The Death of Humanity*, writes: "In the final analysis, then, I am suggesting that the solution to the death of humanity is a revival of Christian love and compassion, a renewed sense that human life has meaning and purpose, because we are created in the image and likeness of God."[45] If there is to be a "revival of Christian love and compassion" it will be because Christians—Roman Catholic, Orthodox, and Protestant men and women who truly trust in Jesus as Lord and Savior—commit themselves seriously and persistently to his Great Commission, to the process of discipling their people, and their children, in his worldview (his teaching), with the goal of helping them actually *obey* all that he commanded.

"Lilies that fester smell far worse than weeds," wrote Shakespeare. Christians who fail to think and act biblically, Christians who appease and perpetuate violence, are more of a stumbling block to the salvation of others than those who claim no faith at all. With repentance, revival and reform, let us hope and pray for a maturity of discipleship such that through us "the fragrance of the knowledge of Christ may spread everywhere" (2 Cor 2.15). Lives are at stake, and the question before us is this: Will the rogue ideas and ideologies of the present day—worldviews that seek to destroy life and beauty—go unchallenged, or will those of us who identify as Christians seek the renewal of mind and life in Christ that builds character and contributes to a culture of life?

In his book, *Lest Innocent Blood be Shed*, philosopher Philip Haillie tells the extraordinary story of the Christian Huguenot community in the southern French village of Le Chambon during World War Two. These committed Christians, despite the difficulties and dangers, opened their hearts and their homes to Jews fleeing Nazi persecution,

---

45. Weikert, *The Death of Humanity*, 21.

and saved the lives of thousands of men, women and children. As Christian people they sought the mind of Christ. They understood that every human life was precious, including those of strangers. And they *acted* accordingly. They were believers who were disciples. Haillie concludes his book with this thought:

> I, who share [Pastor Andre] Trocme's and the Chambonnais' belief in the preciousness of human life, may never have the moral strength to be much like the Chambonnais or like Trocme; but I know what I want to have the power to be. I know that I want to have a door in the depths of my being, a door that is not locked against the faces of all other human beings. I know that I want to be able to say, from these depths, "Naturally, come in, and come in."[46]

To do likewise with the needs that God brings to us is what I pray for and desire for myself, my family, my friends, for other Christian families, and for every Christian fellowship the world over. My paraphrase of the words of Jesus in his parable of the last judgment are, I believe, in keeping with his meaning: "When you have provided drink, food and clothing to those in need, when you have visited the sick, when you opened the door of your heart to the stranger—and to those awaiting birth—you have welcomed me."[47]

A PRAYER

"O Lord Jesus Christ, who didst bid Thy disciples to shine as lights in a dark world, in shame and contrition of heart do I acknowledge before Thee the many faults and weaknesses of which we are guilty who in this generation represent Thy Church before the world; and especially do I acknowledge my own part in the same. Forgive me, I beseech Thee, the feebleness of my witness, the smallness of my charity, and the slackness of my zeal. Make me a worthy follower of Him who cared for the poor and the oppressed, and who could never see disease without seeking to heal it or any kind of human need without turning aside to help."[48]

Amen! May it be so!

---

46. Hallie, *Lest Innocent Blood Be Shed*, 287.
47. My paraphrase of Matt 25.40.
48. Baillie, *A Diary of Private Prayer*, 93.

Bibliography

"Abortion Techniques," National Right to Life. Available from https://news.nrlc.org/abortion/medicalfacts/techniques. Accessed September 11, 2022.

Aikman, David. *Jesus in Beijing*. Washington, DC: Regnery, 2003.

Anderson, Ryan T. and Alexandra DeSanctis. *Tearing Us Apart. How Abortion Harms Everything and Solves Nothing,* Washington, DC" Regnery Publishing, 2022.

Alexander, Leo. *Medical Science Under Dictatorship.* Flushing, New York: Bibliographic Press, 1996.

Allen, Cynthia M. "Black Lives Matter. As we address racism we must remember the unborn ones too." (June 26, 2020), star-telegram.com/opinion/cynthia-m-allen/article.243801797.html.

"Anti-Religious Campaign." *Revelations from the Russian Archives.* (August 31, 2016). Available from loc.gov/exhibits/archives/anti.html.

Applebaum, Anne. *Gulag. A History.* New York: Doubleday, 2003.

———. *Iron Curtain. The Crushing of Eastern Europe 1944–1956.* New York: Doubleday, 2012.

———. *Red Famine.* New York: Doubleday, 2017.

Augustine, *On Christian Doctrine*. Translated by D. W. Robertson Jr. Indianapolis, IN: Bobbs-Merrill, 1958.

Ayers, David J. "Sex and the Single Evangelical." (August 14, 2019). Available at ifstudies.org/blog/sex-and-the-single-evangelical//.

Ayubi, Zahra, Peters, Rebecca Todd, Raucher, Michal, "Religious woman have abortions, too. And many faiths affirm abortion rights." Available at https://nbcnews.com/Think/opinion/religious-women-have-abortions-too.many—faiths-affirm-abortion-rights-ncna1287846, accessed August 4, 2020.

Baillie, John. A Diary of Private Prayer.New York: Charles Scribner's Sons, 1949.

Barcus, Nancy B, *Developing a Christian Mind.* Downers Grove, Illinois: InterVarsity, 1977.

"BBC chooses best children's books of all time—do you agree?" *The Guardian.* Available at https"//com/childrens-books-site/2015/apr/03/best-childrens-book-of-all-time-internaitonal-childrens-books-day.

Barnard, Ann. "Death Toll for Syria Now 470,000." *New York Times.* February 11, 201, nytimes.com/2016/02/12/world/middleeast/death-toll-from-syria-now-470000-group-finds.html.

Barnett, Albert E. "The Second Epistle of Peter. Introduction and Exegesis," In *The Interpreter's Bible. A Commentary in Twelve Volumes,* ed. by George Arthur Buttrick, 177. Nashville, Tn: Abingdon Press, 1957.

Barabanov, "The Schism Between the Church and the World," in Alexander Solzhenitsyn, et al. *From Under the Rubble,* Boston: Little, Brown and Company, Inc. Bantam Books, 1976.

Bartholomew, Craig G. and Michael W. Goheen. *The Drama of Scripture. Finding Our Place in the Biblical Story.* Grand Rapids, Michigan: Baker Academic, 2014.

Bartholomew, Craig G., and Goheen, Michael. *Living at the Crossroads. An Introduction to Christian Worldview.* Grand Rapids, Michigan: Baker Academic, 2008.

Bates, Stephen. "Sweden Pays for a Grim Past,"*The Guardian,* (March 5, 1999). Available at htpps://www.theguardian.com/world/1999/mar/06/stephenbates.

Becker, Jason. *Hungry Ghosts. Mao's Secret Famine.* Toronto: The Free Press. 1996.

Behe, Michael J. *Darwin's Black Box.* New York: The Free Press, 1996.

Berman, Harold J. *Law and Revolution. The Formation of the Western Legal Tradition.* Cambridge, MA: Harvard University Press, Vol I, 1983. Vol II, 2003.

Besancon, Alain. Trans. Ralph C. and Nathaniel H. Hancock. *A Century of Horrors. Communism, Nazism, and the Uniqueness of the Shoah.* Wilmington, DE: ISI, 2007.

Bilger, Micaiah. "Shocking Report Shows 54% of women getting abortions are Christians," Available at www.LifeNews.com/2016/05/13/shocking-report-shows-54%-of-women-getting-abortions-are-Christians.

Binding, Karl and Alfred Hoche. *The Release of the Destruction of Life Devoid of Value.* Leipzig: Felix Meiner, 1920. Republished in 1975 in Santa Ana, CA, with comments by Robert L. Sassone.

Black, Edwin, *War Against the Weak. Eugenics and America's Campaign to Create a Master Race.* New York: Four Walls Eight Windows, 2003.

Blackman, Walt. "Abortion: The overlooked tragedy for black Americans." Feb 25, 2020, azcapitoltimes.com/news/2020/02/25/abortion-the-overlooked-tragedy-for-black-americans.

Boa, Kenneth and Turner, John Alan**,** *Hearts and Minds. Raising Your Child with a Christian View of the World.* Carol Stream, IL: Tyndale House, 2006.

Bonhoeffer, Dietrich**.** *The Cost of Discipleship.* New York: Touchstone, 1995.

Bottom, Joseph and David G. Dalin, eds. *The Pius War. Responses to the Critics of Pius XII.* Lanham, MD: Lexington Books, 2004.

Breitman, Richard. *Official Secrets. What the Nazis Planned, What the British and Americans Knew.* New York: Hill and Wang, 1998.

Brennan, William. *Dehumanizing the Vulnerable. When Word Games Take Lives.* Chicago: Loyola University Press, 1995.

———. *The Abortion Holocaust.* St. Louis, MO: Landmark, 1983.

Brower, Sigmund. *Who Made the Moon? A Father Explores How Faith and Science Agree.* Nashville, Tennessee: Thomas Nelson, 2008.

Brown, John B. Jr., and Robin Fox, eds. *Affirming Life. Biblical Perspectives on Abortion for the United Church of Christ*. Bechtelsville, PA: UCC Friends For Life, 1991.

Brown, Kristi Burton, "Late-term Abortions: It happens and it needs to stop." Available at https://www.liveaction/news/lagte-term-abortion-it-needs-to-stop-in-america/. Accessed September 7, 2022.

Browning, Christopher, *Ordinary Men. Reserve Police Battalion 101 and the Final Solution in Poland*. New York: HarperCollins, 1998.

Brzezinski, Zbigniew, *Out of Control. Global Turmoil on the Eve of the 21st Century*. New York: Charles Scribner's Sons, 1993.

Budziszewski, J. *Written on the Heart. The Case for Natural Law*. Downers Grove, Illinois: IVP Academic, 1997.

Burke, Kevin, with David Wemhof and Marvin Stockwell. *Redeeming a Father's Heart*. Bloomington, IN: Author House, 2007.

Burke, Theresa with David C. Reardon. *Forbidden Grief. The Unspoken Pain of Abortion*. Springfield, IL: Acorn Books, 2007.

Burleigh, Michael. *Sacred Causes. The Clash of Religion and Politics, from the Great War to the War on Terror*. New York: Harper Perennial, 2007.

——— *Moral Combat. Good and Evil in World War II*. London: Harper Press, 2010.

Butterfield, Rosaria *The Gospel Comes with a House Key*. Wheaton, Illinois: Crossway, 2018.

Campbell, Mark. "Five Fears That keep Pastors From Preaching About Abortion." (June 15, 2018) Available at https://focusonthefamily.com/pro-life/pre-born/five-fears-that-keep-pastors-from-preaching-about-abortion.

Catechism of the Catholic Church. New Hope, KY: Urbi et Orbi Communications, 1994.

Center for Medical Progress. "Human Capital." centerformedicalprogress.org/human-capital/documentary-series/. Accessed 9/9/20.

Chang, Iris. *The Rape of Nanking. The Forgotten Holocaust of World War II*. New York: Basic, 1997.

Chang, Jung and Jon Halliday. *Mao. The Unknown Story*. New York: Alfred A. Knopf, 2005.

Charles, J. Darryl. "The Kuyperian Option." *Touchstone: A Journal of Mere Christianity* 31 May/June 2018) 22–28.

"Charles Malik." Available at https://en.wikipedia.org/wiki/chasrles malik. Last edited August 23, 2020.

Clark, Christopher. *The Sleepwalkers. How Europe Went to War in 1914*. New York: Harper Collins, 2013.

"Christianity by country." Available at https://En.wiki.Christianity-by-country. Last edited September 4, 2022.

Clark, Richard. "Planned Parenthood Makes as Much as $23 Million Annually from Selling Baby Body Parts." Available at https://lifenews.com/2015/07/24/planned-parenthood-makes-as-much-as-23-million-annually-from-selling-baby-body-parts. Accessed September16, 2022.

Coleman, Priscilla K. "Abortion and mental health: quantitative synthesis and analysis of research 1995– 2009. British Journal of Psychiatry 199 (September 1011) 180–86, Available at https://Cambridge.org/journal/the-british-journal-of-[psychiatry/article/abortion-and-mental-health-quantitative-synthesis-and-analysis-of-mental-health-published-19952009/E8D.

"Competing Worldviews Influence Today's Christians,." Research Releases in Culture & Media, May 9, 2017. Available at https://www.barna.com/research/competing-worldviews-influence-todays-christians/.

Condon, Guy and David Hazard. *Fatherhood Aborted*. Wheaton, IL: Tyndale House, 2001.

Conquest, Robert. *Reflections on a Ravaged Century*. New York: W. W. Norton, 2000.

Cook, Michael, "Iceland lashed over Down syndrome at UN." Bioedge, February 15, 2022. Available at https://bioedge.org/disability/Iceland-lashed-over-down-syndrome-record-at-un/. Accessed September 15, 2022.

Copan, Paul. *Is God a Moral Monster? Making Sense of the Old Testament God*. Grand Rapids, MI: Baker, 2011.

Cornwell, John. *Hitler's Pope. The Secret History of Pius XII*. New York: Viking, 1999.

Courtois, Stephen, et al., Translated by Jonathan Murphy and Mark Kramer. Consulting Editor, Mark Kramer. *The Black Book of Communism. Crimes, Terror, Repression*. Cambridge, MA: Harvard University Press, 1999.

Covey, Stephen R. *7 Habits of Highly Effective Families*. New York: Franklin Covey, 1997.

———. *7 Habits of Highly Effective People*. New York: Free Press, 1989, 2004.

———. *The Leader in Me*. New York: Free Press, 2008.

Cowles, C. W. et al, *Show Them No Mercy*. Grand Rapids, MI: Zondervan, 2003.

Craig, William Lane. *Reasonable Faith*. Wheaton, IL: Crossway Books, 1993.

Crawford, David and Michael Hanby. "The Abolition of Man and Woman." *The Wall Street Journal* (June 25, 2020) A17.

Currie, Stephen, *The Quest for Freedom: The Abolitionist Movement*. Detroit: Thomson Gale, 2006.

"Dachau," Holocaust Encyclopedia. Available at https://umhmm.or/content/en/article/dachau. n.d.

Darwin, Charles. *The Origin of Species*. London: Penguin, 1968.

Davis, Tom. *Sacred Work*. New Brunswick, NJ: Rutgers University Press, 2005.

Dickson, John. *Humilitas. A Lost Key to Life, Love, and Leadership*. Grand Rapids, MI: Zondervan, 2011. "Didache." In *Lost Scriptures: Books that Did Not Make It into the New Testament,* edited by Bart D. Ehrman, 211–17. New York: Oxford University Press, 2003.

DiMauro, Dennis, *A Love for Life*. Eugene, OR: Wipf & Stock, 2008.

Dorrien, Gary. *Social Ethics in the Making*. Oxford: Wiley-Blackford, 2011.

Dorsett, Lyle W. *A Passion for Souls*. New York: Oxford University Press, 2004.

Dunahoo, Charles H. *Making Kingdom Disciples. A New Framework*. Phillipsburg, NJ: P & R Publishing, 2005.

Dreher, Rod. *The Benedict Option. A Strategy for Christians in a Post-Christian Nation*. New York: Sentinel, 2017.

Earls, Aaron, "7 in 10 Women who Have an Abortion Identify as a Christian," (12/2/21). Available athttps://ResearchLifeway.com/2021/12/03/7-n-10-women-who-have-had-an-abortion-identify-as-a-christian/.

Eckardt, Alice, ed. *In Burning Memory. Times of Testing and Reckoning.*, Oxford: Pergamon, 1993.

———. 'The Pogrom of *Kristallnacht* in Christian Context." In *Burning Memory. Times of Testing and Reckoning,* edited by Alice Eckardt, 57–67. Oxford: Pergamon, 1993.

Eisner, Peter. *The Pope's Last Crusade*. New York: William Morrow/ Harper Collins, 2013.

Ericksen, Robert P. *Theologians Under Hitler.* New Haven, CT: Yale University Press, 1985.

———. and Susannah Heschel, eds. *Betrayal. German Churches and the Holocaust.* Minneapolis, MN: Fortress, 1999.

"Euthanasia Program." Holocaust Encyclopedia. (December 4, 2019). Available at ency.uhmm.org/content/en/article/euthanasia-program.

Evans, Karin. *The Lost Daughters of China. Abandoned Girls, Their Journey to America, and the Search for a Missing Past,* New York: Penguin Putnam, 2000.

Evans, M. Stanton. *The Theme is Freedom. Religion, Politics, and the American Tradition.* Washington, DC: Regnery, 1994.

Fairchild, Mary. "How Many Christians Are in the World Today?" (updated April 6, 2020) Learnreligions.com/christianity-statistics-700533.

Ferguson, Niall. *The War of the World.* New York: Penguin, 2007.

Fisher, Brian. "Why do so many Christians have abortions? *Charisma News.* (August 6, 2013). Available at https://charismanews.com/opinion40519-why-do-so-many-churchgoers-have-abortions.

Flew, Antony with Roy Abraham Varghese. *There Is a God.* New York: Harper Collins, 2007.

Fogelman, Eva. *Conscience and Courage. Rescuers of the Jews During the Holocaust.* New York: Anchor Books, 1996.

Foster, Richard J. *Celebration of Discipline. The Path to Spiritual Growth.* New York: Harper & Row Publishers, 1978.

Fox, Robin. "Historical Perspectives on Abortion," in *Affirming Life. Biblical Perspectives on Abortion for the United Church of Christ,* edited by John B. Brown and Robin Fox, 13–31. Bechtelsville, PA: United Church of Christ Friends For Life, 1991.

Frankl, Viktor E. *Man's Search for Meaning.* Boston, MA: Beacon, 1962, 2006.

Franks, Angela, *Margaret Sanger's Eugenic Legacy.* London: McFarland & Company. 2005.

Freytas-Tamura, Kimiko. "Ireland Votes to End Abortion in Rebuke to Catholic Conservatism." *New York Times,* (May 26, 2018) Available s.

Frielander, Henry, *The Origins of Nazi Genocide. From Euthanasia to the Final Solution.* Chapel Hill, NC: University of North Carolina Press, 1995.

Gamalwadi, Vishal. *The Book That Made Your World. How the Bible Created the Soul of Western Civilization.* Nashville, TN: Thomas Nelson, 2011.Garber, Steven. *The Fabric of Faithfulness. Weaving Together Belief and Behavior.* Downers Grove, Illinois: IVP Books, 2007.

Gardiner, Anne Babeau. "The Ecumenical Molech: the Latest Assault on the Unborn in the Name of the World's Religions," *the Human Life Review* XXX (Spring 2004) 58–65.

Garton, Jean. *Who Broke the Baby.* Minneapolis, Minnesota: Bethany House, 1979.

Gaultney, Katie. "Home education on the rise in Europe." January 1, 2016,https://world.wng.org/2016/01/home-education-on-the-rise-in-europe.

Gellately, Robert. *Lenin, Stalin, and Hitler. The Age of Soviet Catastrophe.* New York: Vintage Books, 2007.

Genovese, Eugene D. *A Consuming Fire. The Fall of the Confederacy in the Mind of the White Christian South.* Athens, GA: University of Georgia Press, 1998.

Gerhardt, Elizabeth. *The Cross and Gendercide. A Theological Response to Global Violence Against Women and Girls.* Downers Grove, IL: IVD Academic, 2014.

Glover, Jonathan. *Humanity. A Moral History of the Twentieth Century.* New Haven: Yale University Press, 1999.

Goldberg, Arthur, "Abortion: Devastatin Impact Upon Black Americans," February 2022. Available at https://Public Discourse.com/2019/02/48594/. Accessed September 16, 2022.

Goldberg, Jonah. *Liberal Fascist.* New York: Doubleday, 2007.

Goldhagen, Daniel Jonah. *A Moral Reckoning. Hitler's Willing Executioners.* New York: Alfred A. Knopf, 1996.

Gonzales v. Carhart." En.wikipedia.org/wiki/Gonzales_v_Carhart.

Gonzalez, Mike and Andrew Olivastro. "The Agenda for Black Lives Matter is Far Different Than the Slogan." July 3, 2020, Available at https://heritage.org/progressivism/commentary/the-agenda-black-olives-matter-far-different-then-the-slogan.

Gorman, Michael J., *Abortion & the Early Church.* Eugene, OR: Wipf and Stock Publishers, 1998.

———.and Ann Loar Brooks. *Holy Abortion? A Theological Critique of the Religious Coalition for Reproductive Choice.* Eugene, OR: Wipf and Stock Publishers, 2003.

Gourevitch, Philip. *We wish to inform you that tomorrow we will be killed with our families. Stories from Rwanda.* New York: Picador. Farrar, Straus and Giroux, 1998.

Graves, Dan, "Founder of World Mission, John Mott." Available at https//www.Christianity.com/church/church-history/timeline/1901–2000/promoter-of-world-missions,john-mott. n.d. Accessed October 24, 2020.

Green, Lisa Cannon "Survey: Women Go Silently From Church to Abortion Clinic." (June 21, 2018) Available at focusonthefamily.com/pro-lifesurvey-women-go-silently-from-church-to-abortion-clinic/.

Gregg, Samuel. *Reason, Faith, and the Struggle for Western Civilization.* Washington, DC: Regnery Gateway, 2019.

Grimes, David, et al. "Unsafe Abortion: the preventable pandemic." World Health Organization. Sexual and Reproductive Health 4, who.int/reproductive. health/topics/unsafe_abortion/articles_unsafe_abortion.pdf. n.d. Accessed 9/22/20.

Grobman, Alex and Danile Landes, eds, *Critical Issues of the Holocaust.* Los Angeles; Simon Wiesenthal Center and Rossell Books of Dallas, TX, 1983, Sections 2 & 3,. pp 16–101.

Grossman, David A. *On Killing. The Psychological Cost of Killing in War and Society.* New York: Back Bay, Little, Brown and Company, rev. ed. 2009.

Guibilina. Alberto, and Francesca Minerva. "After-Birth Abortion: Why should the baby live?" *Journal of Medial Ethics* 39 (2013) 261–63.

Guinness, Os. *Time for Truth. Living Free in a World of Lies, Hype, & Spin.* Grand Rapids, MI: 2000.

———. *Prophetic Untimeliness. A Challenge to the Idol of Relevance.* Grand Rapids, MI: Hourglass Books, 2003.

———. *The Magna Carta of Humanity. Sinai's Revolutionary Faith and the Future of Freedom.* Downers Grove, IL: InterVarsity, 2021.

———. *Unspeakable. Facing Up to Evil in an Age of Genocide and Terror.* New York: Harper, 2005.

Gushee, David P. *The Righteous Gentiles of the Holocaust.* Minneapolis, MN: Fortress, 1994.

———. *The Sacredness of Human Life*. Grand Rapids, Michigan: Wm B. Eerdmans, 2013.

Hague, William. *William Wilberforce. The Life of the Great Anti-Slave Trade Campaigner*. Orlando, FL: Harcourt, 2007.

Haillie, Philip, *Lest Innocent Blood Be Shed*. New York: Harper Perennial, 1979, 1994.

Harris, Sam. *Letter to a Christian Nation*. New York Alfred A. Knopf, 2006. Harrison, Beverly W. *Our Right to Choose: Toward A New Ethic of Abortion* (Boston: Beacon, 1983.

Hartley, Emma. "Sami desire for truth and reconciliation process," in *Politico*. Accessed at https://www./ed/article/sami-reconciliation-porocess-Sweden-minority-multiculturalism-human-rights-discrimination/.

Hendershot, Anne. *The Politics of Abortion*. (New York: Encounter), 2006.

"Herbert Spencer." Available at https://en/wikipedia.org/wiki/Herbert_Spencer. Last edited September 10. 2022.

Herzog, Dagmar, *Sexuality in Europe: A Twentieth-Century History*. Cambridge: Cambridge University Press, 2011.

Hiebert, Paul G. *Transforming Worldviews. An Anthropological Understanding of How People Change*. Grand Rapids, Michigan: Baker Academic, 2008.

Hilberg, Raul. *Perpetrators, Victims, Bystanders*. The Jewish Catastrophe 1933–1945. New York: Harper Perennial, 1982.

Hildebrand, Dietrich Von, *Humility. Wellspring of Virtue*. Manchester, New Hampshire: Sophia Institute 1948, 1997.

———. *My Battle Against Hitler. Faith, Truth and Defiance in the Shadow of the Third Reich*. New York: Image, 2014.

———. *Trojan Horse in the City of God. The Catholic Crisis Explained*. Manchester, NH: Sophia Institute, 1993.

Hilgers, Thomas W. and Dennis J. Horan. *Abortion and Social Justice*. Thaxton, VA: Sun Life, 1972.

Hill, John Lawrence. *After the Natural Law*. San Francisco: Ignatius Press, 2016.

Hitler, Adolf. *Mein Kampf*. Boston: Houghton Mifflin, 1925, 1971.

Hollander, Paul. *From the Gulag to the Killing Fields*. Wilmington, DE: ISI Books, 2007.

Homrighausen, Elmer G. "The Second Epistle of Peter, Exposition." *The Interpreter's Bible*. A Commentary in Twelve Volumes, ed. by George Arthur Buttrick. Nashville, TN: 1957. 12:177–78.

Horowitz, David. *Dark Agenda: The War to Destroy America*. West Palm Beach, Fl: Humanix, 2018.

Houlihan, P. J. "The Churches," https://encyclopedia, 1914–1918-online.net/article/the-churches. Last edited October 22, 2015.

H. R. 36 (114th) 2015: Pain-Capable Unborn Child Protecton Actc. Available at https://govtrack.us/congress/bill/114/hr36#.

Hunt, Irmgard A. *On Hitler's Mountain. Overcoming the Legacy of a Nazi Childhood*. New York: William Morrow, 2005.

Huntington, Samuel P. *The Clash of Civilizations and the Remaking of the world Order*. New York: Simon & Schuster, 1996.

Hvistendahl, Mara. *Unnatural Selection. Choosing Boys over Girls, and the Consequences of a World Full of Men*. New York: Public Affairs, 2011.

Ilibagiza, Immaculee, with Steve Irwin. *Left to Tell. Discovering God Amidst the Rwandan Holocaust*. Carlsbad, CA: Hay House, 2006.

Jacobson, Thomas W. and Wm. Robert Johnson. *Abortion Worldwide Report: 1 Century, 100 Nations, 1 Billion Babies*. Westchester, OH: GLC Publications, 2018.

Jaffa, Harry V., *A New Birth of Freedom*. Lanham, Maryland: Rowan & Littlefield Publishers, 2004.

———. *Crisis of the House Divided. An Interpretation of the Issues in the Lincoln-Douglass Debates, Chicago*: The University of Chicago Press, 1959.

Jenkins, Philip. *The Great and Holy War: How World War I Became a Religious Crusade*. New York: Harper Collins, 2014.

"John R. Mott–Facts." Available at https://NobelPrize.org.NobelMedalAB2020.Sun. Sep2020, https://www.nobelprize.org/prizes/peace/1946/mptt/facts/.

John Paul II, *The Gospel of Life*. Boston, MA: Pauline, 1995.

———. *The Splendor of Truth*. Boston, MA: Pauline, 1993.

Johnson, Abby. *Unplanned*. Colorado Springs, CO: Focus on the Family/ Tyndale House, 2010.

Johnson, Paul. *Modern Times. The World from the Twenties to the Nineties*. New York: Harper Perennial, rev. ed., 1991.

Johnston, David L. "Charles Malik, the UN, and Human Right." Available at humantrustees.org/blog/religionand-human-rights/item/170-charles-malik.

Jones, David Albert. "The Hippocratic Oath II," *The Catholic Medical Quarterly* (February 2006), cmq.org.uk/CMQ/2006/Hippocratic_oath_ii.htm.

Kautsky, Karl. *Terrorism and Communism: A Contribution to the Natural History of the Revolution*. Trans. W. H. Kideridge. London: Allen and Unwin, 1920.

Keller, Timothy. *Making Sense of God. An Invitation to the Skeptical*. New York: Viking, 2016.

Kelsey, Morton. *Can Christians Be Educated? A Proposal for Effective Communication of our Christian Religion*. Compiled and edited by Harold William Burgess. Religious Education, Inc. Birmingham, Al: 1977.

"Khmer Rouge: Cambodia's Years of Brutality," BBS. Available at https:/www.bbc.com/world-asia-pacific-10684399.

Kilpatrick, William and Gregory and Suzanne M. Wolfe, *Books That Build Character. A Guide to Teaching Your Child Moral Values Through Stories*, New York: Simon & Schuster Touchstone, 1994.

King, Martin Luther Jr., "Letter From a Birmingham Jail," reprinted in Peter A. Lillback, *Annotations on a Letter that Changed the World*. King of Prussia, PA: Providence, 2013.

Klee, Ernst, with Willi Dressen and Volker Riess, editors. *The Good Old Days. The Holocaust as Seen by its Perpetrators and Bystanders*. New York: Konecky & Konecky, 1988.

Klusendorf, Scott. *The Case for Life*. Wheaton, IL: Crossway, 2009.

Kontorovich, Eugene. "A Genocide Test Faces the West." *Wall Street Journal*, January 28, 2021, A17.

Koop. C. Everett and Francis A. Schaeffer. *Whatever Happened to the Human Race?* Westchester, Illinois: Crossway, 1983.

Kuby, Gabriele. *The Global Sexual Revolution. Destruction of Freedom in the Name of Freedom*. Translated by James Patrick Kirchner. Kettering, OH: Angelico, 2015.

Kuhl, Stefan, *The Nazi Connection. Eugenics, American Racism, and German National Socialism*. New York: Oxford University Press, 1994.

Larsen, Bjorke. "*Norway's Lutherans Apologize to Gypsies*." Available at https://.www.christianitytoday/ct/200decemberweb-only/560html/.

Leavitt, Steven B. and Stephen D. Dubner. *Freakanomics*. New York: Harper Collins, 2005, 2006.
Le Fanu, James. *Why Us? How Science Discovered the Mystery of Ourselves*. New York: Pantheon, 2009.
Leitenberg, Milton. *Death in War and Political Conflicts in the 20th Century*. Ithaca, NY: Cornell University, 2006.
Lewis, Brenna, "Here's Why Teachers' Unions Support Abortion, Planned Parenthood," studentsforlife.org/2019/07/08/heres-why-teaches-unions-support-abortion-planned-parenthood.
Lewis, C. S. *The Abolition of Man*. New York: Harper San Francisco, 1944, 2001.
———. *Christian Reflections*. Grand Rapids, MI: William B. Eerdmans, 1967.
———. *God in the Dock. Essays on Theology and Ethics*. Edited by Walter Hooper. Grand Rapids, MI: William B. Eerdmans, 1970.
———. *Mere Christianity*. New York: Harper Collins 1952, 1996, 2001.
———. *Miracles. A Preliminary Study*. New York: Macmillan, 1947.
———. *Of Other Worlds. Essays and Stories*. London: Geoffrey Bles, 1966.
———. *The Chronicles of Narnia.* (7 volumes in one). New York: Harper Festival, 2010.
Lifton, Robert Jay. *The Nazi Doctors. Medical Killing and the Psychology of Genocide*. New York: Basic 1986.
Littell, Franklin H. "Reinhold Niebuhr's Christian Leadership in a Time of Testing." In *Burning History. Times of Testing & Reckoning*, edited by Alice L. Eckardt, 95– 107. Oxford: Pergamon, 1993.
Llewellyn, Jennifer, and Jim Southey and Steve Thompson. "Religion in Nazi Germany." Alpha History. Available at https://alphahistory.com/nazigermany/religion_in_nazi_germany. Accessed September 13, 2022.
Lockerbie, D. Bruce, *A Christian Paideia. The Habitual Vision of Greatness*. Colorado Springs, CO: Purposeful Designs Publications, 2005.
Lower, Wendy. *Hitler's Furies. German Women in the Nazi Killing fields*. New York: Houghton Mifflin Harcourt, 2013.
Luthringer, George. *Considering Abortion? Clarifying What you Believe*. (Washington, DC: Religious Coalition for Reproductive Choice, 1992).
Lukianoff, Greg and Jonathan Haidt. *The Coddling of the American Mind*. New York: Penguin, 2018.
Lutzer, Erwin W. *Hitler's Cross*. Chicago: Moody, 1995.
———. *When A Nation Forgets God. 7 Lessons We Must Learn From Nazi Germany*. Chicago: Moody, 2010.
Macaulay, Susan Schaeffer. *For the Children's Sake. Foundations of Education for Home and School*. Wheaton, Illinois: Crossway Books, 1984.
Machen, J. Gresham. *Princeton Theological Review* 11 (1913) 7.
MacKeen, Dawn Anahid. *The Hundred Year Walk. The Armenian Odyssey*. Boston: Houghton Mifflin Harcourt, 2017.
MacNair, Rachel, "Our Pro-Life Future," *First Things* 147 (June/July 2018) 40–46.
Mangalwadi, Vishal. *The Book that Made Your World*. Nashville, TV: Thomas Nelson, 2011.
Marson, James. "A Russian Fights for Stalin's Victims." *The Wall Street Journal*, December 16, 2016, wsj.com/articles/a-russian-fights-for-stalin's-victims.
Marc, Alexander. "Conflict and violence in the 21st century." Available at World Bank group,un.org/pga/wp-content/uploads/sites/10/2010/01/conflict-and-violence-

in-the-21st-century-current-trends-as-observed-in-empirical-research-and-statistics-Alexander-Marc/ n.d. Accessed 9/10/20.

Margolin, Jean-Louis, "China: A Long march into Night," in Stephen Courtois, et. al., translated by Jonathan Murphy and Mark Kramer, *The Black Book of Communism. Crimes, Terror, Repression*. Cambridge, MA: Harvard University Press, 1999.

Marlin. George J. "World War I and the Papacy," The Catholic Thing, (August 2, 2014). Available athttps://www.thecatholicthing.org/2014/08/12/world-war-1-and-the-papacy.

Marsden, George M. "'Mere Christianity' Still Gets a Global Amen." *Wall Street Journal,* March 24, 2016. wsj.com/articles/mere-christianity-still-gets-a-global-amen-1458858161. Accessed October 22, 2020.

Martin, Douglas. "Franklin Littell, Scholar of Holocaust, Dies at 91." *New York Times*. May 30, 2009, Available at https://www.nytimes.com/2009/05/30/us/30littell.html/.

Martyn Lloyd-Jones, D. *Faith on Trial*. Grand Rapids, MI: Baker, 1982.

McElhinney, Ann and Phelim McAleer. *Goznell. The Untold Story of America's Most Prolific Serial Killer*. Washington, DC: Regnery, 2017.

McGrath, Alister. The Big Question. *Why We Can't Stop Talking About Science, Faith and God*. New York: St. Martin's, 2015.

———. *Enriching our Vision of Reality. Theology and the Natural Sciences in Dialogue*. West Conshohocken, PA: Templeton, 2017.

———. *A Fine-Tuned Universe. The Quest for God in Science and Theology*. Louisville, KY: Westminster John Knox, 2009.

———. *The Great Mystery. Science, God and the Human Quest for Meaning*. London: Hodder & Stoughton, 2017.

———. *Mere Apologetics. How to Help Seekers and Skeptics Find Faith*. Grand Rapids, Michigan: Baker, 2012.

———. *Surprised by Meaning. Science, Faith, and How We Make Sense of Things*. Louisville, KY: Westminster John Knox, 2011.

Medawar, Peter. *The Limits of Science*. Oxford: Oxford University Press, 1984.

Mehan, Mary. "Saving Lives through the Churches," *The Human Life Review* XXXI (Spring 2005) 5–32.

Merritt, Jonathan. "Was World War 1 a religious crusade? An interview with Philip Jenkins." Religious News Service. (May 22, 2014) Available at religiousnewsservice.com/2014/05/22/world-war-religious-crusade-interview-Philip-Jenkins.

Metaxas, Eric. *Amazing Grace. William Wilberforce and the Heroic Campaign to End Slavery*. New York: Harper One, 2007.

———. *Bonhoeffer. Pastor, Martyr, Prophet, Spy. Righteous Gentile vs. the Third Reich*. Nashville, TN: Thomas Nelson, 2010.

Meyer, Steven. *Signature in the Cell*. New York: Harper One, 2009.

Mechielsen, Jack. "Preface," in *No Icing on the Cake: Christian Foundations for Education*, edited by Jack Mechielsen. Melbourne: Brookes-Hall, 1980.

Miller, Monica Migliorina. "Severed Ties: How Abortion Dissolvers Feminine Authority." *Crisis*, Vol. 9 (November 1991) 21–26.

Montanaro, Domenico. "Poll: Majority want to keep abortion legal, but they also want restrictions." National Public Radio, Inc [US], Available at npr.org2019/06/07/730185531/poll-majority-want-to-keep-abortion-legal-but-they-also-want-restrictions.

Moreland, J. P. *Scientism and Secularism*. Wheaton, IL, 2018.
Morris, Benny and Drur Ze'evi. *The Thirty-Year Genocide. Turkey's Destruction of its Christian Minorities*. Cambridge, MA: Harvard University Press, 2019.
Morse, Arthur. *While 6 Million Died. A Chronicle of American Apathy*. New York: Ace Corporation, 1968.
Mosley, Patrina, "Planned Parenthood Is Not Pro-Woman." *Family Research Council*, September 27, 2018, www.frc.org›brochure›planned-parenthood-is-not-pro-woman.
Mujahid, Abdul Malik. "On Human Rights, the Democrats Are Silent," *The Wall Street Journal* (November 20, 2019) A17.
Murray, Douglass. "One Hundred Years of Evil." *National Review* LXIX (October 30, 2017). Available at nationalreview.com/magazine/2017/10/30/Russian-revolution-100-year- evil/.
Nagel, Thomas. *Mind & Cosmos: Why the Materialist Neo-Darwinian Concept of Nature is Almost Certainly* False. New York: Oxford University Press, 2012.
Nathanson, Bernard, with Richard N. Ostling, *Aborting America*, Doubleday & Company, Garden City, 1979.
———. *The Hand of God. A Journey from Death to Life by the Abortion Doctor Who Changed His Mind*. Washington, DC: Regnery, 1996.
Naugle, David. *Worldview. The History of a Concept*. Grand Rapids, MI: William B., Eerdmans, 2002.
Niebuhr, Reinhold. *The Nature and Destiny of Man. Volume 1: Human Nature*. New York: Charles Scribner's Sons, 1941, 1964.
Newbigin, Lesslie. *The Gospel in a Pluralist Society*. Grand Rapids, Michigan: William B. Eerdmans Publishing Company, 1989. Geneva: WCC Publications, 1989.
———. "Truth and Authority in Modernity," in *Faith and Modernity*, edited by Philip Sampson, Vinay Samuel, and Chris Sugden, Oxford: Regnum, 1994, 60–88.
Noebel, David A. *Understanding the Times*. Eugene, Oregon: Harvest House, 1994.
Noll, Mark A., *The Scandal of the Evangelical Mind*. Grand Rapids, MI. William B. Eerdmans, 1994.
Noonan, John T. "An Almost Absolute Value in History." In *Morality of Abortion: Legal and Historical Perspectives*, edited by John T. Noonan, 7–59. Cambridge, MA: Harvard University Press, 1970.
———. ed. *The Morality of Abortion. Legal and Historical Perspectives*. Cambridge, MA: Harvard University Press, 1970.
O'Connor, Elizabeth. *The Call to Commitment. The Church of the Savior, Washington, DC*. New York: Harper & Row, 1963.
Ofer, Dalia, and Lenore L. Weitzman, "Women in the Holocaust." Jewish Women's Archive. Available at https://jwa.org/encyclopedia/article/women-in-holocaust.
O' Kane, Caitlin. "New York passes law allowing abortion at any time if mother's health is at risk," Wttps://cbsnews.com/new-york-passes-abortion-bill-late-term-if-mothers-health-is-at-risk-today-2019-11-23/.
de Oliveira, Plinio Corea ."The Church and the Communist State: The Impossible Coexistence," (August 1, 1963). Available at www.tfp.org/the-church-in-the-communist-state-the-impossible-coexistence. "Desmond Tutu—Biographical," obelprize.org/prizes/peace/1984/tutu/biographical/.
Olasky, Marvin. *Abortion Rites. A Social History of Abortion in America*. Wheaton, IL: Crossway Books, 1992.

———. and Herb Schlossberg. *A Christian Worldview Declaration.* Westchester, Illinois: Crossway Books, 1987.

Pabst, Adrian. "Christianity ended the cold war peacefully." *The Guardian.* (November 11, 2009). Available at https://TheGuardian.com//commentisfree/belief/2009/nov/10/religion-christianity.

Palmer, Michael, ed. *Elements of a Christian Worldview.* Springfield, MO: Logion, 1998

Pandey, Kivan. "Selective Abortion Killed 22.5 Million Female Foetuses [sic] in China, India, India, Down to Earth." April 17, 2019. Accessed at https://wwwdowntoearth.org.org.in/news/health/selection=abortion-killed-ss-35-million-foestuses-in-china-india-64043.

Paquelle, Danielle, "Thousands of women were raped during Rwanda's genocide. Now their children are coming of age. (6/16/17)." *Independent.* Available at https://news.independent.co.uk/news/long-read/thousands-of-women-were-raped-during=rwanda's-genocide-now-their-children-are-coming-of-age.

Pavone, Frank. "A Clergyman Answers the Fears Pastors Face as they Address the Issue of Abortion." Edited for Protestants by Gary Thomas. @priestsforlife.org/brochure/face/fearsecumenical. Html.

———. Proclaiming the Message of Life. Cincinnati, OH: Franciscan Media, 2016.

Pearcey, Nancy. *Love Thy Body. Answering Hard Questions about Life and Sexuality.* Grand Rapids, MI: Baker, 2018.

Peck, M. Scott. *The Road Less Traveled.* New York: Touchstone, 1978.

PFI Briefing. "2020 State of Abortion in Pennsylvania." Available at https://pafamily.org/wp-context/2020/05/2020-State-of-Abortion-in-Pennsylvania-Report.pdf/.

"Physicians' Pledge." World Medical Association Declaration of Geneva. September 1948, wma.net/policies-post/wma-declaration-of-Geneva.

Pierson, Anne. Mending Hearts, Mending Lives. Shippensburg, PA: Destiny Image, 1987.

Perrin, Christopher A. *Introduction to Classical Education.* Camp Hill, PA: Classical Academic Press, 2004.

Pinker, Steven. *The Better Angels of Our Nature. Why Violence has Declined.* New York: Viking, 2011.

———"The Enlightenment is Working," *The Wall Street Journal* (February 10–11, 2018) C 1.

Posner, Gerald. God's Bankers, *A History of Money and Power at the Vatican,* New York: Simon & Schuster Paperbacks, 2015.

Potts, Malcom. "A New Ethic for Medicine and Society." *California Medicine* 113 (September 1970) 67–68.

Power, Samantha. *"A Problem From Hell." America and the Age of Genocide.* New York: Harper Perennial, 2002.

Powell, John. *Abortion: The Silent Holocaust.* Allen, TX: Tabor, 1981.

"Public Opinion on Abortion." Pew Research Center Religion and Public Life (Aug 29, 2019). Available at Pewforum.org/fact-sheet/public-opinion-on-abortion.

Prestigiacomo, Amanda. "These 8 States Allow Abortion Up To The Moment Of Birth," (1/30/2019). Daily Wire. Available at https://www.dailywire.com/news/these-8-states-akkiw-abortion-moment-birith-amanda-prestigiacomo.

Pulonov, Alexander, "The problem of religious freedom in later imperial Russia: the case of Russian Baptists." *Journal of Eurasian Studies* 3 (July 2012) 161–67.

Ratzinger, Joseph. *Truth and Tolerance.* San Francisco: Ignatius Press, 2004.

Rausch, David A. *A Legacy of Hatred. Why Christians Must Not Forget the Holocaust.* Grand Rapids, MI: Baker, 1984.

Ray, Brian D. "Homeschooling growing: Multiple Data Points Show Increase 2012 to 2016 and Later." (April 20, 20180. Available at nheri.org/homeschool-population-size-growing.

Reardon, David C. *The Jericho Plan. Breaking Down the Walls Which Prevent Post-Abortion Healing.* Springfield, IL: Acorn Books, 1996.

———*Aborted Women, Silent No More.* Westchester, IL: Crossway, 1987.

Reilly, Robert R. *America on Trial. A Defense of the Founding.* San Francisco: Ignatius, 2022.

"Religious Beliefs in Rwanda," available at https://www.worldatlas.com/articles/religion-beliefs-in-rwanda.html#.

"Religion in the Soviet Union." Available at https://en.wikipedia.org/wiki/Religion_in_the_Soviet Union. Last edited on August 17, 2020.

"Anti-Religious Campaign." *Revelations from the Russian Archives.* (August 31, 2016). Available at loc.gov/exhibits/archives/anti.html.

Rhodes, Aaron. *The Debasement of Human Rights. How Politics Sabotage the Ideal of Freedom.* New York: Encounter Books, 2018.

Rhodes, Richard. *Masters of Death.* New York: Alfred A. Knopf, 2002.

Roach, David. "Reconciliation not a 'finished project' 25 years after historic resolution." Baptist Press, June 20, 2020, baptistpress.com/resources-library/news/racist-reconciliation-not-a-finished-project-25-years-after-historic-resoultion. Accessed October 1, 2020.

Root, Andrew, *Faith Formation in a Secular Age.* Grand Rapids, Michigan: Baker Academic, 2017.

Rosen, Christine, *Preaching Eugenics. Religious Leaders and the American Eugenics Movement.* New York: Oxford University Press, 2004.

Rossi, Lauren Faulkner. *Wehrmacht Priests. Catholicism and the Nazi War of Annihilation.* Cambridge, MA: Harvard University Press, 2015.

Rubenstein, Richard L. *The Cunning of History.* New York: Harper & Row, 1975.

———. and Roth, John K. *Approaches to Auschwitz. The Holocaust and its Legacy.* Atlanta, Georgia: John Knox, 1987.

———. "Waldheim, the Pope and the Holocaust, in Burning Memory. Times of Testing & Reckoning, edited by Alice L. Eckardt, 263–69. Oxford: Pergamon Press, 1993.

Russell-Kraft, Stefanie. *The Nation,* April 11, 2018. Available at https://www.A Christian Argument for Abortion: a Q/A with Pastor Rebecca Todd Peters," Thenation.com/article/a-Christian-argument-for-abortion-aqa-with-rebecca-todd-peters. Accessed September 15, 2022.

"Rwanda: how the genocide happened," May 17, 2011. BBC. Available at https://.com/news/world-africa-1341486. Accessed September 11, 2022.

Rychlak, Ronald J. *Hitler, The War and the Pope.* Huntingdon, IN: Our Sunday Visitor, 2000.

Samuel, Wolfgang W. E. *The War of Our Childhood. Memories of World War II.* Jackson, Missouri: University Press of Missouri, 2002.

Sande, Ken. *The Peacemaker. A Biblical guide to Resolving Personal Conflict.* Grand Rapids, MI: Baker 1991, 1997.

———. Resolving Everyday Conflict. Grand Rapids, MI: Baker, 2011.

Satter, David. "!oo Years of Communism—and 100 Million Dead." *The Wall Street Journal*, November 7, 2017, A 17.

Schaeffer, Francis A. *The God Who is There*. Chicago, Illinois, Intervarsity, 1968.

———. and C. Everett Koop. *Whatever Happened to the Human Race?* Old Tappan, NJ: Fleming H. Revell, 1979.

Schubert, Frank. "Polling on Marriage: the American people continue to support preserving marriage as the union of one," (June 18, 2014). Available at washingtontimes.com/news/2014/June18/polling-on-marriage-the-American-people-continue/.

Sessions, David. "Evangelicals Struggle to Address Premarital Sex and Abortion." July 13, 1917, Available at thedailybeast.com/evangelicals-struggle-to-address-premarital-se-and-abortion/.

"Severe Violations of Human Rights in China," May 5, 2018. Available at https://editorial.voa.gov/a/severe-violations-human-rights-china/4378252,html. Accessed 8/25/22.

Shakespeare, William. *They that have the power to do hurt and will do none*. Sonnet 94, Available athttps://www.poetryfoundation.org/45100/sonnet-94-they-that-have-the-power-to-do-hurt-but-will-do-none. Accessed September 16, 2022.

Shaw, Laura and Erna Korbegovic. Available at https://eugenicsarchive.co/dataabase/documents/d51c2742697b8940a540000009. Accessed September.

Shaver, Jessica. *Gianna*. Colorado Springs, CO: Focus on the Family, 1995.

Shirer, William L. *The Rise and Fall of the Third Reich*. New York: Simon & Schuster, 1987, 1988, 1990.

Sider, Ronald J. *The Scandal of the Evangelical Conscience*. Grand Rapids, Michigan: Baker, 2005.

Siedentop, Larry. *Inventing the Individual. The origins of Western Liberalism*. Cambridge, MA: Harvard University Press, 2014.

Simmons, Paul. "Some Biblical References to Personhood," in *Prayerfully Pro-Choice: Resources for Worship*. Washington, DC: Religious Coalition for Reproductive choice, 2000.

Singer, Peter. *Animal Liberation*, (rev. ed.), New York: Avon Books, 1990.

———. Helga Kuhse, ed. *Unsanctifying Human Life*. Oxford: Blackwell Publishers Ltd, 2002.

Singh, Simon. *Big Bang. The Origin of the Universe*. New York: Harper Perennial, 2004.

Silent No More": An Interview with Georgette Forney, Human Life Review Vo. XLVIII, No. 2 (Spring 2022). 32–36.

Sire, James W. *Naming the Elephant*. Downers Grove, IL: IVP Academic, 2004.

Smith, Christian, with Melinda Lundquist Denton, *Soul Searching*. New York: Oxford University Press, 2005.

Smith, Christian and Pamela Snell. *Souls in Transition*. New York: Oxford University Press, 2009.

Smith, Timothy L. *Revivalism and Social Reform in Mid-Nineteenth-Century America*. Nashville, TN: Abingdon Press, 1957.

Smith, Wesley J., *A Rat is a Pig is a Dog is a Boy*. New York: Encounter, 2010.

———. *The Culture of Death. The Age of "Do Harm" Medicine*. New York: Encounter Books, 2016.

Snay, Michael. *Gospel Disunion. Religion and Separation in the Antebellum South*. New York: Cambridge University Press, 1993.

Snyder, Timothy. *Bloodlands. Europe Between Hitler and Stalin*. New York: Basic Books, 2010.

———. *Black Earth. The Holocaust as History and Warning*. New York: Tim Duggan Books, 2015. Solzhenitsyn, Alexander. *The Gulag Archipelago 1918–1956. An Experiment in Literary Investigation. III-IV*. New York: Harper & Row, 1974.

———. et al. *From Under the Rubble*. Translated b A. M. Brock, et al. Boston: Little, Brown, 1975, Bantam Books, 1976.

———. Templeton Prize lecture. Acceptance Speech by Mr. Aleksandr Solzhenitsyn, May10, 1983, templetonprize.org/laureate-sub/solzhenitsyn-acceptance-speech/.

Somerville, Scott W. "The Politics of Survival: Home Schoolers and the Law." (April 2001), Available at https://.org/content/docs/nche/000010/PoliticsofSurvival.asp.

Sorokowsky, Andrew. "Russian Christianity and the Russian Revolution: What Happened?" *Christian History* 18 (1988). Available at christianhistoryinstitute.org/magazinearticle/russian-christianity-and-the-russian-revolution-what-happened. Accessed September 16, 2022.

Stallsworth, Paul, ed. *The Church & Abortion*. Nashville, TN: Abingdon Press, 1993.

Stanford, Susan M. *Will I Cry Tomorrow? Healing Post-Abortion Trauma*. Old Tappan, NJ: Fleming H. Revell, 1986.

Stark, Rodney. For the Glory of God. *How Monotheism led to Reformations, Science, With-Hunts, and the End of Slavery*. Princeton, NJ: Princeton University, 2003.

Stassen, Glen H, with D. M. Yeager and John Howard Yoder. Authentic Transformation. Nashville, TN: Abingdon, 1996.

———. *A Thicker Jesus*. Louisville, KY: Westminster John Knox, 2012.

Steiner, Jean-Francois. *Treblinka*. Introduction by Terrence Des Pres. New York, NY: Meridian, 1994.

Ten Boom, Corrie with John and Elizabeth Sherrill, *The Hiding Place*. Tappan, NJ: Fleming H. Revell, 1971.

Trueblood, Elton, *The Humor of Christ*. New York: Harper & Row, 1975.

Tshabalala, Vusile. "How many blacks died under apartheid?" Available at http://iluvsa.blopspot.com/2011/06/how-many-blacks-died-under-apartheid.html.

Universal Declaration of Human Rights, Article 3, December 10, 1948/ Available at un.org/en/universal-declaration-human-rights/.a \\ Accessed September 16, 2022.

"Some 25 million unsafe abortions occur each year, UN agency warns," UN News. Available at https://news.un.org/en/story/2017/567312-some-25-million-unsale-abortions-occur-each-yedar-un-agency-warns.

"Summary of Roe v. Wade and other key abortion cases." U. S. Conference of Catholic Bishops Pro-Life Activities. Available at www.usccb.org/issues-and-action/human-life-and-dignity/abortion/Summary-of-Roe-v-Wade-and-other-key—abortion-cases.pdf.

Uwimana, Denise. "Cancilde and Emmanuel. "How far does forgiveness reach?" in *Plough Quarterly* 19 (Winter 2019) 76–78.

———. *From Red Earth. A Rwandan Story of Healing and Forgiveness*. Walden, NY: Plough, 2019.

Van Toai, Doan and David Chanoff. *The Vietnamese Gulag*. New York: Simon and Schuster, 1986.

Von Hildebrand, Dietrich. *My Battle with Hitler*. New York: Image, 2014.

———. *Trojan Horse in the City of God. The Catholic Crisis Explained.* Manchester, NH: Sophia Institute, 1993.

Wainwright, Geoffrey. *Lesslie Newbigin. A Theological Life.* Oxford: Oxford University, 2000.

Warren, Roland. "Pro Abundant Life," https://www.care-net.org/pro-abundant-life. n.d.

Washington, Harriet A. *Medical Apartheid. The Dark History of Medical Experimentation on Black Americans from Colonial Times the Present.* New York: Harlem Moon, 2006.

Weaver, Richard, *Ideas Have Consequences.* Chicago, IL: University of Chicago Press, 2013.

Weigel, George. *The Great War Revisited.* First Things Reprint Series 6 (2014).

Weikart, Richard. *From Darwin to Hitler. Evolutionary Ethics, Eugenics, and Racism in Germany.* New York: Palgrave Macmillan, 2004.

———. *Hitler's Religion.* Washington DC, Regnery History, 2016.

———. *The Death of Humanity and the Case for Life.* Washington, DC: Regnery Faith, 2017.

Weil, Simone. *First and Last Notebooks.* Eugene, OR: Wipf and Stock, 2015.

West, John G. *Darwin Day in America.* Wilmington, DE: ISI, 2015.

Whatley, Monica with Dr. Shawn Whately. *Shaping Hearts and Minds.* Toronto: Eagle and Child, 2016.

"Where are the World's Slaves?" National Geographic. https://blog.education.org/2016/06/01/where-are-slaves-in-the-world/.

Wilberforce, William. *Real Christianity. A Practical View of the Prevailing Religious System of Professed Christians in the Higher and Middle Classes in This Country, Contrasted with Real Christianity.* A Paraphrase in Modern English by Bob Belz. Ventura, CA: Regal, 2006.

Willard, Dallas. *The Great Omission.* New York: Harper One, 2006.

Williams, Juliet. "Planned Parenthood awarded $2.3 million for secret videos." abcnews.go/Health/wireStory/jury-awards-planned-parenthood-million-secret-video-67053926.n.d.

Williams, Laura E. *Behind the Bedroom Wall.* Milkweed Editions 1996.

———. *Abortion. Questions & Answers.* Cincinnati, OH: Hayes, 1985.

Woolman, John. *The Journal of John Woolman, and A Plea for the Poor.* Gloucester, MA: Peter Smith, 1971. Wolterstorff, Nicolas. Gloria Stronks and Clarence Joldersma, editors. *Educating for Life.* Grand Rapids, Michigan: Baker Academic, 2002.

———. *Journey Toward Justice.* Grand Rapids, MI: Baker Academic, 2013.

Wright, N. T. *Following Jesus. Biblical Reflections on Discipleship.* Grand Rapids, MI: William B. Eerdmans, 1994.

Wright, N. T. New York: HarperCollins, 2008. Wright, Walter, "Peter Singer and the Lessons of the German Euthanasia Program." *Issues in Integrative Studies* (2000) No. 18, 27–43.

Yakovlev, Alexander N. *A Century of Violence in Soviet Russia.* New Haven, CT: Yale University Press, 2002.

Yoder, John Howard. *The Politics of Jesus.* Grand Rapids, MI: William B. Eerdmans, 1972.

Name Index

Abel, 141
Abraham, 191
Adam, 141, 158
Alexius I, 87
Alito, Samuel, 211
Althaus, Paul, 89
An, Chi, 57
Andrew, Apostle, 183
Andrews, Lori, 63
Anderson, Ryan, 14, 19, 25
Applebaum, Anne, 41, 85–86
Arkes, Hadley, 12
Athanasius, 157
Augustine, Saint, 153, 156
Aultman, Kathi, 23

Baillie, John, 236
Barabanov, Eugene, 87
Barcus, Nancy, 158–59
Barth, Karl, 90
Bartholomew, Craig, 137–40, 143–44, 146, 216, 230
Becker, Carol, 62
Becker, Jason, 43
Biden, Joseph, 11, 43
Binding, Karl, 38, 54
Black, Edwin, 35–38, 40, 74, 80, 82
Blackman, Harry, 25

Boa, Kenneth, 209, 214, 222
Bodelschwingh, Friedrich von, 83
Bonhoeffer, Dietrich, 91, 173, 188
Bonow, Amelia, 12
Brandt, Karl, 54
Braune, Paul. 83
Brennan, William, 62–63
Brower, Sigmund, 226
Brown, Carol, 15, 57, 223, 235
Browning, Christopher, 72
Brzezinski, Zbigniew, 1, 6, 7, 13, 43, 64, 72
Buck, Carrie, 36
Burke, Kevin, 21
Burke, Theresa, 18, 20
Burleigh, Michael, 46
Bush, George H. W., 56
Bush, George W., 7, 9
Butterfield, Kent, 225
Butterfield, Rosario, 225

Cain, 140, 158
Calvin, John, 13
Camp, Lee (Laura), 101–2, 123–24
Carnegie, Andrew, 35
Chamberlain, Houston Stuart, 45, 68
Charles, J. Darryl, 13
Chesterton, G. K., 81

Chotek, Sophie, 5
Clark, Christopher, 73
Coleman, Patricia, 18, 19
Conquest, Robert, 32–33, 66. 86
Conti, Leonardo, 83
Cook, Michael, 28
Cornelius, 184, 185–87
Cornwall, John , 93
Courtois, Stephen, 41, 44
Covey, Stephen, 195–96, 203, 217

Daleiden, David, 26
Daly, Mary, 111
Darwin, Leonard, 37
Darwin. Charles (Darwinism, Social Darwinists) 2, 27, 34–35, 40, 45–46, 59–61, 71, 78
DeSanctis, Alexandra, 14, 19, 25
Dewey, John, 62
Di Mauro, Dennis, 112–14
Dirac, Paul 97
Dobbs v. Jackson Women's Health, 11–12, 115, 211
Doe v. Bolton, 10, 11, 25, 62
Dorrien, Gary, 79
Draper, William, 55
Dreher, Rod, 233
Dubner, Stephen D., 60

Eckhardt, Alice, 77
Ehrlich, Paul, 56, 57
Engels, Fredrick, 40
Eshilman, Nikolai, 86
Etzioni, Amitai, 228
Evans, M. Stanton, 30
Eve, 141, 158

Ferdinand, Franz, 5
Ferguson, Neil, 5
Fisher, Brian, 123
Fletcher, Joseph, 63, 110–11
Forney, Georgette, 21
Fox, Robin, 103–04
Franks, Angela, 35, 36
Freud, Sigmund, 64
Friedlander, Henry, 39, 54, 82, 83

Gabelein, Frank E. 131, 137
Galen, Clemens August von, 83
Galton, Francis, 3, 34–35, 78

Garton, Jean, 225
Garber, Steven, 98, 231
Gellately, Robert, 43
Gerhardt, Elizabeth, 57
Giubilin, Alberto, 59, 60
Gladden, Washington, 3, 78
Glover, Jonathan, 5
God (Almighty, Creator, Father, Redeemer), 69, 70, 113, 132–38, 165–78, 183–206, 211, 218–19, 221, 230, 233–35
Goheen, Michael, 138–40, 143–46, 216, 230
Goldberg, Arthur, 30
Goldhagen, Daniel, 49, 50
Gorman, Michael, 13
Gosnell, Kermit, 22
Grant, Madison, 28, 53
Grier, Dolores Bernadette, 29
Grobman, Alex, 88
Grossman, David, 67
Guinness, Os, 30, 61
Gushee, David, 75, 77, 100, 116, 127, 166, 175

Habakkuk, 157
Habyarimana, Juvenal, 51
Haeckel, Ernest, 34
Hallie, Philip, 235, 236
Harrison, Beverly, 111
Hegel, G. W. F., 64
Heisenberg, Werner, 97
Hiebert, Paul, 147
Hilberg, Raul, 99
Hildebrand, Dietrich von, 95, 97
Hirsch, Emanuel, 89
Hitler, Adolph, 34, 38–39, 43–45, 47, 54, 88–89, 95, 203
Hoche, Alfred, 38, 52, 54
Hoekendijk, Hans, 188
Hollander, Paul, 41
Holmes, Oliver Wendell, 37
Holy Spirit (Spirit), 167, 172, 178, 182, 184–90, 192, 199–200, 218–19, 221, 233–35
Huntington, Samuel, 160
Hvistendahl, Mara, 55–58

Irenaeus, 174

Name Index

Jacobson, Thomas W., 7, 8, 10, 52, 55, 57
Jaffa, Harry, 27, 62, 193
Jaki, Stanley, 161
James, Saint, 158, 167, 179, 181, 193
Jan, Julius von, 92
Jesus Christ (Savior, Lord, Redeemer, Messiah), 33, 47, 48, 65–66, 68–69, 90, 98, 127–28, 131–58, 163, 165–74, 177–78, 181–96, 198–201, 203–7, 212, 216, 218, 220–21, 230–36
Job, 156–58
John, Saint, 142, 167, 171–72, 193, 201
John Paul II, 87, 128, 231
Johnson, Abby, 23–25, 205
Johnson, Paul, 64, 70
Johnston, William Robert, 7, 8, 10, 52, 55, 57
Justin Martyr, 153

Kautsky, Karl, 41
Kekomaki, Marti, 63
Kelman, Wolfe, 63
Kelsey, Morton, 221
Kilpatrick, William, 226–28
King, Martin Luther Jr, 31, 112
Kissinger, Henry, 56
Kittel, Gerhard, 89
Knauer (child), 39
Koontz, Dean, 59
Koop, Everett, 62
Kornfield, Boris, 87
Kuby, Gabriele, 63–64, 159–60
Kuyper, Abraham, 13

Lader, Lawrence, 109–10
Lanes, Danile, 88
Larson, Bjorke, 82
Laski, Harold J. 37
Leavitt, Steven B., 60
Leitenberg, Milton, 6, 7
Lemkin, Raphael, 106, 107
Lenin, V. I. (Leninism), 34, 43–44
Lewis, C. S., 48, 70, 144, 147, 153, 189, 227–29, 233
Lifton, Robert Jay, 38–40
Lincoln, Abraham, 13
Littell, Franklin, 131–32
Lockerbie, Bruce, 153
Lower, Wendy, 48–49

Luther, Martin, 13, 48

MacArthur, Douglass, 55
Machen, J. Gresham, 130, 162
Malik, Charles, 107, 108, 120
Mao Zedong, 42
Marx, Karl, 40
Mathews, Navin, 218
Mathews, Sanaya, 218
Matthews-Green, Frederica, 17–18
McAleer, Phelim, 22–23
McEllhinney, Ann, 22–23
McGrath, Alister, 156, 161
McKim, W. Duncan, 53
Medawar, Peter, 163
Melanchthon, Philip, 13
Metaxas, Eric, 3
Meyer, Stephen, 161
Miedema, Pieter, 100
Miller, Monica M., 19
Minerva, Francesca, 59–60
Molech, 198
Monger, Karnamaya, 22
Morana, Janet, 21
Morrison, Charles Clayton, 79
Moody, Howard, 109, 110
Mosely, Patricia, 58–59
Moses, 156, 214
Mosher, Steven, 57
Mott, John R., 4

Nathanson, Bernard, 73, 109–10, 205–6
Naugle, David, 160–61
Nechayev, Sergey, 40–41
Newbigin, Lesslie, 117–18, 128–29
Nicodemus, 150
Niebuhr, Reinhold, 92, 93
Niemoeller, Martin, 90, 91
Nietzsche, Fredrich, 44, 45
Noebel, David, 131
Noah, 140
Noll, Mark, 120
Noonan, John, 12, 164–66

Obergefell v. Hodges, 62
Ofer, Dalia, 54
Ohden, Melissa, 15–16
O'Kane, Caitlin, 11
Olasky, Marvin, 12, 52–53, 58, 104, 119
Oliveira, Plinio Corea de, 84

Ostling, Richard, 73

Pacelli, Eugene (Pope Pius XII), 93
Paul, Saint, 13, 39, 47, 68, 86, 138, 143, 149, 151, 163, 167–68, 177–78, 185, 190–93, 196, 200, 235
Pauli, Wolfgang, 97
Pavone, Frank, 12
Pearcey, Nancy, 130, 144
Peck, Scott, 219–20
Pennypacker, Samuel, 81
Peter, Saint 178–79, 182–89, 193–94, 198, 201, 206
Petri, Erna, 49
Pianka, Eric, 60
Pieper, Josef, 64
Pius XI, 93
Pinker, Steven, 1, 5–7, 13–14, 61
Planned Parenthood v. Casey, 11
Planck, Max, 97
Pol Pot, 43, 73
Polkinghorne, John, 161
Pompeo, Mike, 43
Potts, Malcom, 62–63, 105, 108
Powell, Colin, 7
Power, Samantha, 51, 106–7
Pres, Terrence des, 27, 32

Rand, Ayn, 163
Rausch, David, 80
Rauschenbusch, Walter, 3, 78
Ratzinger, Joseph (Pope Benedict XVI), 97
Reagan, Ronald, 12
Reardon, David C., 18, 20–21
Rockefeller, John D III., 35–56
Roe v. Wade, xiv, 10, 11, 14, 30, 62, 216
Rohm Ernst, 92
Rosen, Christine, 78–81
Roth, John, 46–47, 95
Rubenstein, Richard, 46–47, 75, 95, 97
Ruether, Rosemary Radford, 111

Sande, Ken, 201–2
Sanger, Margaret, 36, 58
Satter, David, 43
Schaeffer, Francis, 62, 143, 145
Schlossberg, Herbert, 119

Scholl, Hans, 98, 231
Scholl, Sophie, 98, 231
Schussler, Elizabeth, 111
Serebrovsky, A. S., 43
Seromba, Athanase, 101
Shakespeare, William, xvii, 76, 235
Shirer, William, 68
Sider, Ron, 121–22
Singer, Peter, 54, 59
Smith, Christian, 124–26, 132, 232–33
Snell, Patricia, 126
Snyder, Timothy, 14–15, 41
Solzhenitsyn, Alexander, 41, 47, 66, 69, 86–88
Spencer, Herbert, 2
Stalin, Joseph, 43, 86
Stallsworth, Paul, 179–80, 211
Stark, Rodney, 193
Stassen, Glen H., 68
Strong, Josiah, 3, 78

Tregold, Arthur, 53
Trocme, Andre, 236
Trueblood, D. Elton, 133
Trump, Donald, 11
Turner, John Alan, 209, 214, 223

Ushakov, Alexander A., 85

Ward, Harry F., 78
Warren, Roland, 169
Watson, James, 59, 60
Weaver, Richard, 32, 46–47, 66–67
Weikert, Richard, 35, 39, 45, 47, 59–60, 235
Weil, Simone, 131, 150, 233
Weitzman, Lenore L., 54
West, John G., 71
Wilberforce, William, 3, 213
Willard, Dallas, 66, 75, 116, 171, 189–90
Wilke, J. C., 12; with Mrs. J. C W., 183
Williams, Juliet, 26
Wolfe, Gregory, 226–28
Wolfe, Suzanne, 226–28
Wolterstorff, Nicolas, 166, 174, 232
Wright, N. T., 135, 187

Yakunin, Gleb, 87

www.ingramcontent.com/pod-product-compliance
Lightning Source LLC
Chambersburg PA
CBHW062007220426
43662CB00010B/1254